The Political Economy of Government Auditing

The Political Economy of Government Auditing addresses the elusive quest for greater transparency and accountability in the management of public finances in emerging economies; and, more specifically, it examines the contribution of autonomous audit agencies (AAAs) to the fight against corruption and waste. Whilst the role of audit agencies in curbing corruption is increasingly acknowledged, there exists little comparative work on their institutional effectiveness. Addressing the performance of AAAs in emerging economies, Carlos Santiso pursues a political economy perspective that addresses the context in which audit agencies are embedded, and the governance factors that make them work or fail. Here, the cases of Argentina, Brazil and Chile are examined, as they illustrate the three – parliamentary, court and independent – models of AAAs in modern states, and their three distinct trajectories of reform, or lack of reform. Beyond Latin America, considerations on the reform of government auditing in other countries, developed and developing, are also taken up as, it is argued, while institutional arrangements for government auditing matter, political factors ultimately determine the effectiveness of AAAs. Reforming AAAs, it is concluded, must consider the trajectory of state building, the role of law in public administration and the quality of governance.

An important contribution to the comparative study of governance institutions, and especially those tasked with overseeing the budget and curbing corruption, *The Political Economy of Government Auditing* will be of interest to scholars and students of comparative politics, development studies, administrative law, and public finance, as well as to development practitioners and policymakers in developing countries, donor governments and international institutions.

Carlos Santiso is Sector Manager of the Governance Division at the African Development Bank.

Law, development and globalization

Series Editor: Julio Faundez

University of Warwick

During the past decades, a substantial transformation of law and legal institutions in developing countries has taken place. Whether prompted by market-based policies or the international human rights movement, by the relentless advance of the process of globalization or the successive waves of democratization, no area of law has been left untouched. The aim of this series is to promote cross-disciplinary dialogue and cooperation among scholars and development practitioners interested in understanding the theoretical and practical implications of the momentous legal changes taking place in developing countries.

Titles in the Series:

State Violence and Human Rights
State officials in the South
Andrew M. Jefferson and Steffen Jensen (eds.) (2009)

Forthcoming titles:

Global Perspectives on the Rule of Law
James Heckman and Robert Nelson (eds.) (2009)

Law in the Pursuit of Development
Principles into practice?
Amanda Perry-Kesaris (ed.) (2009)

Marginalized Communities and Access to Justice
Yash Ghai and Jill Cottrell (eds.) (2009)

Social Movements, Law and the Politics of Land Reform
George Meszaros (2009)

Governance Through Development
Poverty reduction strategies and the disciplining of third world states
Celine Tan (2010)

The Political Economy of Government Auditing

Financial governance and the rule of law in Latin America and beyond

Carlos Santiso

Routledge
Taylor & Francis Group
LONDON AND NEW YORK

First published 2009
by Routledge
2 Park Square, Milton Park, Abingdon, Oxon, OX14 4RN

Simultaneously published in the USA and Canada
by Routledge
711 Third Avenue, New York, NY 10017, USA

Routledge is an imprint of the Taylor & Francis Group, an informa business

First issued in paperback 2016

Typeset in Garamond by Keyword Group Ltd

British Library Cataloguing in Publication Data
A catalogue record for this book is available from the British Library

Library of Congress Cataloguing-in-Publication Data
Santiso, Carlos.
The political economy of government auditing: financial governance and the rule of law in Latin America and beyond/Carlos Santiso.
p. cm.—(Law, development and globalization)
ISBN 978-0-415-47773-4
1. Finance, Public—Accounting—Latin America. 2. Finance, Public—Accounting—Law and legislation—Latin America.
I. Title.

HJ9923.L29S36 2009
657'.835045098—dc22 2008049538

ISBN13: 978-0-415-47773-4 (hbk)

ISBN13: 978-1-138-98966-5 (pbk)

For Anja

L'amour est le miracle d'être un tour entendu jusque dans nos silences, et d'entendre en retour avec la même délicatesse: la vie à l'état pur, aussi fine que l'air qui soutient les ailes des libellules et se réjouit de leur danse. Christian Bobin, *Ressusciter,* 2001.

Contents

Figures

Tables

Foreword by Sanjay Pradhan

Governance and the fight against corruption have moved to the centre of the development agenda, as a global consensus has emerged around the notion that good governance is essential to reduce poverty. But citizens of poor countries are not the objects of development experts' agendas and designs. People of developing countries are themselves demanding greater transparency and accountability from their governments. They have recognised that corruption blocks economic development, as it diverts billions of dollars a year that could otherwise be used to reduce poverty and promote economic growth.

The factors causing poor governance go beyond corruption, whether grand or petty. They are rooted in fundamental weaknesses in the social contract between government and the governed, between the state and citizens. As Carlos Santiso's *Political Economy of Government Auditing* eloquently explains, these weaknesses are reproduced in the budget process and, more broadly, in the management of public resources.

A government budget involves more than financial accounts or legislation. It reflects politically-driven choices over the allocation of scarce resources, and among competing policy priorities. In a profound way, budgeting *is* governing, and the budget, a trust that reflects the social pact between the state and citizens. The extent to which the budget accurately reflects the country's policy priorities is an important indicator of the strength of the social contract underpinning the state.

Sadly, that trust is too often breached in many poor, misgoverned countries, where informal practices make a mockery of budget approval and oversight processes which may exist in law. An effective social pact is predicated on the dynamics of power and politics being subjected to a rule of law in fact, not just in form. Persistent corruption is a symptom of weaknesses in the rule of law, along with malfunctioning accountability institutions and integrity systems in the management of public funds. To turn the tide against corruption, strong scrutiny and oversight through parliaments, law enforcement, independent media, and a vibrant civil society is essential.

Dr Santiso usefully explores some of the institutional dysfunctions that undermine integrity in the oversight of public finances. Specifically, he examines the role of independent audit agencies in ensuring that government accounts are clear and understandable, so that the people can hold government to account. This emphasis is well-placed, as transparency in public finances is a potent antidote to prevent corruption and hold government to account for its financial management, while also empowering citizens. Autonomous audit agencies act as 'auxiliary precautions', guarding against abuse and misuse of power, lending credibility to the reliability of government financial information. As Dr Santiso persuasively argues, audit agencies constitute a critical link in a broader system of checks and balances, and a web of accountability relations.

Transparent and accountable management of public resources matters to donor governments and international financial institutions for several reasons. Good financial governance provides the foundation on which to build effective states capable of delivering services to their people. Good financial governance in countries receiving development assistance matters to external financial institutions because it provides assurances that loans and aid will be effectively used for the intended purposes. Just as local citizens rightly demand accountability, so too do taxpayers in donor countries, and shareholders of international financial institutions.

Dr Santiso correctly emphasises the relationship between audit agencies and parliaments as a critical one. Dysfunctions in this relationship often explain why the scrutiny of auditors-general is circumvented or short-circuited. The relevance and credibility of auditors-general depend, to a large extent, on their independence from partisan interests and political meddling, as well as the timeliness of their audit work. Political failures, rather than technical ones, are often behind breakdowns in the systems of control. Audit agencies are sometimes neither as independent nor as effective as they should be because of the political context in which they find themselves. Ultimately, politics often imposes constraints on these agencies; this is an important challenge this book raises, and one for which the answers are far from simple.

The *Political Economy of Government Auditing* is an important contribution to the literature on the political economy of public finance, as well as emerging theoretical perspectives on oversight, accountability, and checks and balances. It underlines the vital role of the state and accountability institutions for economic development. It provides valuable guidance to policymakers in developing countries as they seek to strengthen transparency and accountability in the management of public resources. It will also be useful to development practitioners everywhere, including those in international financial institutions, such as the World Bank Group.

While focused on Latin America, this book offers relevant lessons for all countries and regions, and for those outside the fields of public finance and accounting. Scholars, practitioners and policymakers tackling reforms of the state in developing countries and emerging economies, will find subtle, practical suggestions in these pages on ways to fight corruption by strengthening the institutions of integrity and accountability in the management of public resources. This seems – sometimes – a Sisyphean task, but it is also urgent, necessary and achievable.

Sanjay Pradhan
Vice President
The World Bank Institute
12 November 2008

Foreword
by Leandro Despouy

The *Political Economy of Government Auditing* represents an ambitious effort to assess the real impact of Autonomous Audit Agencies (AAA) on the fight against corruption, as well as their potential for improving the management of public resources.

Focusing on the cases of Argentina, Brazil and Chile, Dr Santiso provides a critical perspective on the performance of the institutions tasked with controlling government, as well as of the various factors which have an impact – positive or negative – on their performance. The book importantly emphasises the critical function of government control and oversight and its crucial impact on the proper functioning of modern states. This heightens the importance of the book and the recommendations it crafts; and whether or not we agree with the book's proposals, they do open up new paths toward the improvement of the scrutiny and control of government.

One of the main contributions of the book is its emphasis on the influence of politics on the effectiveness of the institutions of control and the agencies of oversight. This insight underlines the importance of analysing not just the performance of the agencies of control in isolation, their technical capacities and the specific moment in which they intervene (*ex ante*, concomitantly or *ex post facto*), but also of considering the specific political and institutional context in which these agencies are embedded and act. In particular, it is critical to understand the incentives of decision-makers in the legislative as well as in the executive branch to actually implement the recommendations of audit reports. The book rightly emphasises the crucial importance of co-ordination between the different components of the system of control and oversight in any given country, which include the legislative and judicial powers. This approach is influenced by the ground-breaking concept of 'horizontal accountability' developed by the Argentine political scientist, Guillermo O'Donnell, a concept that has had a tremendous influence, especially in our region. In this context, hegemonic political systems and electoral systems which undermine the connection between the elected and the electorate are by definition detrimental to the development of a culture of control.

The important and challenging task of reforming AAAs constitutes another of the main themes of this book. Favouring gradual reforms over 'big-bang' approaches, the author provides the example of the *Tribunal de Contas da União* (TCU), the Brazilian external audit agency, which chose to espouse a gradual process of reform and adjustment, as one of the more successful cases in the region. Indeed, any reform of AAAs must take into account their institutional trajectory, the level of development of the public administration which it is set to control as well as the administration's adherence to the rule of law and the regulations governing its actions. AAAs thus cannot be reformed or strengthened abruptly or in isolation. To illustrate this point, the author brings up the example of Argentina's *Auditoría General de la Nación* (AGN), considering premature the decision to replace the former National Tribunal of Accounts with a corrective system of control, following the experience of some Anglo-Saxon countries.

Developing a novel index of institutional effectiveness to measure the performance of AAAs mainly based on information available until 2004, the author highlights the historical weakness in the timeliness of the AGN's audit reports, as well as of the impact of their recommendations. He also emphasises the negative impact on government control of two critical factors, namely the increasing weakening of budget institutions, through the overuse of emergency legislation, as well as the incentives generated by the political and electoral systems. Dr Santiso accurately describes some of the challenges that a collegiate decision-making body, traditionally dominated by the ruling party, poses to the functioning of the AGN, particularly in relation to the drafting of its reports. This situation is mirrored in the composition and leadership of the joint audit and public accounts committee of Parliament, which functions as the key intermediary between the AGN and the legislature. Both of these issues give further credence to the need to respect the constitutional requirement of Article 85 of the Argentinean Constitution that the President of the AGN be appointed by the main party of the political opposition, and to guarantee that the actual running of the AGN be in the hands of its President. This requirement enables effective external control by the opposition in a context where, as the author shows, horizontal accountability is weakened.

These considerations also represent the basis of my disagreement with the need for further constitutional reform in this area. What is needed instead is an appropriate regulation of the aforementioned constitutional clause, in order to prevent the governing party from dominating not only the AGN, but the various agencies involved in the process of external control of the public sector and the national administration. In fact, almost 15 years after the constitutional reforms of 1994, we are still lacking an organic law which regulates the structure and functioning of the AGN in accordance with the stipulations of the Constitution. This has generated an improper juxtaposition of normative systems where the actual application of the law sometimes runs counter to the spirit of the constitution, particularly pertaining to the functional independence of the AGN and its effective functioning.

This situation, as well as many of the weaknesses noted by Dr Santiso, confirms the urgent need to change the mechanisms regulating the functioning of the AGN. These adjustments must be carefully planned taking into account the author's assertion that 'it is critical to conceive reforms as a matter "not of achieving an ideal model, but improving the existing model on the basis of available resources and existing restrictions."'

I dare say that if we were to adopt the main recommendations of Dr. Santiso's book, the reforms of the legal framework of the AGN should:

- Strengthen the institutional independence of the AGN, by introducing legislation guaranteeing its functional and financial independence.
- In case the system of a collegiate board is continued – which is not contrary to the spirit of the Constitution although it favours the figure of a President – establish an open process for selecting the auditors-general and the President of the AGN, following for instance the process of appointment of Supreme Court judges established in 2003.
- Establish mechanisms which strengthen the control of the AGN by the opposition, for instance by appointing auditors-general representing the second party of the opposition.
- Strengthen the follow-up of the recommendations of audit reports, through a better coordination with the internal audit mechanisms within the executive under the purview of the SIGEN, and by establishing a mechanism guaranteeing that audit recommendations be promptly considered and adequately treated by the legislature.
- Considering that the AGN cannot impose sanctions, allow it the option to present itself as plaintiff in judicial proceedings and to institutionalise effective channels of collaboration and coordination with the other components of the system of judicial control, in particular the attorney general's office, the federal prosecutor for administrative matters, and the anti-corruption office.
- Expand the scope of the audits in order to respond to the increasing needs for control and oversight of the modern state and extend the jurisdiction of the AGN to all public funds, irrespective of how they are executed.
- Enhance the professionalism and career prospects for civil servants and audit staff.

While it is necessary to advance the aforementioned reforms, some important improvements have nevertheless been made in the past few years since 2002, and which have enhanced the performance of the AGN. For instance, the number of permanent staff has been increased, while the number of short-term contractual staff has been reduced; delays in producing the audit reports of public accounts have also been reduced; in 2008, the AGN approved the public accounts for 2006 and is currently in the process of approving those for 2007. Furthermore, a policy which I, as President of the AGN, have promoted since the beginning of my tenure, has been consolidated, namely the publication of AGN's audit reports on its web page immediately following their approval by the AGN and transmittal to the legislature. This last point has had a tremendous impact, giving more public visibility to the AGN as the agency of external control, while allowing also for more and better social control of the process of government oversight by an informed civil society. The published reports have also become an important source of information and analysis for the press and other media as well as for other control agencies, at the national and provincial level.

In summary Dr Santiso's work not only amounts to a sharp and critical analysis of the strengths and weaknesses of AAAs; it also provides an insightful and courageous contribution to the study of the institutional context in which these agencies are embedded. It offers a road map for transforming these institutions into key actors in the effective control of public finances in order to improve the quality of life of citizens and their confidence in public institutions.

This now rests in the hands of those who decide to move forward with this necessary and unavoidable task.

Dr. Leandro Despouy
President, Auditoría General de la Nación of Argentina
Buenos Aires, Argentina
30 December 2008

Foreword by Terence Nombembe

It is with a great sense of admiration and pride that I note the emergence of significant research work in an area as critically important as the promotion of integrity, transparency and accountability in government finances. Most significant is the evaluation of the role, impact and effectiveness of autonomous audit agencies in this area.

The evaluation of audit agencies is not left only at the level of perception and perhaps untested facts about the weakness and inability of these institutions to fulfil their prescribed role, as well as the general criticism of their inability to curb corruption and reduce waste in government finances. This research is premised on a very important principle of building quantitative measures to evaluate the performance and impact of audit agencies on the manner in which governments manage public finances. There is indeed little comparative research on the functioning and performance of audit agencies, most of which is carried out by the auditors themselves. I would go further to confirm that even the research carried out by the auditors is to a large extent surreptitious and predominantly confined to a select group of audit agencies. I fully concur with Dr Santiso's observation that the emerging literature on fiscal and budget institutions is starting to address some of these shortcomings and is paying greater attention to the political economy of government auditing and financial accountability.

Dr Santiso's research has broader significance, beyond Latin America, informing policymakers seeking to reform audit institutions and strengthen government accountability. Its findings and policy recommendations also resonate in Africa, and with the struggle to strengthen integrity in government finances. The good news is that there is an increasing number and variety of organisations that have begun to demonstrate an active interest in this area. Even more pleasing is the fact that the audit institutions themselves are part of this emerging trend. The critical challenge is to curb and prevent corruption by strengthening the institutions of integrity, such as audit agencies.

In recent years, the United Nations (UN) and the International Organization of Supreme Audit Institutions (INTOSAI) have started reflecting on the *value and benefits of supreme audit institutions*. In 2007, in its congress in Mexico, INTOSAI established a working group to reflect on this issue and report back in 2010 at its congress in South Africa. This is a practical demonstration by the government auditing community of its commitment to quantify the value and benefits of independent auditing of government finances. Through this effort, audit agencies will lead by example and be transparent about the manner in which they respond to stakeholder expectations and citizen demands.

Another initiative that is gathering encouraging momentum relates to the stepped-up efforts by audit agencies to curb corruption. The next joint UN and INTOSAI summit in Vienna in 2009 will focus on this critical challenge of our societies. This will build on the impressive work that has been done by many institutions, including in Africa.

Representatives of African governments, intergovernmental organisations, the business community and civil society attending the First African Forum on Fighting Corruption held in Ekurhuleni, South Africa, in early 2007 adopted a far-reaching declaration and plan of action, endorsed by African heads of state and government in December 2007. They recognized that corruption is a global phenomenon, which prevails in both developed and developing countries. It undermines social cohesion and values, erodes the social fabric of African society, and impacts most profoundly on the poor and most vulnerable. It is encouraging to note that most of the recommendations contained in the *Ekurhuleni Declaration on Fighting Corruption* were reinforced by the Fifth Global Forum on Fighting Corruption and Safeguarding Integrity, in Johannesburg, South Africa in April 2007.

In October 2008, the African Organization of Supreme Audit Institutions (AFROSAI) agreed on groundbreaking recommendations that seek to respond to the very issues raised by Dr Santiso on the general criticism directed towards audit agencies, particularly in Africa. In essence, AFROSAI identified a need for aligning its approach to anti-corruption to that of INTOSAI, providing research, guidance and assistance to audit agencies on the ideal mandate they should have in order to take a proactive role in combating corruption, developing best practices on audit approaches in the fight against corruption. AFROSAI is a central element in the architecture of integrity emerging in Africa.

The research conducted by Dr Santiso extends beyond Latin America, to feed into and complement the work done within the public sector auditing circles, globally and in Africa. I am confident that the momentum that is building within INTOSAI will help respond to the expectations of the stakeholders and the challenges faced by audit agencies as articulated in Dr Santiso's research.

The timing of Dr Santiso's research is particularly opportune to understand the root of the challenges faced by audit agencies and to trigger the appropriate level of response to position audit agencies as indispensable pillars of integrity to improve financial governance and curb corruption.

Terence Nombembe
Auditor-General of the Republic of South Africa
President, AFROSAI
4 November 2008

Acknowledgements

The Political Economy of Government Auditing is based on the author's doctoral dissertation, *Auditing for accountability? Political economy of government auditing and budget oversight in emerging economies* (Johns Hopkins University, 2007) and research carried out in Argentina, Brazil and Chile between 2002 and 2005, as a research fellow in the Argentine Anticorruption Office in 2003, a visiting fellow in the Chilean *Contraloría General de la República* in 2004 and a visiting fellow in CIPPEC in 2005. Policymakers and auditors provided much of the factual information contained in this book. However, the views and interpretations contained in this book are mine alone, having been written in my individual capacities; and should not in any form be attributed to any of the aforementioned institutions.

This is the end of a long journey through knowledge. I am immeasurably indebted to my wife and life-time companion, Anja, for having taken it with me. I dedicate this book to her. Anja has been and remains an unshakable source of love, encouragement and support. In many ways, completing this book is remarrying her, reconfirming the vows we made to each other in the Andean sacred city of Cusco. In addition to enduring my long periods of self-imposed seclusion and permanent scholarly doubt, Anja's infinite love and unrelenting encouragement have improved this work in countless ways, inviting me to look at the bigger picture, at what counts most, and to search for what is missing. I am also immensely indebted to many other people who contributed in significant ways to shape my intellectual upbringing and thirst for knowledge, first and foremost my parents, Magdalena and Angel, and my brother, Javier.

I am immensely grateful to Riordan Roett for his patient academic steering and mentoring throughout my doctoral studies. I am also indebted to Linn Hammergren from the World Bank for her continuous support and unremitting exchanges during my academic journey, providing invaluable advice and thought-provoking stimulation. I am thankful to the Paul H Nitze School of Advanced International Studies (SAIS) for its financial support during my doctoral studies and the Latin American Centre for Development

Administration (CLAD) for awarding me a prize in public sector governance and anti-corruption research in 2005.

My exposure to the challenges of policy reform and institutional development in developing countries and emerging economies has provided an invaluable source of knowledge and inspiration, a reality check. My experience as a governance adviser to the UK Department for International Development (DFID) taught me priceless lessons on the realities of policy and the challenges of reform in emerging economies. I am particularly thankful to Mark Lewis and Sheelagh Stewart for giving me the space to pursue my research and for supporting my fieldwork. In Argentina, I am thankful to Manuel Garrido, Head of the Anticorruption Office (*Oficina Anticorrupción*, OA) of the Ministry of Justice, for hosting me as a visiting fellow in August 2003 and to Miguel Braun, Head of the Fiscal Policy Department of the Centre for the Implementation of Public Policies Promoting Equity and Growth (*Centro de Implementación de Políticas Públicas para la Equidad y el Crecimiento*, CIPPEC) for doing so in April 2005. In Chile, I am grateful to Gustavo Sciolla Avendaño, Comptroller-General of Chile, and Noemi Rojas Llanos, Deputy Comptroller-General of Chile, for hosting me as a visiting fellow in the Chilean Comptroller-General's Office in August 2004, as well as to Patricia Llanos Campos and Hernán Llanos Gonzalez for facilitating my stay.

My gratitude also goes to all those who generously volunteered their time and shared their knowledge to guide me through the intricacies of financial management and government auditing during the field research I undertook in Argentina (Buenos Aires, August 2003 and April 2005), Brazil (Brasilia, September 2003) and Chile (Santiago, January 2004 and August 2004). These include, in Argentina: María Isabel dos Santos Caetano, Roberto Gargarella, Nicolás Raigorodky, Damián Staffa, Nestor Baragli, Juan Carlos Duré, Nicolas Dassen, Gerardo Uña, Oscar Lamberto, Enrique Paixão, Alfredo Fólica, Juan Héctor Rodríguez, Irene Esculi, Francisco Cullen, Eduardo Trombetta, Juan Francisco Morey, Julio Rodolfo Comadira, Miriam Ivanega, Jesús Rodríguez, Roberto Martinere, Jorge Amado, Nicolás Ducoté, María Baron, Daniel Artana, Delia Ferrera Rubio, Eduardo Delle Ville and Juan Pablo Jimenez; in Brazil: Bruno Wilhelm Speck, Jose Eduardo Cardozo, Ernesto Jeger, Luiz Carlos Bresser Pereira, Fernando Henrique Cardoso, Renato Jorge Brown Ribeiro, Claudio Weber Abramo, Carlos Pereira, Bernardo Mueller, Charles Pessanha, Francisco Gaetani, Renato Jorge Brown Ribeiro, Claudio Ferraz, Carlos Mussi and Yasuhiko Matsuda; in Chile: Joaquin Vial Ruiz Tagle, Arturo Aylwyn Azócar, Mario Marcel Cullen, Alejandro Foxley, Edgardo Beoninger Kausel, Patricio Orellano Vargas, Pedro Ortiz Gálvez, Álvaro Ramírez Alujas, Gonzalo Sánchez García-Huidobro, Peter Siavelis, Juan Luis Correa, Eugenio Tuma Zedan, Luna Israel López, Carlos Pardo Bello, Eduardo Azócar, Sebastian Cox, Jorge Aedo Rosales, José del Río Duque, Jorge Frei Toledo, Omar Rebolledo Martínez, Martín Garrido Araya and Ricardo Martner; and in the rest of the world: Allen Schick, Guillermo O'Donnell,

Robert Klitgaard, Anne Mondoloni, Thomas Carothers, Rick Stapenhurst, Vinod Saghal, William Dorotinsky, Barry Anderson, Warren Krafchick, Pablo Alonso, Koldo Echeberría, Ernesto Stein, Carlos Scartascini, Richard Messick, Lynette Asselin, Geoffrey Shepherd, John Williamson, Nick Manning, Mark Kugler, Xavier Comas, Edmundo Jarquín, Eduardo Lora, Perez, Natalia, Ugo Panizza, Pierre Landell-Mills, Geoffrey Shepherd, Carlos Pimenta, Fernando Straface, Mark Payne, Beatriz Boza, Eduardo Morón, Martín Belaúnde, Nelson Schack, Margarita Seminario, Liliana Alfaro, Ben Reilly, Helena Hofbaeur, Aimee Figueroa Neri, James Wesberry, Julie Lynn and Michael Barzelay.

Julio Faundez' enthusiastic support for publishing this book as part of the *Law, Development and Globalisation* series of Routledge-Cavendish has been pivotal in making this book happen. At Routledge-Cavendish, I am immensely grateful for the editorial guidance and assistance of Colin Perrin and Holly Davis.

This book depicts my intellectual journey in the policy and academic worlds, initially focusing on the challenges of democratisation and the reform of politics, to the politics of reform and the strengthening of public finance management. Ironically, at the end of this journey, I stand where I started, recognising that politics matter. I have learned an invaluable lesson during this journey: the challenge of knowledge, making me aware of the gaps in knowledge and the fiction of false certainties. As French novelist Georges Batailles (1897–1962) once wrote, 'this world was given to us as an enigma to solve' ('*Ce monde est donné à l'homme ainsi qu'une énigme à résoudre*'). The thirst for knowledge is, at times, a frustrating exploration, which reveals the many gaps in our knowledge. However, scholarship is more an attitude towards research, rather than an accumulation of knowledge. Like sand in the wind, it is awareness to and curiosity for the unknown. It is an everlasting journey.

Abbreviations

AAA	autonomous audit agency
AGN	Auditoría General de la Nación (Argentine external audit agency)
AGR	Auditoría General de la República
AFROSAI	African Organization of Supreme Audit Institutions
ASF	Auditoría Superior de la Federación (Mexican autonomous audit agency)
CAIGG	Consejo de Auditoría Interna General de Gobierno (Chilean internal audit agency)
CBO	US Congressional Budget Office
CEFP	Centro de Estudios en Finanzas Públicas
CGR	Contraloría General de la República (Chilean external audit agency)
CGU	Controladoria-Geral da União (Brazilian internal audit agency)
CMO	Comissão Mista de Planos, Orçamentos Públicos e Fiscalização (Brazil)
CPMRC	Comisión Parlamentaria Mixta Revisadora de Cuentas (Argentina)
CRS	US Congressional Research Service
DIPRES	Central Budget Office
GAO	US Government Accountability Office
ICRG	International Country Risk Guide
IDB	Inter-American Development Bank
IFAI	Instituto Federal de Acceso a la Información Pública
IMF	International Monetary Fund
INTOSAI	International Organization of Supreme Audit Institutions
PRS	Political Risk Services
SFC	Secretariat of Internal Control
SIGEN	Sindicatura General de la Nación (Argentine internal audit agency)

SIMAFAL	Sistema Integrado Modelo de Administración Financiera para América Latina
TCN	Tribunal de Cuentas de la Nación (Argentine National Tribunal of Accounts)
TCU	Tribunal de Contas da União (Brazilian external audit agency)
MOP	Ministry of Public Works
NAO	UK National Audit Office
UNDP	United Nations Development Programme
WDI	World Development Indicators

In framing a government, which is to be administered by men over men, the great difficulty lies in this: You must first enable the government to control the governed; and in the next place, oblige it to control itself. A dependence on the people is no doubt the primary control on the government; but experience has taught mankind the necessity of auxiliary precautions.

James Madison, *The Federalist Papers* 51, 1788

Chapter 1

Introduction: budget institutions and financial governance

Constant experience shows us that every man invested with power is apt to abuse it ... it is necessary from the very nature of things that power should be a check to power.

Charles de Montesquieu, *The Spirit of the Laws,* 1748: XI, 4.

A good government implies two things: first, fidelity to the object of government, which is the happiness of the people; secondly, a knowledge of the means by which the object can best be obtained.

James Madison, *The Federalist Papers* 62, 1788.

Over the past decade, the fight against corruption and waste has gained prominence in the international debate on the reform of government, in both emerging and industrialised economies. In developing countries, concerns over corruption and calls for good governance impregnate the consensus on how to promote economic development, build effective states and reduce poverty. Calls for improving governance and curbing corruption are central to the global consensus on international development and permanent features in the controversies surrounding the effectiveness of foreign aid in poor countries. The successive financial crises that have hit emerging economies in recent years have highlighted the importance of responsible management of public finances, prudent fiscal policies and robust budget institutions. Repeated corruption scandals and recurrent allegations of misuse of public funds nevertheless question the efficacy of checks and balances and the robustness of oversight in public finance management. In many developing economies, the governance of the budget process is riddled with severe dysfunctions that imperil the integrity of public finances and increase the risk of corruption, ultimately undermining citizens' trust in democracy.

Anchoring fiscal discipline and budget responsibility are key challenges for emerging economies seeking to consolidate public finances and strengthen financial governance. Over the past decade, East and Central European countries have made significant progress to fortify the institutional architecture for government auditing and budget oversight, largely as part of the process of integration into the European Union. In developing countries in Africa and Asia, reform remains elusive and progress tentative, despite the increased support by international financial institutions and donor governments. Latin American and Caribbean countries occupy a middle ground, combining examples of partial success and pending reform. In Latin American presidential systems, the concentration of budgetary powers, the recourse to executive decree, and the frequent delegation of legislative prerogatives have all too often conspired against the anchoring of the institutions of fiscal control and financial oversight.

In this context, the quest for greater transparency and accountability in the management of public finances is of increasing interest and importance to politicians, policymakers, as well as foreign investors and international donors. Autonomous audit agencies (AAAs) have an important role to play in improving financial governance and discouraging corruption in the public sector.[1] They are an integral part of the system of checks and balances,[2] acting as what James Madison referred to as 'auxiliary precautions' overseeing government management of public resources. In Ancient India, the statesman and political philosopher Kautilya recognised the irresistible temptation of public servants:

> Just as it is impossible not to taste honey or poison that one may find at the tip of one's tongue, so it is impossible for one dealing with government funds not to taste, at least a little bit, of the king's wealth [...] Just as it is impossible to know when a fish moving in water is drinking it, so it is impossible to find out when government servants in charge of undertakings misappropriate money. Kautilya (c 350–c 275 BC), cited in Premchand 1999:148.[3]

AAAs are autonomous state organisations tasked with scrutinising public spending and overseeing government finances, usually on behalf of the legislature; they are 'pillars of integrity' (Dye and Stapenhurst 1998) acting as agencies of government restraint within the state. Their main task is to review the robustness and effectiveness of financial management, government accounts and control systems and, therefore, contribute to strengthening those. They help to improve transparency and accountability in the budget process, traditionally dominated by the executive branch, and ultimately to prevent government abuse and misuse of public resources. They audit government finances to provide reasonable reassurances of the reliability of government financial reporting.

Government auditing (internal and external) is a form of control and oversight. Public sector auditing refers to the application of control and oversight techniques to assess the integrity and reliability of government accounting and financial information systems. It is designed to ensure that the public accounts and other financial statements are a truthful reflection of management performance and the patrimonial situation of a public entity. As Speck (2000:27) notes, 'a critical step in the establishment of fiscal control as a specific function resides in the creation of an institution independent of the bureaucracy and tasked exclusively with the financial and patrimonial control of government.'

AAAs are a critical component of the system of checks and balances in financial governance, and contribute to anchoring the rule of law in public administration. They are a central component of what has been labelled the mechanisms of 'horizontal accountability' within the state. Agencies of horizontal accountability provide auxiliary precautions to check executive power, prevent its misuse and redress its abuse. Horizontal accountability refers to the capacity of state agencies to check other state agencies so as to generate mutual restraint. It is primarily concerned with the mechanisms of internal accountability within the state, what Mainwaring (2003:8) refers to as 'intra-state accountability', to ensure that the state restrains itself (Schedler *et al* 1999).[4] O'Donnell (1999:38–9) defines 'horizontal accountability' as:

> the existence of state agencies that are legally enabled and empowered, and factually willing and able, to take actions that span from routine oversight to criminal sanctions or impeachment in relation to actions or omissions by other agents or agencies of the state that may be qualified as unlawful [...] For this kind of accountability to be effective, there must exist state agencies that are authorized and willing to oversee, control, redress and/or sanction unlawful actions of other state agencies.

Horizontal accountability deals exclusively with those actions that 'are undertaken by a state agency with the explicit purpose of preventing, cancelling, redressing, and/or punishing actions (or non-actions) by other state agencies that are deemed unlawful, whether on the grounds of encroachment or of corruption' (O'Donnell 2003:35).

While they possess different mandates, the function of AAAs is to ensure propriety, safeguard integrity, promote probity in the management of public finances and contribute to fostering transparency and accountability in public sector governance. They are pivotal actors in the governance of the budget and the system of fiscal control, providing much-needed checks and balances in the management of public finances. They play an important role in the system of government oversight and accountability and, if effectively deployed, provide critical devices in the fight against corruption.

In performing their tasks, AAAs necessarily interact with the three branches of government. As oversight institutions often acting on behalf of the legislature, they participate in the cycle of legislative accountability, assisting the legislature in holding government to account for the manner in which it manages public finances. They also interact with the executive to ensure that their audit findings are effectively implemented, providing valuable information to government and senior management on the performance of the bureaucracy. A critical link in this regard is the interaction between internal control systems within the bureaucracy and AAAs. Lastly, AAAs entertain relations with the judiciary to sanction non-compliance and enforce accountability on government officials where cases of impropriety or corruption are uncovered. For example, in the court model, AAAs give a final verdict on accounts and are often endowed with self-enforcing sanctioning powers. Where such powers do not exist, the relationship with the judiciary system turns out to be a critical factor to enforce accountability.

The contribution of AAAs to public sector governance is defined both in *positive* (improving government financial management) and *negative* terms (preventing corruption and minimising mismanagement), often reflecting different legal traditions of public management and fiscal control. Depending on their approach to fiscal control, they have preventive, corrective or repressive functions (Barra 2002). AAAs control compliance with financial administration rules and regulations. Their deterrence effect on future misconduct or impropriety therefore depends on the credibility of their control.

There is renewed interest in the contribution of AAAs to the governance of the budget and the oversight of public finances, prompted by calls for greater transparency and accountability in government finances. It is amply recognised that independent auditing of public spending is critical to foster budget transparency, enforce government accountability, and ultimately restrain government's abuse of power and constrain executive discretion in the handling of the public purse. As Siavelis (2000:71) notes, 'at the root of both corruption and administrative inefficiency is government institutions' lack of oversight capabilities.'

External auditing of government finances occupies a critical juncture in executive-legislative budget relations. It should, in principle, contribute to strengthening checks and balances in public finance, restrain executive discretion and support legislative oversight. External auditing aims to preserve the integrity of public finances by checking government's compliance with the mandate enshrined in the budget law approved by parliament. It is thus meant to restrain executive discretion in public budgeting and improve fiscal transparency. While each external audit agency is unique and grounded in the country's trajectory of state building, AAAs participate in the cycle of legislative accountability.

The strengthening of oversight agencies has therefore become a critical feature of the reform of the state in emerging economies and the anchoring of the rule of law in the management of public finances. They were largely overlooked in the first stage of structural reforms of budget processes and modernisation of financial management systems that many emerging countries embarked upon in the past two decades (Santiso 2006a, 2006b, 2004c). This is starting to change. AAAs are now being rediscovered, due, in some part, to the new public management movement and the rediscovery of the budget as a key lever of change and reform in public policies. In developing countries, AAAs are acquiring greater significance in recent years partly because of the considerable increase in foreign aid and the changing modalities through which it is delivered. The emergence of budget support as the preferred aid modality puts further onus on the strength of domestic accountability systems to ensure that foreign aid is used for the purposes intended. Donors are thus providing increased support to the strengthening of developing countries' own systems of external auditing.

Although they have been receiving greater attention in the past decade, outside a small circle of public finance specialists, AAAs still remain one of the few unexplored institutions of the architecture of financial governance and budget oversight. There exists little comparative research on the functioning and performance of AAAs, most of which is carried out by auditors themselves. In particular, the political economy of government auditing and financial accountability has received little attention until recently. The emerging literature on fiscal and budget institutions, to which this book seeks to contribute, is starting to address this shortcoming.

In the course of the 1990s, the focus of the reform of the state has gradually shifted from the modernisation of public administration to the rationalisation of public finances, with a growing emphasis on improving the institutions of economic policy and fiscal governance. The renewed focus on the strengthening and reform of AAAs must be placed in this broader context. A broadening of the reform agenda in public budgeting is noticeable, reflecting the recognition of the limits of an excessive focus on financial management systems within the executive branch of government, such as finance ministries or central budget offices, and semi-autonomous agencies, such as central banks or tax authorities. It is increasingly acknowledged that reforming budgetary systems and financial accountability requires tackling the structural and systemic dysfunctions in the institutions and processes shaping the budgetary process. While first-generation budgetary reforms centred on strengthening the executive functions of government in the management of public finances, second-generation reforms increasingly emphasise the importance of transparency, oversight and accountability. This latter approach necessarily requires engaging with a broader set of institutions and processes beyond the executive, in particular the legislature, oversight agencies, the judiciary and civil society.

The reform agenda has embraced broader goals, blending macroeconomic discipline with social concerns and pro-growth efforts. In fiscal matters, from an initial focus on improving economic efficiency and achieving aggregate fiscal discipline, the reform agenda now emphasises efficiency, effectiveness, transparency and accountability (Schick 1998; Premchand 1999). In the fiscal arena, initial reforms have focused on improving the managerial functions of the executive branch. This was often achieved by granting the executive greater discretion over economic policy and insulating key agencies of economic governance from political interference, in particular finance ministries, central banks, and tax authorities. In recent years, as the result of the recognition of transparency and accountability, financial governance reforms now involve a broader set of institutions beyond the executive, in particular legislatures, oversight agencies and agencies of 'horizontal accountability' (O'Donnell 1998, 2003). It is now amply recognised that tackling structural dysfunctions in the public sector necessarily requires a broader understanding of the governance context and the influence of political institutions on fiscal performance. Experience and evidence suggest that political factors have a determining influence on public budgeting.

These evolving agendas have been shaped by the need to strengthen 'horizontal accountability' and improve the quality of democracy, as reflected in the manner in which public resources are managed and accounted for. 'Horizontal accountability' refers to 'the existence of state agencies that are legally enabled and empowered, and factually willing and able, to take actions that span from routine oversight to criminal sanctions or impeachment in relation to actions or omissions by other agents or agencies of the state that may be qualified as unlawful' (O'Donnell 1999:38).[5]

Many emerging economies are characterised by so-called 'delegative' forms of democratic governance and structural weaknesses in the system of checks and balances (O'Donnell 1994); this is reflected in a weak separation of powers, the concentration of budgetary powers, and the delegation and, at times, the surrendering of fiscal prerogatives by the legislature. All of these trends have conspired against the democratisation of the budget process by broadening the scope for government discretion and leaving it unchecked and unrestrained. This is especially dangerous when it comes to the management of public finances, undermining the credibility and predictability of the budget as a strategic planning instrument. Moreover, these factors have hampered the development of robust oversight agencies and 'horizontal accountability' institutions within the state (O'Donnell 1998, 2003; Mainwaring and Welna 2003).

The 'delegative democracy' argument is a potent tool for explaining the severe dysfunctions in budget institutions and the structural weakness of control, oversight and accountability mechanisms. The 'delegative democracy' argument was articulated by Guillermo O'Donnell (1994) to describe the nature of democracy and the quality of governance in Latin America. It argues that accountability gaps are particularly acute in presidential systems of government with a high degree of executive discretion in public budgeting and structural weaknesses in the mechanisms of internal control and external restraint. It also suggests that the risk of corruption tends to increase with the degree of executive discretion.[6] The consequences of strong presidents and weak legislatures on administrative efficiency and corruption have not been thoroughly analysed.

Thus, tackling structural dysfunctions in public budgeting necessarily requires a broader understanding of the politics of the budget process, including the institutions and incentives shaping it. Anchoring horizontal accountability in public financial management constitutes a critical challenge to the second stage of state reform in emerging economies and entails grappling with the political economy of public finances and more particularly the role of oversight institutions in the governance of the budget. The new-found interest in political economy analyses of economic reform and financial management emphasises the role of political institutions and electoral incentives in both the making and implementation of budget policy.

New institutional economics (North 1990) and political economics (Persson and Tabellini 2000, 2001) have improved our understanding of the influence of political institutions on economic outcomes. The advantages and risks of government's discretion, insulation and delegation in economic policy have been the subject of intense controversy and fertile debates in political science and institutional economics, providing valuable insights into the credibility of economic policy. The institutional perspective has nevertheless only started to be applied to financial governance and budget institutions. More research is required to decipher the interaction between formal and informal institutions and the gap between formal rules and informal practices which pervade the budget process.

In this context, AAAs have largely been overlooked in the reform of the budgetary processes and the modernisation of financial management systems that many emerging countries have embarked upon in the past two decades (Santiso 2006a, 2006b, 2004c). This is starting to change. Although they have been receiving greater attention in the past decade, outside a small circle of public finance specialists, AAAs remain one of the few unexplored institutions of the architecture of financial governance and budget oversight. There exists little comparative research on the functioning and performance of AAAs, most of which is carried out by auditors themselves. In particular, the political economy of government auditing and financial accountability has received little attention until recently. The emerging literature on fiscal and budget institutions, to which this book contributes, is starting to address this shortcoming.

Little is known about what determines the effectiveness of AAAs. While the role of audit agencies in curbing corruption and improving financial governance is increasingly acknowledged, developing countries and emerging economies struggle to reform and strengthen these agencies. There exists scant comparative research on what explains the effectiveness of independent auditing of government finances and the performance and institutional trajectory of AAAs in developing countries. AAAs remain among the least studied institutions of economic governance in social sciences and comparative politics. How relevant are AAAs for improving fiscal governance and curbing corruption? What explains the effectiveness of AAAs in emerging economies? Does the choice of institutional design and their legal tradition matter? How can AAAs be strengthened and reformed?

While AAAs are amply acknowledged as central actors in the governance of the budget, they are often weak institutions failing to fulfil their prescribed role, contested organisations criticised for their inability to curb corruption and reduce waste in government finances. In developing countries in particular, there is often incredulity regarding their ability to stand up to government, as they are often accused of being captured by the ruling party or, at least, viewed as acquiescent to the government. Admittedly, their task is a sensitive and often a dangerous one, in particular in contexts characterised by strong-men rule and authoritarian politics. Furthermore, AAAs are particularly hard-to-reform organisations, anchored in institutional and legal traditions. Their reform has proved particularly elusive in developing countries (Dorotinsky and Floyd 2004).

Building on earlier findings on the role of budget institutions in fiscal performance, this book models and measures the effectiveness of AAAs in emerging economies. It develops a quantitative index to evaluate their performance and gauge their impact on financial governance and fiscal oversight, based on a set of 10 Latin American countries. Resorting to agency theory and comparative political economy, it analyses the contribution of AAAs to mitigating the twin challenges of legislative delegation and government oversight in public financial management.

The research tests the explanatory power of alternative institutional arrangements for external auditing of government finances. It delves into the political economy of government auditing and budget oversight to explain the root causes of institutional dysfunctions, placing AAAs in the broader political and institutional context in which they are embedded. It weighs the influence of two sets of factors underpinning organisational performance: *internal governance factors* linked to the choice of institutional arrangements for independent auditing and oversight of government finances (what we term the institutional design hypothesis); and *external governance factors* linked to the broader governance context in which AAAs are embedded, in particular the nature of the political system, the dynamics of executive-legislative relations, and the culture of the public administration, in particular in terms of its adherence to the rule of law (what we term the political economy hypothesis).

The book looks at the three alternative models for organising the external audit function in modern states, illustrating each one of them by case study. Using a principal-agent analytical framework, it contrasts the institutional trajectories of AAAs in Argentina, Brazil and Chile, which illustrate the three main models of AAAs.[7] The first model, the board model, is one followed by the Argentine National Audit Office (*Auditoria General de la Nación*, AGN) which is an autonomous body linked to the legislature and with a collegiate decision-making structure. The second model, the court model, is followed by the Brazilian Federal Tribunal of Accounts (*Tribunal de Contas da União*, TCU), which is a quasi-judicial body with a collegiate decision-making structure similar to that of courts of justice. The third model, the monocratic model, is the one exemplified by the Chilean Office of the Comptroller General (*Contraloría General de la República*, CGR), which is an independent state agency headed by a single auditor-general with ample powers and prerogatives.

We argue that, while the choice of institutional arrangements for government auditing matters, political economy factors ultimately condition the effectiveness of AAAs. External rather than internal governance factors have greater explanatory power on agency performance, rooted in broader political factors, the nature of the political system, and the strength of the rule of law in government. The cause of agency failure is most often linked to either poor institutional design or adverse political economy (often a combination of both). Dysfunctions in government auditing and fiscal control are systemic, rather than agency-specific or linked to the choice of institutional design. What matters most, therefore, is the quality of the AAA's insertion in the system of fiscal control and financial oversight. In particular, the efficacy and fluidity of the agency's links with its main principal, the legislature, are critical to explain its effectiveness (or lack thereof). Strengthening external oversight of public finances necessarily entails revisiting the governance of the budget and enhancing the systems of checks and balances. Thus, AAAs face political constraints, as well as technical constraints.

The performance of AAAs thus depends on a series of intertwined factors, including their institutional arrangements, legal powers, resource endowments and institutional location. This research reveals the paradox of independence of AAAs: while AAAs have to be sufficiently independent to act autonomously, their effectiveness ultimately depends on the quality and fluidity of their relations with the other components of the system of checks and balances, and the strength of the rule of law in financial administration. As critical checks on government, AAAs are particularly vulnerable to political interference seeking to defuse and neutralise them. As we will see in this book, AAAs ultimately depend on the political system in which they are embedded and the balance of political forces; in other words: politics matter.

In many countries, AAAs require reforming, rather than strengthening; much reform has indeed occurred in recent years, often gradual and, at times, radical (such as in Argentina in 1992, Mexico in 2000, Nicaragua in 2000 and Honduras in 2002). We therefore also investigate the political economy of the reform of AAAs: Why and how do AAAs reform themselves from within or are reformed from the outside? Which reform strategy is likely to bear the greatest fruits? Reforming and strengthening AAAs have proved difficult. Paradoxically, AAAs are characterised by a 'hyperactive paralysis' as they seek to redefine their role in the architecture of fiscal governance and enhance their contribution to oversight of public finances; many reforms happen but little change occurs.

AAAs are *par nature* conservative and inertial organisations in institutional terms: their function is to preserve the law, their development is largely path-dependent and, as a result of their very nature, they are difficult to reform or reshape. External government auditing is, essentially, an institution in transition. In that evolving context, AAAs have difficulty recasting themselves in the broader architecture of public sector governance and fiscal control. This research agenda is particularly relevant to those few countries, especially in Sub-Saharan Africa, such as Angola or Mozambique, where they are being established. In such cases, the choice of institutional design is often a controversial one, but is strongly influenced by the legal traditions of the former colonial power. However, the analysis of this book reveals the limits of institutional design and constitutional engineering for improving the performance of external auditing of government finances.

The cases of Argentina, Brazil and Chile, which are examined in this book in more detail, illustrate three main pathways to reform (or lack thereof). While the Argentine case provides an example of failure *of* reform, the Chilean case offers an example of the failure *to* reform. Whereas the Brazilian case illustrates the promises of gradual reform based on successive adjustments, the Argentine case warns against the dangers of radical reform based on the institutional transplant of exogenous models. This book thus demonstrates that standard reform strategies based on institutional transplant of exogenous models and changes in the agency's internal governance are likely to fail. External factors, such as the functioning and the strength of checks and balances, the robustness of legislative oversight and fiscal control, and the balance of budgetary powers between the executive and legislature, matter greatly. Ultimately, as we will show, effective reform must be couched in the longer trajectory of institutional change of the country, the nature of its public financial management system, the strength of budget institutions and fiscal traditions, and, more generally, the strength of the state itself and its adherence to the rule of law.

These findings have important implications for policymakers seeking to strengthen financial governance and reduce fiduciary risk, as well as for donor governments and international financial institutions supporting these efforts through technical assistance and financial aid.[8] This book contributes to the emerging body of literature on the role of fiscal institutions in financial governance and, in particular, the role of oversight agencies in financial accountability.

The book is structured in eight main chapters. After this introductory section, Chapter 2 discusses the political economy of government auditing, highlighting the importance of the governance context for the effectiveness of external auditing systems. Chapter 3 looks at the institutional arrangements for external auditing. It discusses the concept of financial accountability, devises a conceptual framework and develops a quantitative index to gauge the performance of AAAs in 10 Latin American countries. The following three chapters compare and contrast the trajectories of the three models of AAAs, as applied to different political and governance contexts in Argentina, Brazil and Chile, respectively. Chapter 7 provides a comparative analysis of different models of AAAs and pathways to reform. It also presents the key findings and policy implications of the research. Chapter 8 concludes the analysis and indicates ways forward for further enhancing our knowledge and understanding of the independent auditing of government finances and the role of AAAs in improving public financial management and curbing corruption.

Chapter 2

Political economy of budget oversight and external auditing

Some officials handle large sums of money: it is therefore necessary to have other officials to receive and examine the accounts. These inspectors must administer no funds themselves. Different cities call them examiners, auditors, scrutinizers and public advocates.

Aristotle, cited in Day and Klein, 1987:9.

The modernization of government financial management is a central part of the institutional reforms and the modernisation of government in emerging economies. In recent decades, developed and developing countries alike have sought to reform the state and improve public sector governance following various strategies. There have thus been successive waves of reform, following the latest fads in development thinking, first focusing on civil service reform and subsequently on public management reform. The latest wave centres on the budget, both as a key policy process reflecting political arbitrages between competing priorities; but also as a key lever for the structural reform of the state and as a key driver for the modernisation of public sector governance.

This latest wave of reform underscores the importance of efficient budgetary systems for the effective delivery of public services. It underlines the critical nature of functioning oversight systems and their role in ensuring transparency and accountability in the management of public resources. As such, it also integrates political considerations, placing the reform of the budget in the broader context of the accountability relations between citizens and the state. Hence, the existence of modern, functioning external oversight systems matters not only to build capable states, but also to consolidate democracy. In Latin America, the functioning of democracy is criticised and contested because of the persistence of exclusionary politics, opaque public finances, and the lack of accountability of governments. External scrutiny of government and oversight of its finances represent the Achilles heel of Latin American democracies' struggle to consolidate.

Efforts to modernise fiscal control systems and budget-oversight institutions are integral components of public finance reforms. It is increasingly acknowledged that promoting external oversight of public finances necessarily entails enhancing the systems of checks and balances governing the budget process. This chapter delves into the broader political context in which AAAs evolve and the political economy of budget oversight and government auditing.

Modernising government through budget reform

The strengthening of external auditing thus participates in the broader context of the consolidation of democracy, the reform of the state and the modernisation of government. Any discussion of the role and performance of AAAs must therefore be couched in the broader debate on the modernisation of public management and the conduct of economic policy. As Haggard and Kaufmann (1995) note, successful economic reform entails a fundamental paradox: while the state is to withdraw from policy interventions and become leaner, the transition usually requires nimble and robust political institutions that are capable of implementing policy effectively and efficiently. It also requires a capable bureaucracy responsive to shifts in government priorities and accountable to citizens.

The renewed interest in the state has been prompted by the need to reform it.[1] Effective reform requires building the capacity to pursue it. As Gerald Caiden (1994:111) points out, 'countries most in need of state reform are least able to implement it.' Similarly, the renewed interest in AAAs stems from the need to reform them and improve their effectiveness. Many of the difficulties facing emerging economies originate from institutionally weak states as well as excessive executive power. The political economy challenge of building effective public sector capacity in emerging economies, where the civil service is a major source of patronage, is that it is precisely the institution tasked with carrying out structural reforms, the bureaucracy, that must be reformed (Geddes 1994; Grindle 1996; Tendler 1997). As Tanzi (2000a:445) argues:

> between their creation and their final implementation, fiscal decisions go through many stages at which mistakes, indifference, passive resistance, implicit opposition, and various forms of principal-agent problems may distort the final outcome

The central question, therefore, is not the size of the government, but the methods of government. While a rules-based bureaucracy does not necessarily guarantee an effective and efficient public sector, it is generally believed to be an essential enabling condition. Legal predictability and judicial security require rules (constitutions, laws and regulations) that are credible, predictable and consistently enforced. Therefore, for Tanzi (2000b:16), 'the quality of the public sector will depend to a considerable extent on the existence of controls and enforcement mechanisms.' In the area of government financial management, these mechanisms include internal control, external auditing and judicial review. From this perspective, compliance with rules and performance in achieving results are not antithetical; they are intrinsically linked.

In Latin America, structural reforms have been implemented to varying degrees of success and with varied intensities of eagerness (Santiso 2004a, 2003; Lora 2001; Lora and Panizza 2002). Reform failure has given way to reform fatigue. These trends have prompted policymakers to revisit the prevalent Washington Consensus (Kuczynski and Williamson 2003).[2] Nevertheless, and despite the general disillusion with the Washington Consensus' reform agenda, policymakers now accept that fiscal prudence and budget responsibility are the necessary (albeit insufficient) foundation for growth and development. This new-found conviction reveals a learning curve and the emergence of pragmatic policies blending social concerns with fiscal discipline. It is also reflected in the efforts to rationalise budgetary systems, modernise public finance management, and anchor fiscal responsibility.

Figure 2.1 illustrates the region's institutional weakness. It shows that the observed quality of governance institutions is below what would be expected considering the region's levels of per capita income. There are, nonetheless, important variations across countries.

In the mid-1990s, to palliate these shortcomings, second-generation economic reforms were pursued to tackle governance weaknesses and institutional dysfunctions. While first-generation economic reforms were aimed at

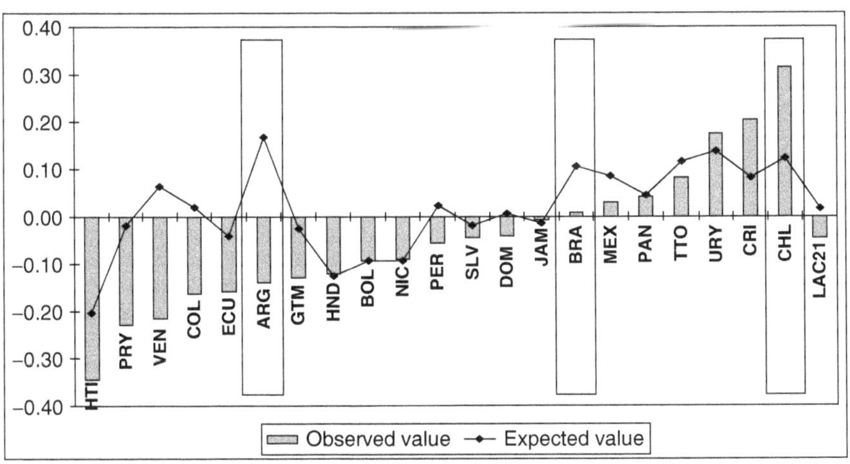

Figure 2.1 Institutional quality in Latin America and the Caribbean (2002).
Source: Adapted from Echeberría 2004 and Straface 2005.

stabilising the economy and launching structural adjustment, second-generation reforms have broader goals, seeking to strengthen governance and institutions (Naím 1995).[3] Table 2.1 captures the challenges of second-generation reforms, in particular in terms of the changes in the modes of governance and the methods of government they require.

The second stage of the reform of the state entails reforming the methods of government and the styles of policymaking. The very nature of second-generation reforms thus requires functioning institutions, and credible and predictable policies. While first-generation economic reforms focus on reforming policies, second-generation reforms seek to transform the institutions that sustain these. In other words, while first-generation economic reforms mainly concern the *content* of economic policies, second-generation reforms emphasise the *process* of policy implementation (or the lack of it). First-generation economic reforms have improved economic policy and fiscal

Table 2.1 From first to second generation reforms

	First Generation	*Second Generation*
Main objectives	Crisis management: reducing inflation and restoring growth; Contingency reforms	Improving social conditions and competitiveness; maintaining macroeconomic stability; structural reforms
Instruments	Drastic budget cuts, tax reform, price liberalisation, trade and foreign investment liberalisation, deregulation, social funds and safety nets, autonomous contracting agencies, privatisation	Civil service reform, restructuring of social ministries, judicial reform, modernising the legislature, upgrading regulatory capacity, improving tax collection, large-scale privatisation, restructuring central-local government relationships
Actors	Presidency, economic cabinet, central bank, multilateral financial institutions, private financial groups, foreign portfolio investors	Presidency and cabinet, legislature, civil service, judiciary, unions, political parties, civil society and media, state and local governments, private sector, multilateral financial institutions
Main challenge	Macroeconomic management by an insulated technocratic elite	Institutional development highly dependent on middle management in the public sector and on the cohesion of civil society
Main focus	Economic reform: economic liberalisation and market economy	Economic development: capable state and enabling environment

Source: Lavielle *et al* 2003:5.

discipline; they have not necessarily improved the performance of the public sector. The post-Washington Consensus nevertheless marks the rediscovery of institutions of governance and focuses on improving the *effectiveness* of public sector institutions and the *performance* of public policies. It underscores not only the need to restructure and rethink the state, but also to revisit the methods of government and the modes of governance. However, oversight institutions in general and AAAs in particular have been neglected by first-generation economic reforms and overlooked by second-generation reforms.

The reform of the budget is increasingly being considered as a pivotal lever for reforming the state. There has been a gradual shift in strategies for reforming the state in recent years, from an initial focus on public administration and civil service reform, to a greater emphasis on budget reform and public financial management. The budget is a central policy process, reflecting countries' policy priorities and delicate arbitrages between competing policy goals. Financial control and audit systems are among the weakest links in the public finance chain and a major impediment to good governance and financial accountability (Dorotinsky and Floyd 2004).

Heredia and Schneider (2003) offer a useful typology of public sector governance reforms, which include civil service reforms, managerial reforms, and accountability reforms. While civil service reforms have progressed most and managerial reforms are being tried, accountability reforms have just begun to be addressed. While these three types of reform often overlap in practice, their ultimate objectives are quite distinct. *Civil service* or Weberian *reforms* aim to enhance the management of human resources in state bureaucracies through the introduction of rigorous rules of career management. *Managerial reforms* are designed to increase the efficiency of the public sector by introducing market-based management techniques such as contracting-out, decentralisation and results-based management.

By seeking to enhance independent oversight of public finances, external auditing mainly contributes to the third type of reforms, *accountability reforms*, whose main objective is to enhance external control and internal restraint in the bureaucracy. In this model, 'the problem is excessive power in the executive administration, and the cure is greater democratic control, transparency, and accountability' (Heredia and Schneider 2003:8). Accountability reforms are designed to restrain executive discretion, constrain bureaucratic arbitrariness and prevent abuse. The role of legislatures, oversight agencies and civil society is critical in this type of bureaucratic reform.

New approaches to public sector governance have been developed to redress state failure and bureaucratic inefficiency. The trend in public policy is to move away from rigid compliance with formal bureaucratic rules, to the achievement of policy objectives, reflected in the increased focus on performance auditing over compliance control. The paradigm of new public management first articulated by Osborne and Gaebler (1992) proposes 'reinventing the state'; rather than dismantling and 'rolling back the state', through the privatisation of state assets, the contracting out of service delivery, and downsizing the civil service. New public management proposes a reform of the methods of government and the modes of governance. The objective is to reduce the role of the state as a direct provider and producer of goods and services and transform it into a regulator of public services.[4]

This shift in emphasis, in turn, increases the significance of oversight systems to ensure that government is held to account for its performance; it also privileges *ex post* forms of accountability, over *ex ante* methods of control; thereby giving greater flexibility to public managers in the implementation of policy. New public management proposes transforming the Weberian rules-based bureaucracy into results-oriented public management, making the transition from routine control to contractual delegation. Instead of emphasising procedures, new public management emphasises performance; instead of control through strict adherence with formal rules, it frames accountability based on results. Ultimately, new public management is about new forms of bureaucratic accountability (Echeberría *et al* 2005).

New public management is also transforming public budgeting and government financial management. It transforms existing norms, rules, processes and objectives of budget and government financial management. Results-based management is usually accompanied by performance-based budgeting, which tightens the link between performance and resource allocation by introducing systems to monitor public sector performance (Diamond 2003; Schick 1990). It has the potential to improve efficiency in the delivery of public services. It provides a useful input into strategic planning and medium-term frameworks.[5] However, as Moynihan (2003:1) notes:

> While performance information offers benefits to governments, it cannot eliminate the inherently political nature of budgeting [...] Performance information is just one consideration in the political process of budgeting, it gives decision-makers information they need for evidence-based policy-making.

Managing for results necessarily requires strengthening the mechanisms of oversight and accountability. By providing reliable and timely information on budget performance, performance-based budgeting is a potent instrument to improve transparency and accountability in government, and, ultimately, to inform policy choices. Financial reporting therefore has a strategic political meaning. The information that AAAs provide is critical in this context, certifying the reliability of government financial information and assessing the performance of the public sector.

Improving the way in which the bureaucracy monitors compliance with formal rules and measures performance with management objectives requires reliable accounting systems and credible auditing institutions. These must provide accurate and timely information on government finances and state performance in order to inform policy. However, while government accounting and internal auditing systems are essentially managerial functions designed to control the bureaucracy and enhance its efficiency, external auditing by independent agencies is designed to independently scrutinise government and hold it accountable for the manner in which it manages public resources.

In Latin America, as Schick (2003) puts it, new public management is 'an idea whose time has come but whose implementation has not'.[6] Evans (1995:17) argues that, in Latin America as in many developing countries, 'real bureaucracy is in scarcity, not excess [...] Ineffective states are characterized precisely by the lack of predictable, rule-bound, bureaucratic norms and relations within the state apparatus.' For Schick (1998:129–30), the critical challenge of state reform in Latin America resides in its reconstruction rather than its reinvention and achieving this requires a solid system of control and oversight:

> no country should move directly from an informal public sector to one in which managers are accorded enormous discretion to hire and spend as they see fit [...] Modernizing the public sector means establishing reliable external controls.

Reform progress in Latin America has been mixed and impact difficult to ascertain (Spink 1998), with countries struggling to establish first an effective state and a rule-based bureaucracy (Echeberría *et al* 2005; Bresser Pereira *et al* 2004). According to measures of bureaucratic efficiency developed by Longo (2005, 2003), Latin American countries perform poorly. This index, reproduced in Figure 2.2, reveals Latin America's underperformance, with a few exceptions such as Brazil and Chile.

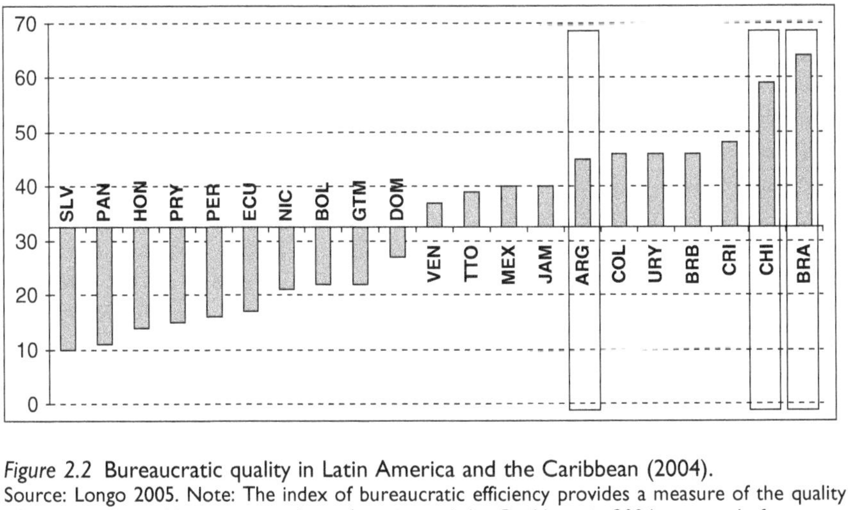

Figure 2.2 Bureaucratic quality in Latin America and the Caribbean (2004).
Source: Longo 2005. Note: The index of bureaucratic efficiency provides a measure of the quality of civil services in 21 countries in Latin America and the Caribbean in 2004, on a scale from zero to 1000. It is composed of five sub-indices measuring: (i) the degree of efficiency; (ii) meritocracy; (iii) structural consistency; (iv) functional capacity; and (v) integrative capacity.

The initial enthusiasm with new public management has thus progressively given way to scepticism about its general applicability. New public management tends to assume that some form of state capacity already exists, that 'policy is authoritative and that the budget is credible, in other words, it presumes the existence of formal budget institutions' (Schick 1998, 2000). It also assumes the existence of a rule-based bureaucracy or a state that has a fair degree of autonomy. These, however, are largely missing in most developing countries, which continue 'to suffer from a severe lack of control and oversight that renders performance-management a premature task.'[7]

Restraining government and controlling corruption

The renewed interest in oversight institutions in general, and audit agencies in particular, also emanates from concerns for improving governance and curbing corruption. Public sector governance is primarily concerned with two key dimensions of the state: capacity (the ability to design and deliver policies) and accountability (transparency, answerability and responsiveness to citizens).[8] The role played by governance institutions in economic policy has achieved the status of conventional wisdom, not only in economic history, but also in economic development (World Bank 1997). Growing theoretical and empirical evidence shows that political institutions decisively influence policy outcomes by shaping the incentives politicians face. Three institutional features of economic policymaking are particularly important for budget oversight and external auditing: the *exercise of executive authority*, the *insulation of economic policy formulation* and the *balance of power between the executive and the legislature in budgetary matters*. These variables relate to the central dilemmas of delegation of powers in economic policy. Undoubtedly, the concentration of executive power has allowed for the kind of decisive decision-making required to implement radical reforms by overcoming collective action dilemmas. Centralised executive authority helps overcome policy stalemates and executive-legislative deadlocks. However, it has also enabled impatient executives to circumvent institutional constraints. As Haggard and Kaufmann (1995:10) note:

> such discretionary authority is two-edged: if unchecked over the long run, it can undermine effective economic management by creating uncertainty. In the short run, however, centralization of authority has been crucial for economic reform in both authoritarian and democratic regimes.

A fundamental tension between democratic governance and economic reform concerns the styles of policymaking that have characterised the initiation of market reforms. The modes of governance and the methods of government that characterised first-generation reform are no longer adequate to sustain these reforms and launch second-generation reforms. Following the seminal work of Haggard and Kaufmann (1992 and 1995) and Carey and Shugart (1998), an important trend of the political economy literature argues that the styles of government and the modes of governance that enable the swift adoption and implementation of first-generation economic reforms are essentially antithetical to those required to embark on second-generation economic reforms and to consolidate democratic governance (Santiso 2004b).

The isolation and insulation of economic policymaking has implied the concentration of power in the presidency and the (*de facto* or *de jure*) delegation of legislative authority to powerful executives governing by decree. As such, the delegative nature of policymaking in many emerging economies has significantly altered the balance of power between the executive and the legislature, including in the budget process. For various reasons (a minority government, a fragile government coalition or legislative ineptness), legislatures concede governments' broad latitude to use decree powers, reflecting an inability or an unwillingness to oversee legislative delegation and restrict government discretion.

A central question concerning the value of government by decree is whether and to what extent the government is acting within the boundaries of the rule of law and the legislative authority delegated to it by the legislature. More often than not, executives exceed their delegated powers and usurp legislative authority, especially in public budgeting. Executives are largely left unchecked by legislatures with little powers, capacity or incentives to restrain them. This method of government tends to undermine the institutions of accountability over the long term (Haggard and Kaufmann 1995), legal rules and norms are bent and circumvented. Moreover, excessive discretionary power of the executive, through, for instance, the abuse of executive decree authority or legislative delegation of budgetary powers, is likely to increase unpredictability in government policymaking and undermine the rule of law in public financial management.

In Latin American presidential democracies, executive discretion is not only the preferred tactic to launch economic reform in times of crisis; it has also become the preferred method for governing the economy in normal times, turning into an 'addiction to decrees' in many countries. Argentina is symptomatic of the abuse and misuse of executive decree authority in public finances (Uña *et al* 2004; Ferreira Rubio 2000; Ferreira Rubio and Goretti 1998). In Brazil too, executive decrees were often resorted to until their use was partly tamed in 2001 (Figueiredo and Limongi 1997). As Oxhorn and Ducatenzeiler (1999:32) accurately notes, 'rule by decree, or *decretismo*, is a symptom of the weakness of state institutions in relation to civil society, rather than their strength.'

Government by executive decree, while an asset in the initial phase of economic reform, progressively becomes a liability in the second stage of economic reform (Bambaci 1999; Bambaci *et al* 2002). The central dilemma is then how to retain the advantages of strong executive authority while at the same time providing the institutional checks and balances that guarantee accountability and oversight. To a great extent, therefore, an objective of second-generation reforms is to reassert the mechanisms of accountability and the systems of checks and balances.

Independent auditing of government finances, as well as legislative oversight of the budget are precisely meant to provide constraints on executive discretion in public budgeting. A strand of the public finance literature emphasises the role of AAAs as 'veto gates' or 'accountability points' in public finance management, in particular through the use of *ex ante* forms of administrative control, contributing to preventing and controlling corruption. The political economy literature further argues that the existence of *checks and balances on executive discretion* increases the credibility of policies and government's commitment to those. Henisz (2004:1) demonstrates that 'checks and balances that limit the discretion of policy-makers reduce the volatility of government expenditure and revenue.' For Henisz (2000, 2004), 'veto gates' in policymaking act as accountability mechanisms checking executive discretion and thereby enhancing policy credibility. Panizza (2001:312) finds that 'checks and balances in the political system (measured by the index of political constraints) are associated with higher institutional quality.'

Oversight institutions in general and AAAs in particular have been neglected by first-generation economic reforms and overlooked by second-generation reforms. While important reforms have been introduced in the institutions of economic governance, such as central banks, finance ministries and tax authorities, AAAs have largely remained untouched. The renewed interest in government auditing stems, in part, from the recognition of their potential contribution to anchoring fiscal responsibility and improving public management in the second stage of reform.

The experience of Latin America clearly shows the limits of expeditious decision-making and the consequent need to strengthen the mechanisms of accountability and the institutions of integrity in the management of public finances (Santiso 2003, 2001). Numerous authors have focused on how political institutions can affect economic performance by establishing credible commitment to economic policies (Shugart and Mainwaring 1997; Mainwaring and Shugart 1997; Haggard and McCubbins 2001). A particular problem of public policy in presidential systems is the trade-off between the credibility of policies and the discretion of government. These questions are of special relevance to the management of public finances. They highlight the importance of political institutions in the making and implementation of public policies and the role of oversight agencies as credibility devices (Stein *et al* 2005). They underline the role of transparency and accountability to enhance the quality of public policies and the credibility of government financial management.

A commonly used proxy indicator for the quality of institutions is adherence to the rule of law. The strength of the rule of law is a key variable for explaining the quality of democracy and economic performance (Barro 2000). Rule of law in public finances refers to adherence to the rules and procedures governing the budget process and the management of public resources. External auditing, and in particular compliance auditing, contributes to anchoring the rule of law in public budgeting; it is designed to ensure that government complies with applicable budgetary rules and financial legislation. Figure 2.3 illustrates the quality of the rule of law in Latin America and the Caribbean in 2002. It reveals an important gap between the region's expected and actual performance. While Chile outperforms its expected value, considering its level of per capita income, Argentina and Brazil significantly underperform.

Recent research into the political economy of public policy shows that the effectiveness of institutional constraints on executive discretion is likely to be influenced by the nature of executive-legislative relations. There exists abundant empirical evidence linking well-functioning political institutions to better economic outcomes. The governance literature finds a strong correlation between the quality of governance and economic performance in an expected manner.[9] It shows that economic performance, as measured by per capita incomes, and the quality of governance, as measured by aggregate governance indicators developed by the World Bank,[10] are positively correlated across countries and over time.

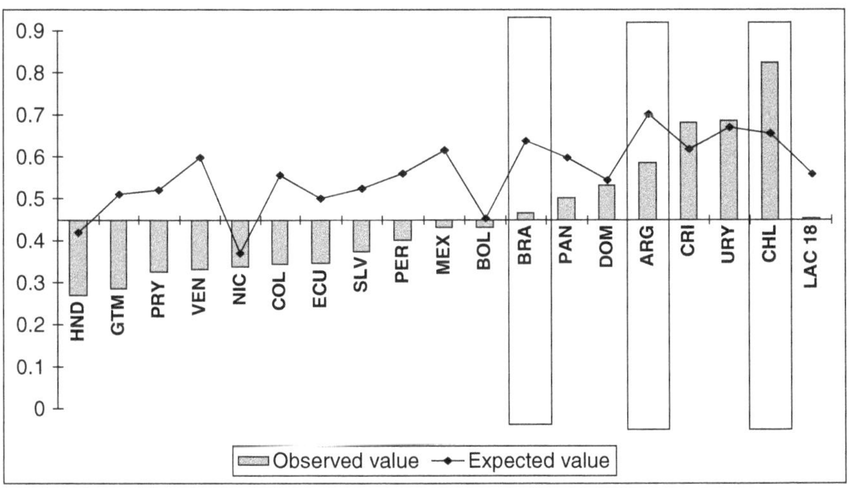

Figure 2.3 Rule of law in Latin America and the Caribbean (2002).

Source: Adapted from Straface 2005. The cluster evaluating the adherence to 'the rule of law' measures the extent to which agents have confidence in and abide by the rules of society. These include measures of the perceptions of the incidence of crime, the effectiveness and predictability of the judiciary, and the enforceability of contracts (Kaufmann *et al* 2002).

There are two important caveats to this research, however. First, most authors use a narrow set of proxy indicators for measuring the quality of institutions, essentially the security of property rights and the prevalence of the rule of law.[11] Second, while correlation is strong, causality remains uncertain and it is difficult to ascertain with confidence. Do political institutions promote economic growth or does growth spur institutional development? Existing evidence on forward and backward linkages between institutional quality and economic development is mixed. Chong and Calderón (2000) suggest that institutional quality promotes economic growth and, in turn, economic growth generates institutional quality, but that the influence of institutional reforms on economic performance takes more time than the reverse influence of economic growth on institutional quality. However, Kaufmann *et al* (2005:2) argue that 'most of the correlation between governance and per capita income reflects causation from the former to the latter.' Rodrik *et al* (2002:11) conclude that 'the estimated direct effect of institutions on incomes is positive and large.' In any event, bad governance leads to lower incomes.

A key concern driving the renewed interest in strengthening checks and balances in public finance management is the endemic corruption that still pervades many developing countries. Anchoring transparency and accountability in the governance of the budget is a central thrust of current efforts at strengthening the institutions of integrity. The governance agenda is particularly concerned with the pernicious effects of corruption on both the quality of institutions and the pace of growth. Corruption, generally defined as the abuse and misuse of public office for private gain, often leads to the privatisation of public policy and the capture of public institutions. Figure 2.4 shows the pervasiveness of corruption in Latin America and the Caribbean.

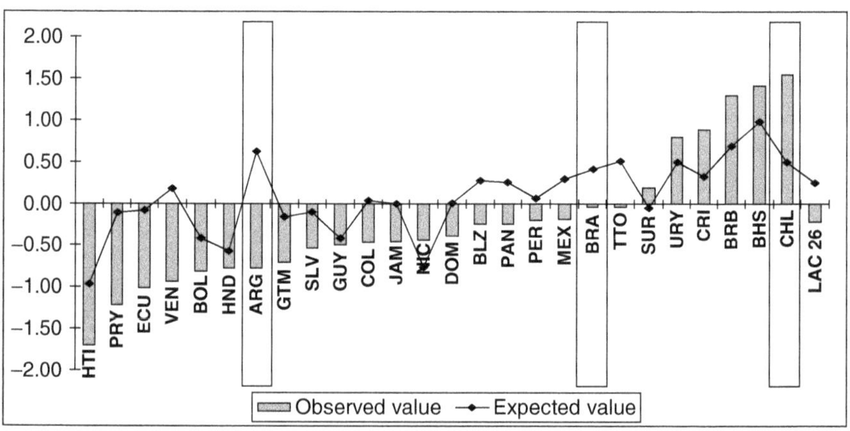

Figure 2.4 Corruption control in Latin America and the Caribbean (2002).
Source: IDB 2005:90.

Corruption is worse than it should be, considering the region's level of per capita income.

However, the corruption literature is generally more concerned with the consequences, rather than the causes, of corruption (Rose-Ackerman 1978; Mauro 1995). Indeed, Campos *et al* (1999) argue that the extent to which corruption is harmful to economic growth may depend on the structure of corruption, as well as its predictability. If corruption is predictable and reliable, it does not adversely affect agents' expectations. This 'predictable' corruption is thus viewed by some as less harmful than arbitrary corruption.

The anti-corruption agenda highlights the role of oversight agencies in the prevention of corruption. It singles out in particular the contribution of AAAs to the control of corruption and waste in public finances, as their mission is precisely to prevent, detect and deter corruption practices in government finances. Rose-Ackerman (1999) and Klitgaard (1988) show that corruption can be addressed through various types of institutional reforms, in particular through those aimed at restraining bureaucratic discretion and strengthening external oversight. According to Rose-Ackerman (1999:43), executive 'discretion must be both limited and managed' and the most effective deterrent to corruption is a credible, apolitical monitoring system. Agencies of restraint anchored in core state institutions such as AAAs, legislative committees, and independent judiciaries are vital foundations for effective anti-corruption strategies (Santiso 2007d). These agencies, however, are embedded in a broader system of checks and balances whose effectiveness depends on the effectiveness of the separation of powers. Understanding the dynamics of corruption and the politics of anti-corruption is critical to ascertain the relevance and impact of AAAs and the political economy context in which they are embedded.

An important insight of the comparative political economy literature concerns the limits of technical approaches to institutional reform. This research suggests that technical solutions alone cannot solve political problems. It also criticises reform strategies which narrowly focus on organisational change, rather than institutional reform and the 'rules of the game' underpinning organisational effectiveness. As Kaufmann and Kraay (2002:214) argue, 'specific institutional reforms need to depart from a narrow focus on traditional public sector management and an excessive focus on legal fiat or on rules-based measures.' Persson and Tabellini (2000) underline the decisive influence of political incentives, electoral rules and party systems on institutional quality and public-spending patterns (such as the size of government, government deficits, and the composition of public spending).[12] Models from this literature also predict that rent-seeking corruption in the public sector is likely to be more prevalent under presidential systems than under majoritarian electoral systems with large-district magnitude (Persson *et al* 2002; Lederman *et al* 2001).

Government auditing and budget politics

Budgeting is governing (Wildavsky and Swedlow 2001).[13] A broader political economy perspective is therefore required to fully capture the role of AAAs in the governance of the budget and the politics of public finances. As Scartascini and Stein (2004:2) underscore:

> understanding the budget process and the incentives of the multiple agents that participate in this process is a key ingredient for any fiscal reform seeking lasting results in terms of improvements in fiscal discipline and efficiency in the use of public resources.

The role, functioning and effectiveness of AAAs in the oversight of public finance and the governance of the budget can only be understood if placed in the broader political and institutional context in which AAAs evolve. These considerations include the balance of political powers, the dynamics of executive-legislative budget relations, and the informal norms shaping formal institutions. In particular, a political economy perspective uncovers the tensions and trade-offs between, on the one hand, the centralisation of budget systems and the concentration of budgetary authority within the executive and, on the other hand, the importance of the mechanisms of transparency, oversight and control in fiscal policy and financial management.

The governance of the budget is hereafter defined as encompassing the interests and incentives of individuals and institutions governing the formulation, approval, execution and oversight of the budget.[14] It includes four main stages: the formulation of the budget by the executive, its review and adoption by the legislature, its implementation by the executive, and its control by oversight agencies and the legislature. The budget is not only the legal authorisation by the legislature to the executive to raise revenue and deploy expenditure. It is also an instrument of control and accountability used by the legislature over the executive, and by the executive over the bureaucracy. Indeed, progressively the budgeting literature is broadening its scope, from an original focus on the dynamics of public budgeting within the executive (interactions between finance ministries and spending agencies), to the interactions between the executive and the legislature along the different stages of the budget process. This broader political economy perspective of the budget process is captured in Figure 2.5. Table 2.2 provides an overview of the main public sector agencies participating in the governance of the budget in 18 Latin American countries. It situates AAAs in the broader system of executive-legislative relations and the cycle of legislative accountability.

AAAs play a critical role in the budget process, especially during its latter stages. In particular, they help reduce the risks of excessively centralised

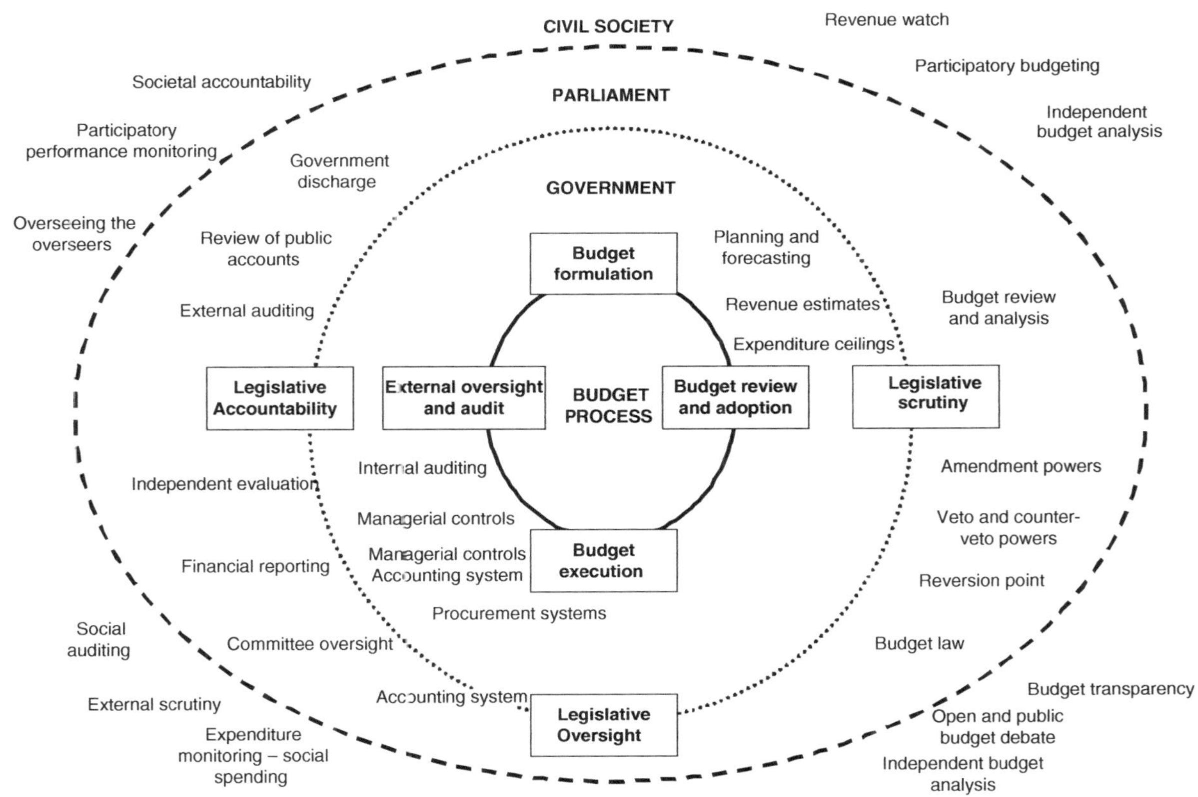

Figure 2.5 Political economy of the budget process.
Source: Santiso 2005a.

Table 2.2A Institutional framework of fiscal governance in Latin America

	Central budget office of the ministry of finance	*Integrated system of financial management*	*Accounting office*	*Internal audit agency*	*External audit agency*
Argentina	Oficina Nacional de Presupuesto (ONP), Subsecretaría de Presupuesto, Secretaría de Hacienda, Ministerio de Economía	SIDIF 1992	Contaduría General de la Nación (CGN), Subsecretaría de Presupuesto, Secretaría de Hacienda, Ministerio de Economía	Sindicatura General de la Nación (SIGEN), 1992	Auditoria General de la Nación (AGN), 1992v
Bolivia	Viceministerio de Presupuesto y Contaduría (VMPC), Ministerio de Hacienda	SAFCO-SIIF 1986	Contaduría General del Estado (CGE), Secretaría Nacional de Hacienda, Ministerio de Finanzas		Contraloría General de la República (CGR), 1990
Brazil	Secretaria de Orcamento Federal (SOF), Ministerio do Planejamento, Orçamento e Gestão	SIAFI 1986	Secretária do Tesouro Nacional (STN), Órgão Central de Contabilidade	Secretaria Federal de Controle Interno (SFCI), Corregedoria-Geral da União, Presidência da República, 2001	Tribunal de Contas da União (TCU), 1992
Chile	Direccion de Presupuesto (DIPRES), Ministerio de Hacienda	SIGFE 2000	Contraloría General de la República (CGR)	Consejo de Auditoria Interna General del Gobierno (CAIGG), Presidencia de la República, 1997	Contraloría General de la República (CGR), 1964
Colombia	Dirección General del Presupuesto (DGP), Ministerio de Hacienda y Crédito Público	SIIF 2004	Contaduría General de la Nación (CGN), Ministerio de Hacienda y Crédito Público	Consejo Asesor de Control Interno, Presidencia de la República, 1998	Contraloría General de la República (CGR), 1993

Costa Rica	Direccion General de Presupuesto Nacional (DGPN), Ministerio de Hacienda	SIGAF 1996	Contabilidad Nacional (CN), Ministerio de Hacienda		Contraloría General de la República (CGR), 1994
Dominican Republic	Oficina Nacional de Presupuesto (ONP), Secretaría de Estado de Finanzas (SEF)	SIGEF 998	Contraloría General de la República (CGR), Secretaría de Estado de Finanzas		Cámara de Cuentas de la República (CC)
Ecuador	Subsecretaría de Presupuestos (SP), Ministerio de Economía y Finanzas	SIGEF	Dirección de Contabilidad (DC), Ministerio de Finanzas y Crédito Público		Contraloría General del Estado (CGE), 2002
El Salvador	Dirección General de Presupuesto (DGN), Ministerio de Hacienda	SAFI 1993	Dirección General de Contabilidad Gubernamental (DGCN), Ministerio de Hacienda		Corte de Cuentas de la República (CCR), 1995
Guatemala	Dirección Técnica del Presupuesto (DTP), Ministerio de Finanzas	SIAF-SAG 1998	Dirección de Contabilidad del Estado (DCE), Ministerio de Finanzas Públicas		Contraloría General de Cuentas (CGC), 2002
Honduras	Dirección General de Presupuesto (DGP), Secretaría de Finanzas		Contaduría General de la República (CGR), Secretaría de Finanzas		Tribunal Superior de Cuentas (TSC), 2002
Mexico	Subsecretaría de Egresos (SSE), Secretaría de Hacienda y Crédito Público	SICGP 1985	Unidad de Contabilidad Gubernamental e Informes sobre la Gestión Pública, Subsecretaría de Egresos (SSE), Secretaría de Hacienda y Crédito Público	Subsecretaría de Control y Auditoria de la Gestión Pública, Secretaria de Contraloría y Desarrollo Administrativo (SECODAM, 1983-2003) Secretaría de la Función Pública (2003-)	Auditoría Superior de la Federación (ASF), 2000

Continued

Table 2.2A Institutional framework of fiscal governance in Latin America—Cont'd

	Central budget office of the ministry of finance	*Integrated system of financial management*	*Accounting office*	*Internal audit agency*	*External audit agency*
Nicaragua	Dirección General de Presupuesto (DGP), Ministerio de Hacienda y Crédito Público	SIGFA 1993	Dirección General de Contabilidad Gubernamental (DGCG), Ministerio de Hacienda y Crédito Público		Contraloría General de la República (CGR), 1979, 2001
Panama	Dirección de Presupuestos de la Nación (DIPRES), Ministerio de Economía y Finanzas	SIAFPA 1992	Direccion Nacional de Contabilidad (DNC), Ministerio de Economía y Finanzas; and Contraloría General de la República (CGR)		Contraloría General de la República (CGR), 1984
Paraguay	Dirección General de Presupuestos (DGP), Subsecretaría de Estado de Administración Financiera, Ministerio de Hacienda		Dirección General de Contabilidad Pública (DGCP), Ministerio de Hacienda	Auditoría General del Poder Ejecutivo, Presidencia de la República, 1999	Contraloría General de la República (CGR), 1994
Peru	Dirección Nacional de Presupuesto Público (DNPP), Viceministerio de Hacienda, Ministerio de Economía y Finanzas	SIAF-SP 1994	Contaduría Publica de la Nación (CGN), Ministerio de Economía y Finanzas		Contraloría General de la República (CGR), 2002
Uruguay	Oficina de Planeamiento y Presupuesto (OPP), Presidencia de la República	SIIF (1996)	Contaduría General de la Nación (CGN), Ministerio de Economía	Auditoría Interna de la Nación (AIN), Ministerio de Economía y Finanzas, 1996	Tribunal de Cuentas de la República (TCR), 1997
Venezuela	Oficina Nacional de Presupuesto (ONAPRE), Ministerio de Finanzas	SIGECOF (1995)	Oficina Nacional de Contabilidad Pública (ONCP), Ministerio de Finanzas	Superintendencia Nacional de Auditoría Interna (SNAI), Ministerio de Finanzas	Contraloría General de la República (CGR), 2001

Table 2.2B Institutional framework of fiscal governance in Latin America—Cont'd

	Parliamentary structure	*Legislative budget committee (lower and upper chamber, where applicable)**	*Legislative public accounts committee**	*Legislative budget office*
Argentina	Bicameral	FC: Comisión de Presupuesto y Hacienda (House); Comisión de Presupuesto y Hacienda (Senate)	FC; JC: Comisión de Parlamentaria Mixta Revisora De Cuentas de la Administración	no**
Bolivia	Bicameral	SC: Comisión de Hacienda (House); Comisión de Hacienda, Política Económica y Crediticia (Senate)	SC: Comisión de Hacienda, Comite de Presupuesto, Política Tributaria y Contraloría (House)	no** (Oficina Técnica Económica de Presupuesto, OTEP, House)
Brazil	Bicameral	FC; JC: Comissão Mista de Planos, Orçamentos Públicos e Fiscalização (CMPOF)	SC; JC: Comissão Mista de Planos, Orçamentos Públicos e Fiscalização (CMPOF)	yes*** (Consultoria de Orçamento e Fiscalização Financeira, House; Consultoria de Orçamentos, Fiscalização e Controle, Senate)
Chile	Bicameral	FC; JC: Comisión Especial Mixta de Presupuestos; Comisión de Hacienda (House); Comisión de Hacienda (Senate)	FC: Comisión de Hacienda (House); Comisión Revisora de Cuentas (Senate)	yes (Unidad de Asesoría Presupuestaria del Congreso Nacional, Senate)
Colombia	Bicameral	SC: Comisión Cuarta (House); Comisión Cuarta (Senate)	FC: Comisión Legal de Cuentas (House)	no*** (Oficina de Asistencia Técnica Legislativa, OATL)
Costa Rica	Unicameral	FC: Comisión Hacendario (National Assembly)	FC: Control del Ingreso y el Gasto Público (National Assembly)	yes
Dominican Republic	Bicameral	SC: Comisión de Finanzas (House); FC: Comisión de Presupuesto (Senate)	SC: Comisión de Finanzas (House); Comisión de Finanzas (Senate);	no

Continued

Table 2.2B Institutional framework of fiscal governance in Latin America—Cont'd

	Parliamentary structure	*Legislative budget committee (lower and upper chamber, where applicable)**	*Legislative public accounts committee**	*Legislative budget office*
Ecuador	Unicameral	SC: Comisión Especializada Permanente de lo Tributario, Fiscal, Bancario y Presupuestario (National Congress)	FC: Comisión Especializada Permanente de Fiscalizacióon y Control Politico (National Congress)	no
El Salvador	Unicameral	SC: Comisión de Hacienda y Especial del Presupuesto (Legislative Assembly)	SC: Comisión de Hacienda y Especial del Presupuesto (Legislative Assembly)	no
Guatemala	Unicameral	SC: Comisión Finanzas Públicas y Moneda (Congreso de la República)	SC: Comisión Finanzas Públicas y Moneda (Congreso de la República)	no
Honduras	Unicameral	FC: Comisión Ordinaria de Presupuesto (National Congress)	SC: Comisión Ordinaria de Presupuesto (National Congress)	no
Mexico	Bicameral	SC: Comisión de Presupuesto y Cuenta Pública (House)	SC: Comisión de Presupuesto y Cuenta Pública (House); SC: Comisión de Vigilancia of the ASF (House)	yes (Centro de Estudios en Finanzas Públicas, CEFP)
Nicaragua	Unicameral	SC: Comisión de Asuntos Económicos, Finanzas y Presupuesto (National Assembly)	SC: Comisión de Asuntos Económicos, Finanzas y Presupuesto (National Assembly)	yes (Dirección General de Análisi y Seguimiento del Gasto Público)
Panama	Unicameral	FC: Comisión de Presupuesto (Legislative Assembly)	FC: Comisión de Presupuesto (Legislative Assembly)	yes
Paraguay	Bicameral	FC; JC: Comisión Bicameral de Presupuesto; Comisión de Presupuesto (House);	FC: Comisión de Cuentas y Control de Ejecución Presupuestaria (House)	no

Peru	Unicameral	FC: Comisión de Presupuesto y Cuenta General (Congress)	FC: Comisión de Presupuesto y Cuenta General; and Comisión de Fiscalización y Contraloría (Congress)	no*** (Centro de Investigacion Parlamentaria)
Uruguay	Bicameral	FC: Comisión de Presupuestos (House); Comisión de Presupuesto (Senate)	SC: Comisión de Presupuestos (House); Comisión de Presupuesto (Senate)	no
Venezuela	Unicameral	SC: Subcomisión de Presupuesto, Comisión Permanente de Finanzas (National Assembly)	FC: Comisión Permanente de Contraloría	yes (Oficina de Asesoría Económica y Financiera de la Asamblea Nacional, OAEF)

Source: Author compilation, as of December 2004.

Notes: *: FC: full committee; SC: sub-committee of finance and economic committee; JC: special joint committee of both chambers of parliament; **: Under consideration; ***: Legislative advisory capacity not exclusively assigned to budgetary matters.

systems, especially in presidential systems of government, and contribute to enhancing the credibility of financial information. The budget literature does include consideration of the transparency of public finances, but tends to limit it to the veracity and reliability of government financial information (an important issue in itself). It nevertheless tends to pay lesser attention to the demand for greater fiscal transparency and the role of parliament and civil society. In that context, AAAs have a critical role to play to improve budget transparency. Their very *raison d'être* is to provide reasonable assurance on the reliability of government financial statements. External audits are meant to ascertain the accuracy and reliability of government accounts. The oversight role of legislatures, through its budget and public accounts committees in particular, is also critical to increase the demand for financial accountability. Recent research by Saporiti and Streb (2003) suggests that effective checks and balances in the budgetary process help curb political budget cycles.[15] Political budget cycles will be highest in countries with low checks and balances or low observance of the rule of law.

The 'common pool dilemma' of public finance argues that the actors of the budgetary game all have an incentive to over-spend and under-tax, leading to sub-optimal fiscal outcomes.[16] Even though politicians and policymakers may prefer government as a whole to maintain aggregate fiscal discipline in the interest of long-term sustainability, they face multiple spending pressures from specific constituencies. As a result, there tends to be an upward bias in public expenditure, not necessarily offset by increased taxes. The costs of extra spending are borne by all while the benefits are usually concentrated (Weingast *et al* 1981). The 'tragedy of the commons' can be minimised by assigning control over the budget to agents with incentives to internalise the costs of government programmes. This function is usually assigned to the finance ministry and, within it, the central budget office (Schick 2001). Under those institutional arrangements, typically enshrined in the countries' constitutions or organic budget law, the central budget office of the finance ministry becomes the guardian of budgetary rectitude and fiscal discipline.

Drawing on Alesina *et al* (1996), Stein *et al* (1998:3) argue that 'budget procedures which include constraints on the deficit, introduce hierarchical elements into the budget process, and are more transparent, lead to lower deficits and lower debt'. Institutional arrangements most likely to reduce fiscal pressures on public spending involve some form of centralisation of the budget process, provided by a strong finance ministry, negotiated fiscal rules and budget targets within the executive, as well as a constrained role of the legislature in the budgetary process.

There are, nevertheless, important risks associated with centralised budgetary arrangements. Four key risks can be underscored. First, hierarchical budget arrangements tend to allow for excessive executive discretion in public budgeting, especially in presidential systems. They thus impede the consolidation of the mechanisms of accountability in governmental financial management. Second, unchecked executive discretion in public budgeting undermines the credibility of the budget as an instrument of strategic planning. It hampers the consolidation of predictable budgetary processes with clear procedures and consistent rules. The combination of the constitutional powers of the president, the use and abuse of decree authority by the executive, the delegation of budgetary powers by the legislature and the constraints of legislative budgetary prerogatives, all contribute to reinforcing executive dominance in the budget process and lessen legislative oversight.

Third, hierarchical budget institutions tend to over-emphasise aggregate fiscal discipline over other goals of public budgeting. As described by Schick (1998), the three main objectives against which the performance of public finance management systems should be evaluated are: aggregate fiscal discipline; allocative efficiency or strategic prioritisation of public expenditure; and operational efficiency, reflected in the efficient and effective use of resources in the implementation of strategic priorities.

Fourth, centralised budgetary systems tend to be less transparent, which makes fiscal discipline and expenditure control harder to achieve. This is a particularly acute problem considering the quasi-monopoly of the executive on public financial information. Legislatures' access to budgetary information is believed to be a critical factor to enhance financial scrutiny (Wehner 2004). The extent to which the legislature has access to reliable and timely budget information and budget research capacity, especially through quality and timely audit information, is a major determinant of the effectiveness of government financial accountability.

Budget transparency is particularly deficient in Latin America; indeed, it is the weakest feature of budget systems in the region. There exists an important gap between formal rules and informal practices, between the quality of the legal framework for public budgeting and adherence to it (Lavielle *et al* 2003). According to the survey data reproduced in Tables 2.3 and 2.4, while the quality of the legal framework in Argentina, Brazil, Chile, Mexico and Peru is generally sound, perceptions of budget transparency are poor.

Table 2.3 Budget transparency in Latin America (aggregate index)

Country	*Assessment of legal framework*	*Perceptions index*	*Aggregate index (unweighted)*
Argentina	7.0	5.1	6.1
Brazil	6.4	5.1	5.8
Chile	7.3	5.9	6.6
Mexico	5.1	5.0	5.1
Peru	6.0	3.7	4.9

Source: Lavielle *et al* 2003:5.

Note: The index of perceptions is an average on a scale of 1 to 10, of not transparent to transparent.

Table 2.4 Budget transparency in Latin America (disaggregate index)

	Phases of the budget (scale 1–5)				
	Most transparent				*Least transparent*
Formulation	Chile	Mexico	Argentina	Peru	Brazil
Average	3.36	2.67	2.57	2.47	2.47
Approval	Chile	Argentina	Brazil	Mexico	Peru
Average	2.80	2.79	2.63	2.44	2.39
Execution	Chile	Argentina	Brazil	Peru	Mexico
Average	3.16	2.71	2.40	2.38	2.36
Oversight and auditing	Chile	Brazil	Mexico	Argentina	Peru
Average	3.07	2.31	2.27	2.19	1.89
Economic information	Chile	Argentina	Brazil	Mexico	Peru
Average	3.53	3.15	3.15	2.75	2.66

Source: Based on Lavielle *et al* 2003:3.

This research reveals, in particular, that legislative oversight and external auditing are perceived as particularly deficient. These are precisely the phases of the budget in which the parliament ought to be most assertive.

Lack of fiscal transparency and budget accuracy has been shown to have adverse consequences on financial management, corruption control, and government accountability. According to the International Monetary Fund (IMF), 'transparency in government operations is widely regarded as an important precondition for macroeconomic fiscal sustainability, good governance, and overall fiscal rectitude' (Kopits and Craig 1998:1). There are several ways of enhancing transparency, such as establishing more transparent procedures, which generate more and better fiscal information. Transparency is also increased by the possibility of independently verifying public accounts. This is where AAAs have an important role to play.

One approach to assessing the role of external audit in the broader governance context is the principal-agent framework applied to public finance management. Two principal-agent relationships are apparent in terms of the transparency challenges in public finance management. The first is embedded in the principal-agent relations between the government and the bureaucracy, where the former needs to oversee the latter. This challenge concerns the need to anchor fiscal transparency within the bureaucracy. The second principal-agent relationship concerns the executive and the legislature and the oversight of the former by the latter.

The legislature, as the principal of its agent, the executive, needs to have access to relevant information in a timely and effective manner in order to exercise its oversight role. As mentioned previously, its oversight of government financial management entails important monitoring costs as a result of the asymmetries of information with the executive. Thus, AAAs, by providing information on government financial management, help fill this gap. Nonetheless, when fiscal information is available it is not necessarily acted upon. This finding suggests that it is action on existing information by budget-oversight institutions that is lagging, not necessarily the availability of information itself.

The mechanisms to ensure that the budget has been complied with, both in formal and substantive terms, have indeed been the subject of limited scrutiny. 'Auxiliary precautions', to paraphrase James Madison (1788), are required to ensure both that the fiscal information provided by the executive is credible and reliable and that budget outcomes adequately comply with the provisions of the budget law as approved by the legislature. Audit systems perform these critical functions; internal audit systems within the executive (in the context of government-bureaucracy principal-agent relationships) and external audit systems between the executive and the legislature (in the context of legislature-government principal-agent dynamics).

The literature distinguishes between two approaches to legislative oversight and bureaucratic control, which can be applied to the analysis of AAAs: 'police patrol' and 'fire-alarm' oversight. In the first type of oversight, the legislature actively seeks evidence of misbehaviour by government agencies, looking for trouble as a method of control as does a prowling patrol car. In fire-alarm oversight, the legislature waits for signs that agencies are improperly executing policy and uses complaints to trigger concern that the agency is misbehaving. Police-patrol oversight is a form of routine oversight, while fire-alarm oversight is essentially ad hoc.

Routine 'police patrol' oversight and ad hoc 'fire alarm' oversight have both preventive and corrective functions. 'Police patrol' oversight tends to emphasise *ex ante* control seeking to deter corruption by detecting it, while 'fire alarm' oversight emphasises *ex post* control reacting to evidence of corruption after the fact. While mostly complementary, both types of oversight have different logics, one of restraint and the other of sanction. In the field of public finances, external auditing is a form of routine 'police patrol' oversight, while legislative enquiry commissions are a form of ad hoc 'fire alarm' oversight.

Wehner (2004) also distinguishes between *ex ante* and *ex post* financial scrutiny by legislatures, noting that legislatures in parliamentary systems following the Westminster model tend to develop few capacities for *ex ante* budget oversight but strong capacities for *ex post* financial scrutiny, in particular via strong legislative public accounts committees and effective AAAs. Presidential systems, on the other hand, tend to put greater emphasis on *ex ante* oversight and compliance control, reflecting greater competition and conflict between the executive and the legislature.

Morgenstern and Manzetti (2003:135) argue that legislative budget oversight depends on the 'degree to which the legislative branch has developed the technocratic institutions necessary for ensuring the financial and administrative accountability of the president and executive-controlled bureaucratic agencies'. Whether the legislature has developed these institutions depends on legislators having the political incentives to use them effectively. In other words, for accountability to be effective, the legislature needs both the means and motives for exercising oversight effectively.

Routine oversight is inherently difficult to mobilise, a factor that negatively affects the effectiveness of AAAs and the routine 'police patrol' oversight they provide. Legislators tend to have fewer incentives to engage in 'police patrol' oversight, given its high political costs and usually low return (McCubbins and Schwartz 1987). They have greater incentives to engage in oversight that affects them directly, that is, oversight that has an effect on their constituencies and their potential for re-election. A 'fire alarm' system is more politically attractive because it tends to be more visible and attract media attention. Furthermore, while both a 'fire alarm' and 'police patrol' oversight are equally informative, legislators will prefer the former because it enables them to avoid paying the costs associated with routine 'police patrol' oversight and delegating some of their powers to autonomous oversight agencies (McCubbins and Schwartz 1987). However, 'governmental oversight deals not only with outright, direct, and deliberate corruption but also with inefficiency rooted in simple bureaucratic bottlenecks and misunderstanding of the law' (Siavelis 2002:76). Routine oversight is required not only to punish corruption when it occurs, but also to deter it and improve public management, especially in technically difficult terrains such as monetary policy, fiscal policy or public budgeting. The routine oversight performed by AAAs is indeed critical for making legislative oversight work.

Government accountability and public finances

The delegation of powers and resources from principals to agents creates a desire in the principal for a flow of accountability in the opposite direction. As Monks and Minow (1991:75) remark, 'accountability is what makes delegate authority legitimate; without accountability, there is nothing to prevent abuse.' Accountability is primarily concerned with how to control the exercise of power in order to establish credible constraints on the abuse of power and checks on the misuse of authority. Accountability is, therefore, 'the institutionalization of mistrust' (O'Donnell 2003).

Auditing systems help mitigate the accountability dilemmas of legislative and bureaucratic delegation by providing assurances to the principal (the legislature) that the terms of the delegation have been complied with, both in form (compliance with rules and procedures) and in substance (compliance with objectives and performance). External auditing of government finances as well as legislative oversight of the budget are to provide constraints on executive discretion in public budgeting. A strand of the public-finance literature emphasises the role of AAAs as veto gates in public-finance management, in particular through the use of *ex ante* forms of administrative control.

Some authors argue that enforcement and sanctions are intrinsic elements of accountability. As Schedler (1999:17) underscores, 'inconsequential accountability is not accountability at all.' These authors argue that the credibility of any restraint mechanism rests on its direct enforceability as a self-binding mechanism (Schedler 1999:1). According to this view, to be credible, AAAs should be endowed with sanctioning powers, which they can impose directly and autonomously without the intervention of another state power or agency.

Others, however, distinguish between *direct* and *indirect* sanctioning powers, noting that 'some mechanisms of accountability rely exclusively on answerability without necessarily having the capacity to impose sanctions' (Mainwaring 2003:13). Thus, according to this view, while accountability cannot exist without means of redress, it does not necessarily require direct, legally ascribed sanctioning power. Core accountability relations therefore do not necessarily entail the power to impose sanctions *directly*. Rectification can be achieved *indirectly* by the sanctions enforced by those state agencies possessing sanctioning powers.

While accountability does entail the power to sanction non-compliance with rules, oversight is primarily concerned with controlling, informing and restraining. We argue that AAAs are *oversight agencies* or agencies of restraint, and not *accountability institutions*. According to this view, audit agencies essentially act as auxiliary institutions to legislatures, which are ultimately responsible for enforcing accountability and imposing political sanctions on the government. The theory holds that in an ideal world, political accountability for corruption and mismanagement should be enforced by the legislature on the executive, while managerial accountability for waste and underperformance ought to be enforced by the executive on the bureaucracy.

These agencies need to function in synergy to have a systemic impact. However, the central paradox of oversight agencies resides in the fact that their effectiveness depends both on their autonomy, which is required to effectively pursue their control and restraining functions, and on their linkages to the other agencies part of the system of accountability within the state. Ultimately, accountability is an integrated system of control whose credibility depends on the quality of the linkages and synergies between the different components of the system of checks and balances.

Realistic expectations about the effectiveness of each agency taken individually and acting in isolation are thus warranted.

However, AAAs are also linked to citizens in that they derive some of their power from the weight of public opinion and the media. The information they make available to the public informs citizens regarding agency performance and abuses, and their investigations and prosecutions can potentially influence voting. In fact, the trend is for AAAs to develop a direct relationship with society, reflected in the pressure to make their audit findings publicly available. The debate on the publicity of audit findings nevertheless raises the question of who is the ultimate principal of AAAs, the legislature or the public. The recent emphasis on societal accountability and citizen oversight further advocates the role of AAAs as agents of the public.

Accountability relations in public finances differ substantially in presidential and parliamentary systems of government. Unlike in parliamentary systems where the accountability relationship is broadly linear from the electorate to the bureaucracy, presidential systems are characterised by triangular relationships of delegation and accountability. Figure 2.6 illustrates the dynamics of government accountability and offers a simple framework to understand accountability relations in presidential systems. It situates auditing systems in the broader system of delegation and accountability in public finance management. Internal audit systems provide government with

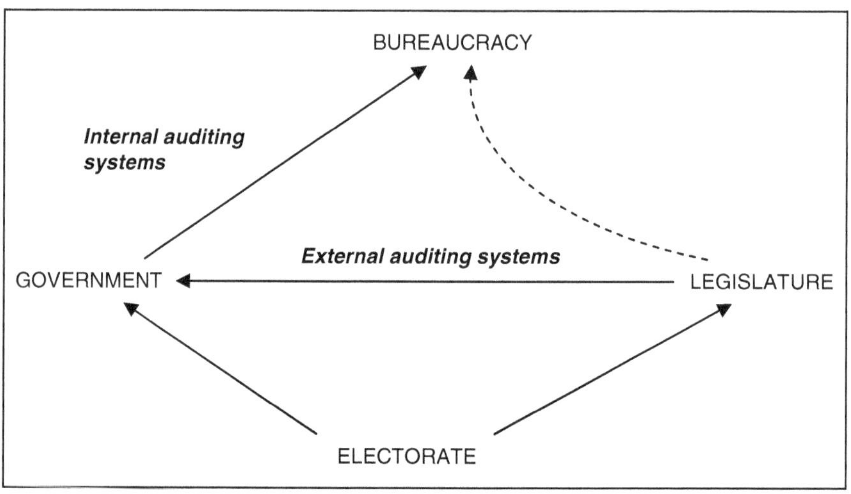

Figure 2.6 Delegation and accountability in presidential systems.
Source: Adapted from Moreno et al (2003:88). Arrows indicate the direction of a delegation relationship running from principal to agent. Accountability relationships run in the opposite direction, with agent accountable to the principal; double-headed arrows indicate horizontal exchange.

an oversight mechanism to control the bureaucracy, while external auditing systems provide the legislature with an instrument to check the executive.

Countries seeking to strengthen government auditing as a whole typically encounter two sets of problems: (i) how to coordinate internal control systems within the executive; and (ii) how internal and external controls relate to each other (Diamond 2002a). AAAs greatly rely on the information internal audit units provide them with; and therefore the institutional arrangements for organising internal audit systems affect the credibility of AAAs. Nevertheless, the choice of institutional arrangements varies greatly between countries. To address the coordination problem, several countries, such as Argentina, Chile, Brazil and Mexico, have created central coordination mechanisms to oversee departmental and agency internal control systems. These are often established within the purview of the finance ministry or the presidency (as in Chile) or as semi-autonomous agencies (as in Argentina). In a few cases, such as Peru, responsibility for coordinating and supervising internal control systems has been transferred to the external audit agency.

In Argentina, the 1992 law on financial administration created the superintendence for internal audit and control, the *Sindicatura General de la Nación* (SIGEN), under the authority of the presidency. In Brazil, since 2002, the *Controladoria-Geral da União* (CGU) supervises the internal control system. In Chile, a central supervisory agency for the internal control system was established in 1997, the *Consejo de Auditoría Interna General de Gobierno* (CAIGG), as part of President Frei's pledge to enhance internal controls within the public sector upon assuming office in 1994. The CAIGG is an advisory body to the president composed of seven advisers and a secretary-general. Between 1994 and 2001, 130 internal control and audit units were created, totalling 200 such units now operational. Nevertheless, the Chilean external audit agency continues to oversee the government accounting system.

In Venezuela, the 1995 organic law for financial administration transferred the internal audit function to government agencies under the supervision of a superintendence for internal audit and control (Moreno 2001). The external audit agency assumed the standard role of *ex post* external auditing. The new organic law of the system of fiscal control of 2001 and the organic law for financial administration of 2000 confirmed this institutional arrangement. Similarly, in Colombia internal auditing was revamped in the early 1990s and, in 1996, an advisory council for internal control was created as a consultative organ of the president's office. Conversely, in Peru, the new organic law for the national system of control adopted in 2002 has strengthened the role of the external audit agency as the supervisory body of the internal audit function.[17]

The strengthening of external auditing systems in recent years inserts itself in the intensification and rationalisation of legislative budget oversight.

The experience of the US is instructive. The US Congress has significantly developed its institutional capacity to oversee budget execution through the Congressional Research Service (CRS), Congressional Budget Office (CBO) and the Government Accountability Office (GAO). The GAO, then called the General Accounting Office, was established in 1921, as part of the modernisation of the budgetary process set forward by the Budget and Accounting Act of the same year to address the disarray in federal public finances after the First World War. It is an independent, non-partisan agency that supports the legislature in its oversight of government finances. Often referred to as a 'Congressional watchdog', it was established 'to support the Congress in meeting its Constitutional responsibilities and to help improve the performance and ensure the accountability of the federal government for the benefit of the American people.'[18]

Its role has nevertheless significantly evolved over the years, as a result of conflicts between the executive and the legislature over the budget. Successive reforms of the US budgetary system follow a pendulum logic between executive discretion and legislative oversight in the distribution of budgetary powers. A feature of recent reforms has been the emphasis on increasing financial oversight and external scrutiny of the government's performance, especially since the adoption of the Government Performance and Results Act in 1993 and the Government Management Reform Act in 1994. The legislature continuously sought more and better information on how well government programs were meeting their stated objectives. As Bourdin (2001) notes, the objective was not gaining greater budgetary powers for the legislature, which are already extensive, but rather increased legislative capacities to scrutinise the budget and oversee government performance. To reflect its new role, the GAO's name was changed to the Government Accountability Office in 2004.

Reforming external audit agencies

External auditing arrangements exhibit important differences across countries and over time. They continuously evolve, sometimes in radical ways following abrupt changes of systems, and sometimes in piecemeal fashion reflecting gradual changes within systems. In general, however, institutional arrangements for external auditing are 'sticky' and path dependent. They only evolve gradually and show a great deal of inertia. Except in a few cases of radical reform such as in Argentina in 1992 and in Mexico in 2000, changes tend to occur *within* existing systems.

Latin American countries are symptomatic of the many dysfunctions of fiscal control systems. The nature and functioning of presidential political systems have prevented the consolidation of robust institutions of restraint, oversight and accountability. Latin American presidential systems of government experiment with a democratic deficit, which is particularly acute in public budgeting and financial governance. Latin American 'delegative democracies' (O'Donnell 1994) are characterised by important failures in the systems of checks and balances, which undermine the mechanisms of oversight and accountability. The concentration of budgetary powers in the executive, the recourse to executive decrees for managing public finances, and the frequent delegation of legislative budget prerogatives conspire against the anchoring of transparency, oversight, and accountability in public financial management.

While the *raison d'être* of AAAs is not questioned, their relevance and effectiveness is. In Latin America, AAAs are often discredited and contested organisations because of their perceived inability to dent endemic corruption and improve the efficacy of public spending. Moreover, they are particularly hard-to-reform organisations, showing great difficulty in adjusting to shifting executive-legislative budget relations and adapting to new trends in public sector governance. Nevertheless, financial control, accounting systems and auditing structures in Latin America have undergone important reforms over the past decade in the context of the modernisation of financial governance (Diamond 2002b). Table 2.5 provides an overview of recent reforms, including the revision of organic budget laws and financial administration regulations, the adoption of budget transparency laws and fiscal responsibility legislation, or the review of fiscal control and government auditing frameworks. Partly at the insistence of international financial institutions, Latin American countries have significantly upgraded their financial information, management and accounting systems (Dorotinsky and Matsuda 2002; Asselin 1999).[19] Important reforms have occurred in Argentina, Brazil, Chile, Colombia, Costa Rica, Ecuador, El Salvador, Guatemala, Mexico, Nicaragua, Panama, Paraguay, Peru, Dominican Republic, Uruguay and Venezuela.

This reform effort is the latest wave of reform. A first wave occurred in the 1920s with the introduction of modern public budgeting and financial management systems following the recommendations of the missions led by Princeton Professor Edwin Kemmerer to Latin America between 1917 and 1930, which were backed by the US (Drake 1989).[20] These reforms contributed to the rationalisation of financial administration and re-equilibration of executive-legislative budget relations, largely in favour of the executive. It was during that period that modern AAAs emerged in the Andean region (Colombia 1923, Chile 1927, Ecuador 1927, Bolivia 1928, Peru 1930). In particular, they advanced strong comptroller-generals' offices to provide central accounting for government institutions. Under this system, accounting officers present public accounts to the comptroller-general for verification of their legality and regularity.[21]

Table 2.5 Financial governance reforms in Latin America

Country	*Fiscal Governance*	*Fiscal Transparency*			*Fiscal Responsibility*	*Fiscal Accountability*
	*Organic budget law; organic financial administration law**	*Access to public information law*	*Habeas data*	*Law on fiscal transparency*	*Law on fiscal responsibility**	*Law on fiscal control*
Argentina	1992, 1997	**(2002)	1994	1999	1999, 2001, 2004	LAFCSP Law 24156 (1992)
Bolivia	1990 (1997)	(2004) 2005		2004		SAFCO Law 1178 (1990, , 1999, 1997)
Brazil	2001		1988	2000	2000	Law 10180 (2001)
Chile	1975				***	LOAFE Decree 1263 1975
Colombia	2004	1985	1997	2003	2003	Laws 43 (1993) and 2145 (1999))
Costa Rica	2001	**				LAFPP Law 8131 (2001)
Dominican Republic	1969	2004				LOPSP (1969)
Ecuador	1977	2004	1996	2002	2002	Decree 1429 (1977, 1990)
El Salvador	1995					LOAFE Decree 516 (1995)
Guatemala	1997		1995			LOP Decree 101-97 (1997)
Honduras	1976, 2004	**(2003)			2004	LOP Decree 407-76 (1976)
Mexico	1976	2002	2002			LFSF Law (2000)
Nicaragua	2005 (1987)		1995			LOCGRSCAP Decree 625 (1981, 1984, 2000) and LAFRP (2005)
Panama		2002	2002	2002	2002	
Paraguay	1999	2004	1992			LAFE Law 1535 (1999)
Peru	2004	2002	1993	1999, 2003	1999, 2003	LOSNCCGR Law 27785 (2002)
Uruguay	1999					TOCAF Decree 95 (1991, 1999)
Venezuela, R B de	2000, 2003		1999		2003	LOAF SP (2000) and Decrees 2621 and 2268 (2003)

Source: Author's compilation, as of December 2005.

* Joint World Bank-IMF Country Budget Law Database, complemented by Web-based research of the countries' ministries of economy and finance. ** Under

As a result, AAAs in Andean countries were modelled after their US counterpart and were given responsibility for the oversight of government control systems, including internal and external controls and accounting systems. They became powerful institutions tasked both with overseeing government and maintaining public accounts. However, conferring these two tasks to the same agency generated tensions, as:

> one arm of the [AAA] prepared the accounts of agencies, which were audited by another arm of the [AAA] in its report to parliament. This puts the [AAA] in a somewhat ambiguous position – as auxiliary organ of the legislative branch in charge of both the internal and external controls over the execution of central government expenditures (Diamond 2002a:15).

A second wave, also promoted by the US, occurred in the 1960s when most countries were under military rule. It led to the modernisation of budgetary systems in several countries (Brazil 1964, Uruguay 1962, Chile 1975, Mexico 1976). A third wave of reforms started in the late 1980s with the support of international financial institutions (Santiso 2006a, 2006b, 2004d) in the wake of the financial crises in the region. It largely followed the precepts of the Washington consensus (Santiso 2004a, 2004b). This wave saw important changes in AAAs, for example in Argentina in 1992, Mexico in 2000, Nicaragua in 2000 and Honduras in 2002.

These reforms were informed by new findings on the influence of political institutions on fiscal performance and the role of budget institutions in financial governance, including the rehabilitation of parliaments in the scrutiny of public finances even in countries with highly centralised budgetary systems such as Chile (Santiso 2008a, 2008b, 2006c, 2006d) The renewed focus on strengthening government auditing and reforming audit agencies must be placed in this broader context.

The budget literature demonstrates that institutional arrangements for public budgeting do matter. It finds theoretical and empirical evidence to suggest that budget institutions influence fiscal outcomes and that centralised budgetary systems are more likely to generate fiscal discipline and lead to smaller budget deficits (Alesina *et al* 1996; Stein *et al* 1998).[22] Concentration of budget powers in the executive, it is argued, makes it 'more likely to enforce fiscal restraint, avoid large and persistent deficits and implement fiscal adjustments more promptly' (Alesina and Perotti 1996:7).[23]

However, as discussed previously, executive discretion in public budgeting carries important risks. The separation of powers, the concentration of budgetary powers, and the legislative delegation of fiscal prerogatives have broadened the scope for government discretion in public finances. This difficult combination tends to leave executive discretion unchecked. It hampers the development of robust oversight agencies and 'horizontal accountability' institutions capable of restraining the state (O'Donnell 1998; Schedler *et al* 1999; Mainwaring and Welna 2003). Latin American expeditious modes of economic governance are particularly harmful to the management of public finances, undermining the credibility of the budget as a strategic planning instrument. As a result of this new knowledge, financial governance reforms now involve a broader set of fiscal institutions beyond the executive, in particular legislatures (Santiso 2008a, 2008b, 2006c, 2006d), oversight agencies (Santiso 2008c, 2007b, 2007c, 2006e; Dove 2002), and other mechanisms of accountability within the state (Santiso 2004b)

Chapter 3

Institutional arrangements for external auditing

Modern states organise their external audit function in different ways, adopting different models for setting up an AAA. These choices reflect different trajectories of state building and legal traditions in public administration. Their place and role in the broader architecture of the state and the systems of checks and balances differ from country to country. A key issue that preoccupies scholars, practitioners and policymakers is which of these institutional models is most effective in deterring corruption and improving governance in the public sector.

This chapter therefore conceptualises the different models of AAAs and situates them in the broader context of the governance of the budget and the rule of law in public financial management. It delves into the logics of delegation, oversight and accountability in public financial management and develops a conceptual framework to gauge the effectiveness of AAAs in budget governance. The analytical model draws on a principal-agent analytical framework and the concepts of delegation and oversight in executive-legislative budget relations. Based on this discussion, this chapter develops a typology of AAAs based on their key attributes, features and functions. It describes the three alternative institutional arrangements for organising the external audit function in modern states and offers four criteria to assess their performance.

Conceptualising government auditing

By overseeing public spending and checking government finances, government auditing systems (internal and external) are a form of control and oversight designed to restrain executive discretion in public budgeting and mitigate the risks of legislative delegation in public finances. They control compliance with fiscal rules and financial regulations. Their deterrence effect on future misconduct or impropriety depends on the credibility of their control.

There has nevertheless been a general shift in fiscal control systems over the last two decades, from an initial concern with controlling compliance (emphasising sanctions and punishment through quasi-judicial control) to a new emphasis on auditing performance (emphasising the achievement of results and the improvement of management). AAAs' core business resides in ensuring compliance with legal and financial regulations through *compliance auditing*. In recent years, 'new public management' has emphasised their role in improving the efficiency, effectiveness and economy of public spending, expanding their mandates to *performance auditing*.

However, the legalistic culture of control that tends to prevail in Latin America and other developing countries tends to put greater emphasis on the compliance with formal rules, rather than the achievement of results and the improvement of performance. Compliance auditing still pervades the culture of control and the bureaucracy generally perceives AAAs as controllers seeking to constrain and punish it, rather than advisers seeking to improve public management. These prevailing attitudes tend to generate uncooperative and confrontational behaviour between the AAA and the bureaucracy. As a former head of the Argentine AAA laments, 'the opposition is more interested in controlling government rather than improving public management and bureaucratic performance.'[1]

While each AAA is unique and grounded in the country's trajectory of state building, AAAs participate in the cycle of legislative accountability. AAAs generally act as auxiliary institutions to legislatures, assisting the latter in the performance of their oversight functions in budget and financial matters. To fulfil its accountability responsibilities, the legislature must ensure that the executive complies with the provisions of the budget law it approved. Legislative oversight 'concerns whether, to what extent and in what way Congress attempts to detect and remedy violation of legislative goals' (McCubbins and Schwartz 1987:426). AAAs perform routine oversight of government finances corresponding to what McCubbins and Schwartz (1987) refer to as 'police patrol' oversight. This form of external control is distinct from the ad hoc 'fire alarm' oversight undertaken by special legislative inquiry commissions, often set up to investigate allegations of corruption.

The agency model of delegation and accountability, most commonly used in the literature of public sector governance (Przeworski 1999; Kettl 1999), provides a useful framework to decipher the dynamics of executive-legislative relations and legislative oversight of the executive (Mainwaring and Welna 2003). In general, AAAs act as 'agents' of the legislature in the oversight of government. Legislatures delegate some of their oversight functions to specialised agencies in order to oversee government more effectively. The effectiveness of legislative budget oversight depends on the 'degree to which the legislative branch has developed the technocratic institutions necessary for ensuring the financial and administrative accountability of the president and executive-controlled bureaucratic agencies' (Morgenstern and Manzetti 2003:135). This, in turn, depends on legislators having the political incentives to use these institutions effectively. In other words, for accountability to be effective, the legislature needs both the means and motives for exercising oversight effectively.

The delegation of legislative oversight powers is different from the delegation of legislative budget powers to the executive, whereby legislatures delegate their powers to tax and spend to the executive. It is also distinct from the more traditional delegation of bureaucratic powers to specialised agencies, whereby governments delegate executive functions to autonomous executing agencies. Internal auditing systems insert themselves into the government-bureaucracy principal-agent relationships. They provide assurances to the government that the bureaucracy has effectively implemented the policies it has set.

Oversight agencies play a critical role in mitigating the risks of delegation. There are two broad types of delegation: legislative delegation and bureaucratic delegation. In the former type, the legislature delegates some of its attributions to the executive, generally the president, or to independent agencies in the bureaucracy (Kiewert and McCubbins 1991; Carey and Shugart 1998). The latter type of delegation occurs within the executive, between the government and the bureaucracy, through the delegation of presidential prerogatives to autonomous bureaucratic agencies (Geddes 1994; Willis 1996). Bureaucratic delegation to administrative enclaves consists of creating autonomous or semi-autonomous public agencies, most often through special legislation. These public agencies enjoy some degree of protection from political interference. The delegation of executive functions to executing agencies puts further onus on the mechanisms of regulation and accountability. As a result, government accounting and auditing acquire a new meaning, becoming mechanisms of managerial oversight. AAAs perform key oversight functions, helping to mitigate some of the dilemmas of both types of delegation, helping government control the bureaucracy and assisting the legislature in its scrutiny of government.

Comparative research in political science and public administration has devoted considerable attention to the conditions under which politicians take the seemingly counter-intuitive decision to delegate powers and responsibilities to autonomous agencies. Bureaucratic delegation to independent agencies is often suggested as an effective strategy to implement structural reforms. Its objectives are to improve agency performance through reducing political interference and insulating the administrative apparatus from the constraints of regular public service employment. The delegation of bureaucratic powers to autonomous agencies increases the costs of policy reversal and, as a result, increases the credibility of policy. Legislative delegation is accompanied by '*auxiliary precautions*', to paraphrase Madison (1788), in the form of institutionalised mechanisms for overseeing government and holding it to account. As Haggard (2000:43) recognises:

> the process of delegation is a central one in democratic systems: modern democracy would be impossible without it. Thus the issue is not whether

or not to delegate, but how delegation can be structured to maximize both efficiency and accountability.

First-generation reforms relied heavily on the insulation of key institutions of economic governance and the isolation of technocratic elites from political interference. Based on rational choice theories, delegation of policymaking powers to independent agencies is often considered as a remedy for the politically motivated inefficiencies in government and the hindrances of parliamentary politics. Observers believe that these reforms can improve performance even in conditions of poor governance, creating 'pockets of efficiency' (Geddes 1994) or 'islands of excellence' (Grindle 1996). Independent central banks (Cukierman *et al* 1992) or autonomous revenue authorities provide two examples of such insulation strategies (Taliercio 2003, 2004).

Successful examples of delegation notwithstanding, there are important caveats. First, delegation is not risk-free, both for the principal who decides to delegate (in terms of loss of control) and for the agencies themselves (in terms of greater exposure to capture). Second, AAAs evolve in changing political contexts. The political conditions that led to their creation are not necessarily sufficient to sustain their autonomy over time and even guarantee their survival. These agencies can be neutralised in several ways to render them inconsequential. Third, delegation with discretion has tended to atomise the state in a plethora of autonomous institutions with weak accountability mechanisms. The magnitude and complexity of principal-agents relations hinder policy coordination.

Nevertheless, the logic of AAAs differs from that of autonomous tax authorities or independent central banks in radical ways. While governments' delegation of powers to specialised agencies is designed to improve the implementation of policy, the legislatures' delegation of oversight powers to autonomous oversight agencies is designed to restrain government more effectively. They are most often institutionally and constitutionally linked to the other two powers (legislature and judiciary), as part of the systems of division of powers. AAAs are oversight agencies tasked with monitoring compliance with delegation rules governing the budget in an impartial and timely manner (Dove 2002). As such, they are part of the system of checks and balances. They generally possess some degree of discretion over the instruments they use and the arrangements they adopt. Their head exercises some measure of judgment in the definition of tasks and the distribution of resources.

AAAs can thus be conceived as auxiliary institutions helping the principal (generally the legislature) enforce accountability on its main agent (the executive) in the management of public resources through routine oversight. The creation of autonomous agencies nevertheless generates another set of principal-agent dilemmas, between the legislature and the AAA. Under the model of the cycle of accountability in the budget process illustrated in Figure 3.1, the legislature approves the budget, the executive implements

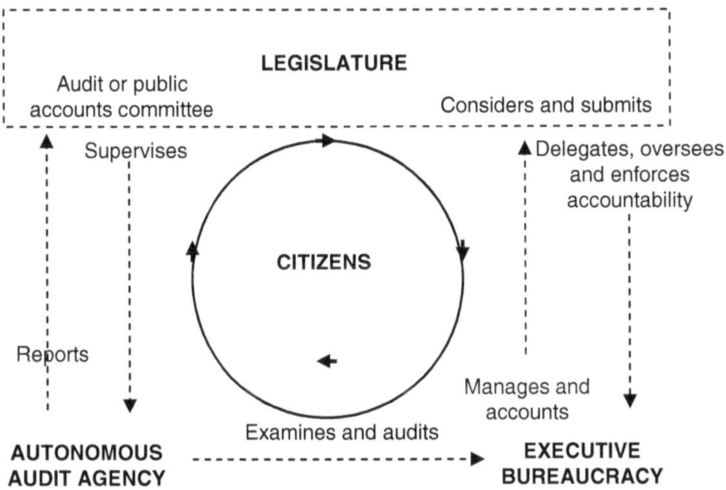

Figure 3.1 Accountability cycle in public finance management.

it and the AAA reports to the legislature to ascertain whether the resources have been used for the purposes intended. The legislature delegates some of its oversight powers to the AAA to control government more effectively.

Typology of audit agencies

Features and functions of AAAs vary across countries and have evolved over time. Different institutional arrangements exist for organising the external audit function in modern states. What roles AAAs actually play in financial oversight naturally depends on their structure and processes, as well as the resource endowments, legal powers and political instruments they possess.

The 1977 Lima Declaration of Guidelines on Audit Precepts of the International Organization of Supreme Audit Institutions (INTOSAI) indicates that 'internal audit services are established within government departments and institutions, whereas external audit services are not part of the organizational structure of the institutions to be audited' (Section 3.1). The external audit agency must nevertheless examine the effectiveness of internal auditing systems and structures. The relationship between the internal control system and external audit is extremely close, as the quality of each affects the other.

External audit ensures that planning, budgeting and spending conform to a country's laws, pursue the objectives defined by the legislature and government, and achieve meaningful impact. As the Lima Declaration states:

> the concept and establishment of audit is inherent in public financial administration as the management of public funds represents a trust.

> Audit is not an end in itself but an indispensable part of a regulatory system whose aim is to reveal deviations from accepted standards and violations of the principles of legality, efficiency, effectiveness and economy of financial management early enough to make it possible to take corrective action in individual cases, to make those accountable accept responsibility, to obtain compensation, or to take steps to prevent – or at least render more difficult – such breaches. (Section 1)

Standard typologies of AAAs classify them according to their institutional features and functions and include three ideal types of AAAs: (i) the monocratic model; (ii) the court model; and (iii) the board or collegiate model:[2]

- The *monocratic model* is that of an AAA headed by a single auditor-general and generally acting as an auxiliary institution to the legislature, albeit with ample autonomy. Under this model, AAAs focus on *ex post* auditing, rather than *ex ante* control, and emphasise financial and performance auditing over compliance control, Chile being an exception. The controls they perform seek to correct rather than penalise. This model is prevalent in Anglo-Saxon countries such as the US, the UK and Canada, and, in Latin America, in Chile, Colombia, Mexico and Peru, Chile nevertheless being an outlier.
- The *court model* is that of a collegiate court of auditors or tribunals of accounts, endowed with quasi-judicial powers in administrative matters, often acting as an administrative tribunal.[3] The quasi-judicial features and functions of the court model privilege legal and financial compliance over performance auditing. The links with the legislature are weaker than in the monocratic model; yet those with the judiciary are also ambiguous. As a result, there is often uncertainty as to who is the agency's principal. Roman law countries such as France, Italy and Spain, and, in Latin America, Brazil and El Salvador follow this model.[4]
- The *board model* is an institutional hybrid. It is an agency with collegial decision-making similar to that found in tribunals, headed by a board of auditors, but without jurisdictional authority or quasi-judicial powers. Under this model, the AAA emits an audit opinion on the reliability and probity of government accounts, usually for the legislature to consider. Germany, the Netherlands, Sweden, and, in Latin America, Argentina and Nicaragua follow this model.

All three models share a central common feature: their independence from the executive. They are also linked, to varying degrees, to the legislature. The court model has closer ties to the judiciary, as in the case of the Brazilian TCU, the board model to the legislature, as in the case of the Argentine AGN, and the monocratic model to the bureaucracy, as in the case of the Chilean CGR. Figure 3.2 illustrates the typology of AAAs and situates the cases of Argentina, Brazil and Chile within it.

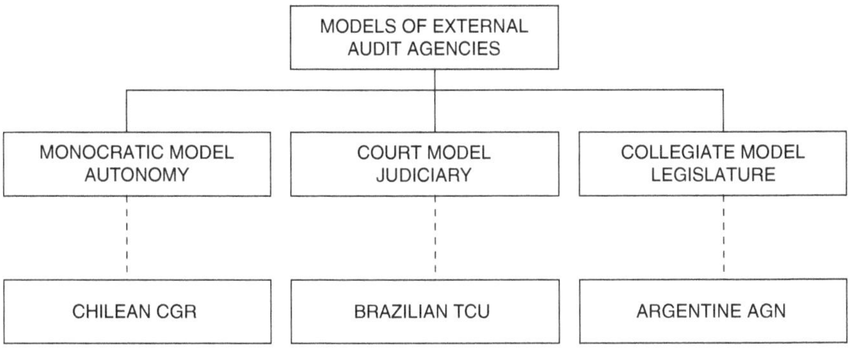

Figure 3.2 Typology of AAAs.

International auditing standards underscore that for the external audit process to function effectively and impartially, AAAs must be independent from the executive. Nevertheless, to have a meaningful impact on bureaucratic behaviour, they must also develop close working relationships with the bureaucracy they audit. Furthermore, as oversight agencies with limited sanctioning powers, they must also develop effective linkages with those institutions with the powers to bring government to account, namely the legislature and the judiciary.

In practice, AAAs are unique hybrids and do not fit easily in the traditional model of separation of powers. Each AAA combines elements of the three different models described above. Key variations between agencies include the timing of control (whether *ex ante* or *ex post* control), its nature (whether emphasising compliance or performance auditing), its effects (the intensity of follow-up of audit recommendations), as well as its status (the legal standing of audit rulings). Comparative analysis of institutional arrangements for fiscal governance and legal frameworks for external auditing in Tables 2.2 and 3.1, respectively, reveals the great variety of functions these perform, as well as the difference in institutional arrangements.

Typology of audit methods

AAAs' approaches to fiscal control also vary across countries and have evolved over time. INTOSAI's 1977 Lima Declaration articulates the principles of government auditing. In its preamble, it states that AAAs seek 'the proper and effective use of public funds, the development of sound financial management; the proper execution of administrative activities; and the communication of information to public authorities and the general public through the publication of objective reports'.[5] The nature of external auditing of government

Table 3.1 Legal framework of external audit agencies (as of December 2004)

Country	*Constitutional provisions*	*Financial administration law or Organic budget law*	*Organic law (where applicable)*	*Antecessors (after independence)*
Argentina Auditoria General de la Nación, AGN	Constitution of 1994, art 85	Ley de administración financiera y de los sistemas de control del sector público, 24156, 1992; Ley Complementaria Permanente de Presupuesto, 1997		Tribunal de Cuentas de la Nación, 1956
Bolivia Contraloría General de la República, CGR	Constitution of 1967, art 154-155	Ley de Administración y Control Gubernamentales, SAFCO, 1990	Ley Orgánica de la Contraloría General de la República, 1977; Reglamento para el Ejercicio de las Atribuciones de la Contraloria General de la República, 1992	Tribunal Nacional de Cuentas, 1883; Contraloría General de la República, 1928.
Brazil Tribunal de Contas da União, TCU	Constitution of 1988, art 71-75 and 161	Law 10180, 2001	Lei Orgânica do Tribunal de Contas da União, 1992	Tribunal de Contas da União, 1891
Chile Contraloría General de la República, CGR	Constitution of 1980, art 87-89	Ley Orgánica de Administración Financiera, LOAF, 1975	Ley de Organización y Atribuciones de la Contraloría General de la República, 1953, reformed in 1964	Contaduría Mayor y Tribunal de Cuentas, 1839; Tribunal de Cuentas, 1888; Contraloría General de la República, 1927
Colombia Contraloría General de la República, CGR	Constitution of 1991, art 267-268	Law 819, 2003	Law 42 (reformulated), 1993; Law 106, 1993; amended 1999, 2000	Contaduría General de Hacienda, 1821; Corte de Cuentas, 1847; Departamento de Contraloría, 1923

Costa Rica Contraloría General de la República, CGR	Constitution of 1949, art 183-184	Ley de Administración Financiera de la República y de Presupuestos Públicos, 2001	Ley Orgánica de la Contraloría General de la República, 1951, 1994	Tribunal de Cuentas, 1825; Centro de Control, 1945; Contraloría General de la República, 1949
Dominican Republic Cámara de Cuentas de la República, CCR	Constitution of 1966, art 78-81 and 107	Ley Orgánica de Presupuesto para el Sector Público, 1969	Ley 10-04, 2004	Cámara de Cuentas de la República, 1942
Ecuador Contraloría General de la República, CGR	Constitution of 1998, art 121-122 and 211-213	Ley Orgánica de Administración Financiera y Control, LOAFYC, 1977 (1986, 1993)	Ley Orgánica de la Contraloría General del Estado, 2002	Contaduría General de Hacienda, 1822; Tribunal de Cuentas, 1861; Contraloría General del Estado, 1927
El Salvador Contraloría General del Estado, CGE	Constitution of 1983, art 195-199	Ley Orgánica de la Administración Financiera del Estado, 1995	Ley de la Corte de Cuentas de la República, 1995, 2002	Tribunal Superior de Cuentas, 1872; Auditoría General de Hacienda, 1930; Corte de Cuentas de la República, 1939
Guatemala Contraloría General de Cuentas, CGC	Constitution of 1985, art 232-236	Ley Orgánica de Presupuesto, 1997	Ley Orgánica de la Contraloría General de Cuentas, 2002	Tribunal y Contaduría Mayor de Cuentas, 1824; Tribunal y Contraloría de Cuentas, 1945, 1948

Continued

Table 3.1 Legal framework of external audit agencies (as of December 2004)—Cont'd

Country	*Constitutional provisions*	*Financial administration law ororganic budget law*	*Organic law (where applicable)*	*Antecessors (after independence)*
Honduras Tribunal Superior de Cuentas, TSC	Constitution of 1964, reformed in 2002, arts 222–227	Ley Organica del Presupuesto, 1976	Ley Orgánica del Tribunal Superior de Cuentas, 2002	Tribunal de Cuentas, 1928; Contraloría General de la República, 1956
Mexico Auditoría Superior de la Federación, ASF	Constitution of 1917, reformed 1999, arts 73, 74, 78 and 79	Ley de Presupuesto, Contabilidad y Gasto Público Federal, 1976 (1995)	Ley de Fiscalización Superior de la Federación, 2000	Contaduría Mayor de Hacienda, 1824, 1963, 1978
Nicaragua Contraloría General de la República, CGR	Constitution 1987, 1995, 200, arts 154–157	Ley del Régimen Presupuestario, 1988, 1991Ley de administración financiera y del presupuesto público (Law 550, 2005)	Ley Orgánica de la Contraloría General de la República y Systema de Control gubernamental, 1979, Law 361 2000	Tribunal Supremo de Cuentas de la República, 1900; Tribunal de Cuentas, 1930, 1966
Panama Contraloría General de la República, CGR	Constitution of 1972, 1978, 1983, arts 275–276	Ley de Presupuesto, 1999	Ley Orgánica de la Contraloría General de la República, 1984	Visitador Fiscal, 1904; Tribunal de Cuentas, 1904; Agente Fiscal, 1918; Oficina de Contabilidad y Contraloría, 1930; Contraloría General de la República, 1942

Paraguay Contraloría General de la República, CGR	Constitution of 1992, arts 281–284	Ley de Administración Financiera del Estado, 1999	Ley Orgánica y Funcional de la Contraloría General de la República, 1994	n.a
Peru Contraloría General de la República, CGR	Constitution of 1993, art 82	Ley marco de la Administración Financiera del Sector Público, 2003; Ley General del Sistema Nacional de Presupuesto, 2004	Ley del Sistema Nacional de Control y de la Contraloría General de la República, 2002	Tribunal Mayor de Cuentas, 1823; Contraloría General de la República, 1929, 1964
Uruguay Tribunal de Cuentas, TC	Constitution of 1996, arts 208–213	Ley de Contabilidad y Administración Financiera, TOCAF, 1991 (1999)	Texto Ordenado de Contabilidad y Administración Financiera, 1997	Comisión de Cuentas, 1830, 1834; Tribunal de Cuentas, 1934
Venezuela Contraloría General de la República, CGR	Constitution of 2000, arts 287–291	Ley Orgánica de la Administración Financiera del Sector Público, LOAF, 2003	Ley Orgánica de la Contraloría General de la República y del Sistema Nacional de Control Fiscal, 2001; Ley Orgánica del Poder Ciudadano, 2001	Contraloría de la Nación, 1938; Contraloría General de la República, 1961

Source: Author compilation based on the external audit agencies' website; Respondanet of the America's Accountability and Anticorruption Project (AAA) (2005) *Banco de Datos Administración Financiera y Auditoría Gubernamental América Latina y el Caribe* (www.respondanet.com; 8 March 2005); Political Database of the Americas (1998) *Comparative Analysis of Audit Institutions* (www.georgetown.edu/pdba/Comp/Control/control.html; 20 March 2005); University of Salamanca, Instituto Interuniversitario de Estudios de Iberoamérica y Fortugal (2005) *Database on Parliaments in Latin America* (http://iberoame.usal.es/legislativo/legislativos/basededatos/basededatos.htm; 22 March 2005); as well as Santiso (2004c), UNDP (2004) Moreno *et al* (2003), Payne *et al* (2002:228–31); Petrei (1998).

finances is shaped by four main factors: (i) the type; (ii) timing; (iii) scope; and (iv) enforceability of audits.

Types of audits

Fiscal control can be preventive, corrective or punitive (Barra 2002). Their principal function is to audit the legality and regularity of financial management and accounting.[6] AAAs guarantee the accuracy and reliability of government financial reporting through *financial audits* and ensure compliance with legal and financial regulations through *compliance audits*. Compliance control is concerned with the formal adherence to the legal rules and financial regulations framing the budgetary process. These functions include checking the government's compliance with the mandate given by the legislature through the budget law. In recent years, AAAs have broadened their audit methods to assess the efficiency, effectiveness and economy of public spending through *performance audits*. Performance control is concerned with the substantive compliance with the objectives of the budget law and the manner in which public resources have been deployed.

The general trend is towards a greater emphasis on preventive and corrective functions through increased reliance on *ex post* performance auditing. Undoubtedly, increased emphasis on performance and results is necessary to overcome the inefficiencies of procedure-driven bureaucracies, especially in civil law countries. However, it should not replace the need to uphold standards of integrity and probity necessary to combat corruption, especially in countries where the rule of law is weak. These two forms of accountability should complement, rather than substitute one another. Nevertheless, performance auditing is hindered by the legalistic culture of control that still prevails in Latin America, which privileges formal compliance with legal rules over substantive accountability for managerial objectives.

Timing of audits

Fiscal control can occur before (*ex ante*) or after (*ex post*) the fact. *Ex ante* auditing verifies the legality of administrative actions before they are implemented, thereby acting as a potential veto on administrative discretion. *Ex post* auditing examines administrative actions after their implementation. *Ex ante* and *ex post* forms of accountability differ in their relative focus on prevention or correction, including punishment. Some scholars see accountability essentially as an *ex post* phenomenon while others argue that, to be meaningful, it should occur before, during and after the exercise of public authority (Elster 1999; Schmitter 1999).

The timing of compliance control is a subject of intense controversy in the audit profession. While performance auditing can only be *ex post*, compliance auditing can be either *ex ante* or *ex post*. Concerning internal audit and control systems, it is generally agreed that one of their core functions is to perform *ex ante* compliance controls. There is, however, disagreement over the extent to which AAAs should have any *ex ante* compliance control functions. *Ex ante* compliance control, often criticised as co-administration by the bureaucracy, gives the AAA veto power over administrative actions. It converts the AAA into a 'veto player' in the implementation of public policy, endowed with the power to question or nullify administrative acts (Tsebelis 2002). Nevertheless, it is generally accepted that AAAs should focus on *ex post* forms of control, including through compliance control and performance auditing.

This controversy over the timing of compliance control illustrates a fundamental tension between two different philosophies of government auditing. AAAs are torn between two concerns: a *liberal concern* for limiting and restraining executive power, which is best achieved through *ex ante* compliance control, and a *managerial concern* with improving public sector management, which is best achieved through performance auditing. While both these functions are important, the relative emphasis on one or another dimension will depend on the stage of development of the budgetary system, the quality of the bureaucracy and the prevalence of the rule of law. However, they are unlikely to be compatible in the same organisation (Speck 2000).

Enforceability of audits

An important controversy in accountability theories and the literature on oversight agencies centres on the enforcement of audit rulings and the sanctioning powers of audit agencies, especially AAAs. This debate has both theoretical and policy implications. It is central to our understanding of the distinctive roles of oversight agencies and accountability institutions. Accountability necessarily implies a measure of answerability (providing an account for actions undertaken) and enforceability (punishment or sanctions for poor performance or illegal actions) (Goetz and Jenkins 2001, 2004). Some authors argue that enforcement and sanctions are intrinsic elements of accountability and that 'inconsequential accountability is not accountability at all' (Schedler 1999:17). According to this view, without enforcement mechanisms, AAAs only impose soft constraints and ambivalent incentives. Consequently, to be credible, AAAs should be endowed with sanctioning powers, which they can impose directly and autonomously without the intervention of another state power.

We take a different view, however, distinguishing oversight agencies from accountability institutions. We argue that AAAs are essentially *oversight agencies* which depend on accountability institutions to enforce accountability on government. *Accountability institutions* are those state powers endowed with the constitutional prerogatives to hold government to account. In the constitutional model of separation of powers, those accountability institutions are the legislature and the judiciary. As Moreno *et al* (2003:117) observe, 'agents cannot hold other agents accountable, only their principals can.' Only the government's principal, the legislature, can enforce accountability on its agent. The function of oversight agencies such as AAAs is to provide the information required by the government's principal. For Allen and Tommasi (2001:356), 'auditors are authorized only to *report* what they have found. They must rely on others to *correct* the reported problems.'

Oversight and accountability

While accountability cannot exist without means of redress, it does not necessarily require oversight agencies to be endowed with direct, legally ascribed sanctioning power. Rectification can be achieved *indirectly* through those state institutions possessing sanctioning powers and the ability to enforce accountability on government. Mainwaring (2003) and Kenney (2003) distinguish between *direct* and *indirect* sanctioning powers, noting that 'some mechanisms of accountability rely exclusively on answerability without necessarily having the capacity to impose sanctions' (Mainwaring 2003:13).[7]

This understanding of the role of oversight agencies reinforces the conceptualisation of AAAs as auxiliary agencies to the legislature in the oversight of government finances.[8] It also underscores the critical importance of the synergies between the components of the architecture of fiscal control. In particular, it defines financial accountability as a system and a process, rather than the responsibility of a single organisation. *In fine*, AAAs are only a component, albeit a critical one, of a broader system of checks and balances in public financial management. As O'Donnell (1999:39) underscores:

> if [AAAs] are to be effective, they can very rarely function in isolation ... effective horizontal accountability is not the product of isolated agencies but of networks of agencies. In particular, their ultimate effectiveness depends on decisions by courts and legislatures to enforce government accountability.[9]

Therefore, a central paradox of AAAs resides in that their effectiveness depends both on their independence from government and the efficacy of their functional linkages with the legislatures and the courts. AAAs must also cultivate their relations with the public in general and the media in particular. The question thus becomes not whether AAAs should be independent, but rather how much independence is enough and how much is too much.

Measuring effectiveness

AAAs have great difficulty in defining meaningful indicators to measure their performance and ascertain their impact on public finances at the macro level, even in developed countries. In some cases, they measure their effectiveness in terms of outputs, devising quantitative indicators such as the number of cases they receive, review and resolve; the number of reports and recommendations they issue; the number of public testimonies (in the press) and hearings (in the legislature, either standing committees hearings or inquiry commissions hearings) they give; or the number of their recommendations that are actually acted upon by the bureaucracy or followed through by the legislature through remedying legislation.[10] Nevertheless, while some of these measures are available in some developed countries, they are largely unavailable in emerging economies.

An indicator of organisational performance monitored by some AAAs is the economy they generate, directly or indirectly, as a result of their control. For example, the US GAO claims to have generated US$44 billion in direct savings in fiscal year 2004 (US GAO 2005). With an annual budget running at US$464 million, these savings translate into a US$95 return for every dollar invested in the US GAO. Similarly, the UK NAO calculates that it saved £515 million in 2004, exceeding its targeted return of £8 for every £1 invested in itself (UK NAO 2005). In Brazil, the TCU estimated the impact of 'decisions that resulted in potential savings for the treasury' at R$3.2 billion for fiscal year 2002 (TCU 2003:25). It calculated the cost-benefit ratio for its work, estimating it at about R$6.8 of savings for every R$1 invested in the TCU. In 2002, the budget of the TCU included both its appropriation from the budget (R$583 million, representing 0.08 per cent of the federal budget) and the fines and salary retentions it imposes (R$756 million). The TCU therefore estimated that it generated potential savings of R$3.2 billion as a result of the preventive audit work by promoting a more efficient use of public funds.

However, there are critical problems with these quantitative indicators, which render comparative analyses adventurous. First, the data are incipient and inconsistent. Only a few AAAs venture into collecting and monitoring quantitative performance data. In Chile, for example, the annual reports of the CGR, while containing information on outputs and activities, contain little information on impact and savings. Second, the data, when they do exist, generally lack substantiation and rigor. For example, in Brazil, the method used for calculating potential savings remains undisclosed and obscure (TCU 2000 a and b). Third, there generally is a lack of clarity in the definition of such indicators, in particular those relating to savings generated. Available indicators tend to blend together direct (sanctions, fines and retentions) and indirect (recommendations for alternative uses of public spending in public contracts) savings, and actual (effectively collected) and potential (recommended to be imposed) savings.

Fourth, the methodological foundations of the data are often questionable, in particular because of the absence of counterfactual evidence. Speck (2000: 192, author translation) notes that the measurement of savings generated by the external audit agency is guided 'by the need to legitimise the existence of the institution, rather than gauge its efficiency and effectiveness,' in a context where AAAs are questioned (Bourdin 2001). The purpose of these exercises is to improve the agencies' legitimacy and visibility in the eyes of the public. Fifth, and more fundamentally, while such measures of impact do constitute worthy efforts to measure the agencies' effectiveness and set and monitor targets, they fail to capture their systemic impact on the quality of fiscal governance and financial management. Numerous interviews conducted in Argentina, Brazil and Chile and elsewhere confirm that policymakers and audit experts, including within the AAAs, have voiced scepticism concerning the reliability of such measures of performance.

Thus, little remains known of the agencies' ultimate impact on public finances and fiscal governance. For instance, there seldom exist robust systems to monitor the impact of audit reports on new legislation, such as the number of times audit reports are used as a basis for legislative initiatives designed to remedy a situation uncovered by audit findings. Agencies tend to focus on overly detailed and sometimes irrelevant micro issues, such as irregularities in procedures and individual bureaucrats' behaviour, and thus often fail to uncover systemic dysfunctions at the macro level. There is indeed a perceived need for macro indicators of performance that are policy relevant. At the same time, however, AAAs risk becoming a victim of overly ambitious expectations, partly because of their inability to clearly delineate their mission. For instance, it is unrealistic to expect that AAAs alone can prevent corruption in public finances or public procurement.

To gauge the impact of AAAs on financial governance, we construct a quantitative index of AAAs' institutional effectiveness in ten Latin American countries and correlate it with proxy indicators of fiscal performance and budget quality. The index is constructed along the four key attributes of AAAs: (i) their independence from the executive; (ii) the credibility of audit findings; (iii) the timeliness of audit reports; and (iv) the enforcement of audit recommendations.

Independence

Formal independence of AAAs is measured by reviewing constitutional and legal provisions along three main dimensions of independence: institutional (constitutional and legal guarantees), individual (guarantees for the auditor-general and the agency's staff), and financial independence.[11] This indicator is inspired by Taliercio's research on tax agencies and his definition of institutional autonomy centring on governance mechanisms and managerial features (Taliercio 2004, 2003).

It is important to underscore that this is an indicator of *formal* independence, which does not entirely capture the influence of informal rules and practices. Complementary information is thus required to measure public and expert perceptions of the credibility of audit work. Table 3.2 summarises and systematises the institutional arrangements for structural independence of AAAs in ten Latin American countries. It reviews the formal laws, rules and regulations providing for AAAs' independence, based on constitutional provisions, organic fiscal-control law establishing the external audit agency and, where applicable, the organic financial-administration law and organic budget law, as of August 2005.

Credibility

The effectiveness of AAAs hinges upon the technical quality and institutional credibility of their audit findings and the manner in which they are attained. Audit processes must lead to clear findings and articulate cost-effective recommendations, supported by convincing evidence and an effective communication strategy (Allen and Tommasi 2001:356–7). Compared to the sub-index of independence, which largely relies on formal rules, the sub-index of credibility relies on perceptions and thus provides a useful complement. Perceptions of credibility are particularly low, with a regional average at 0.29, with Peru receiving the lowest score (0.12) and Costa Rica the highest (0.48). Interestingly, there is an important disconnect between the measure of formal independence and the perceptions of credibility, which seems to suggest the existence of a wide gap between formal role and actual practice. The correlation coefficient between the two sub-indices is slightly above 0.30, but not statistically significant. The indicator of credibility of audit findings is derived from the survey data of the *Index of Budget Transparency* for 2003 (Lavielle *et al* 2003).[12]

Timeliness

Timeliness is critical to ensure that audit findings are relevant and influence policymaking. Excessive delays make audit reports irrelevant and often inconsequential to sanction mismanagement or prevent corruption. Financial information is believed to be relatively more transparent during the formulation and approval stages, but less so during the execution and control stage. Interestingly, existing perception data show that financial opacity is greater during the control stage of the budget process than in any other stages of the budget cycle. This perception partly reflects the greater degree of *ex ante* scrutiny of the budget during its review and approval in the legislature. There has traditionally been less openness and scrutiny during the later stages of the budget process, in particular its *ex post* control, once executed. This finding underscores important flaws in the *ex post* external scrutiny of the budget, partly under the responsibility of AAAs.

Lack of transparency in the execution stage is linked to the degree of discretion of the executive in the implementation of the budget, including its

Table 3.2A Formal independence of external audit agencies in Latin America

Country	*Stated autonomy*	*Legal: Constitutional status*	*Financial: Budgetary independence*	*Judicial: Immunities and privileges*
Argentina AGN	Functional and financial independence	Yes, as a legislative institution	Drafts its budget proposal for consideration by the parliament's public accounts committee and transmitted to the executive	
Bolivia CGR	Operational, technical and administrative autonomy	Yes	Drafts its budget that the ministry of finance must incorporate in the executive's proposal without modification	Immunities of Supreme Court judges
Brazil TCU		Yes	Drafts its budget with President's approval and within the limits set by the executive budget	Irremovable; immunities of Supreme Court judges (STJ); Can retire with full benefits after 5 years in office
Chile CGR	Autonomous institution	Yes (since 1943)		Irremovable; immunities and prerogatives of superior court judges
Colombia CGR	Technical entity with administrative and budgetary autonomy	Yes	Drafts its budget proposal two months before beginning of fiscal year; submits it to the central budget office for inclusion in the executive's budget proposal; Charges a 'fee' to the audited agency; is overseen by the Auditoría General de la República, AGR.	
Costa Rica CGR	Functional and administrative independence	Yes, auxiliary institution to legislature	Drafts its budget and submits it to the executive in May	Irremovable; immunities of superior court judges
Dominican Republic CCR	Technical body with administrative, operational and budgetary autonomy	Yes, as instrumental legal personae	Budget proposal drafted by a special commission composed of representatives of the CCR, Senate, and Chamber of Deputies; included in the executive's budget proposal; cannot be decreased from one year to another.	Immunities of judges

Ecuador CGE	Technical body with administrative, budgetary and financial autonomy	Yes	Drafts its budget; submits it to the finance ministry; fixed percentage of 5% of state income	
El Salvador CCR	Functional, administrative and budgetary independence from executive	Yes	Drafts its budget proposal; submits it to the executive for inclusion in its budget proposal; Legislature can amend in consultation with the President of the CCR and the finance ministry.	
Guatemala CGC	Decentralised technical institution, with functional, technical and administrative independence	Yes	Drafts its budget proposal, submission to the executive and legislature; cannot be less than 0.7% of the budget	Immunities of appellate court judges
Honduras TSC	Functional and administrative autonomy	Yes		
Mexico ASF	Technical and managerial autonomy	Yes	Drafts its budget proposal which is then considered by the Chamber of Deputies' ASF Oversight Committee ('Comisión de Vigilancia')	

Table 3.2B Formal independence of external audit agencies in Latin America—Cont'd

Individual: Personal independence				
Nomination procedures		*Term of office*	*Removal procedures*	
Proposal	*Designation*		*Accusation*	*Dismissal*
Legislature – three nominated by Chamber of Deputies, three by Senate, on a proportional basis; seventh nominated as President of the Board by the main opposition party in legislature	Legislature – six auditors designated by joint resolution of both chambers; seventh auditor general designated President of the Board by joint resolution of the Presidents of both chambers	8 years, renewable	Legislature	Legislature – same procedures as designation
Senate – slate of three approved by absolute majority of two thirds of its members	Executive – President	10 years	Legislature – Chamber of Deputies	Legislature – Judgment of responsibilities by the Supreme Court and Senate vote by absolute majority of two thirds
Mixed – six nominated by the legislature; three nominated by the President with Senate approval, two of which must be chosen within the TCU and its Public Ministry; President of the TCU elected by peers	President, with prior consent of Senate	President and Vice-President: 1 year (renewable once); Members: indefinite, until 65 years old	Judiciary – Superior Court of Justice (Superior Tribunal de Justiça, STJ)	Judiciary – Superior Court of Justice (Superior Tribunal de Justiça, STJ), two thirds majority

President – Designated by President subject to agreement of Senate by simple majority	President	Indefinite, until 75 years old	Legislature – Chamber of Deputies	Legislature – Senate by two thirds majority, ratified by President
Legislature – from list of three presented by Constitutional Court, Supreme Court and State Council (one each)	Legislature	4 years (parallel to president's term)	Legislature or State Council ('Consejo de Estado')	Judiciary – Supreme Court, after previous accusation of national prosecuting attorney
Legislature – 2 years after the beginning of presidential term	Legislature	8 years, renewable indefinitely	Legislature	Legislature – Chamber of Deputies – two thirds majority
President – slate of three	Senate	4 years	Legislature – Chamber of Deputies by three quarters majority	Legislature – Senate by three quarters majority
Legislature – slate of candidates selected by two thirds majority	President – from list presented by Legislature by special majority (67/100)	4 years	Legislature – one quarter of its members initiate impeachment proceedings	Legislature
Legislature	Legislature	3 years, renewable	Legislature	Legislature – simple majority
Postulation committee nominates six candidates (two thirds vote)[a]	Legislature – two thirds majority	4 years, non-renewable	Legislature (mental incapacity, crime, negligence)	Legislature

[a] Composed of representatives of university deans of accounting and auditing departments throughout the country and an equal number of representatives chosen by the National Assembly of Economists, Accountants, Auditors and Business Administrators.

Continued

Table 3.2B Formal independence of external audit agencies in Latin America—Cont'd

Individual: Personal independence				
Nomination procedures		*Term of office*	*Removal procedures*	
Proposal	*Designation*		*Accusation*	*Dismissal*
Legislature	Legislature – two thirds majority	7, non-renewable	Legislature	Judiciary – Supreme Court trial
Legislature – slate of three candidates chosen by the Chamber of Deputies ASF Oversight Committee	Legislature – Chamber of Deputies by two thirds majority of those present in voting	8 years, renewable once	Legislature – Chamber of Deputies' ASF Oversight Committee initiates impeachment	Legislature – Chamber of Deputies by two thirds majority of those present in voting

Source: Author compilation based on the external audit agencies' websites; Respondanet of the America's Accountability and Anticorruption Project (AAA) (2005) *Banco de Datos Administración Financiera y Auditoría Gubernamental América Latina y el Caribe* (www.respondanet.com; 8 March 2005); Political Database of the Americas (1998) *Comparative Analysis of Audit Institutions* (www.georgetown.edu/pdba/Comp/Control/control.html; 20 March 2005); University of Salamanca, Instituto Interuniversitario de Estudios de Iberoamérica y Portugal (2005) *Database on Parliaments in Latin America* (iberoame.usal.es/legislativo/legislativos/basededatos/basededatos.htm; 22 March 2005); as well as Santiso (2004c), UNDP (2004) Moreno *et al* (2003: 126–7), Payne *et al* (2002:228–31); and Petrei (1998). Notes: (b) Originates in the 'Poder Ciudadano' branch of government, composed of the National Public Defender of Human Rights, the Comptroller General, the Public Minister, and the Public Prosecutor

reallocation during execution. Interestingly, the most transparent stage of the budget process seems to be its review and approval by the legislature, a perception that confirms that public debate on budget priorities in the legislature promotes budget transparency and fiscal openness. Indeed, the budget becomes open to public scrutiny and political debate at this stage. The proxy indicator for the timeliness of external audit findings, which also relies on perception surveys, is also derived from the *Index of Budget Transparency* for 2003 (Lavielle *et al* 2003).

Enforcement

Lack of adequate follow-up of audit findings and enforcement of audit recommendations is a principal cause of ineffectiveness. Audit findings are inconsequential if audit recommendations are not acted upon by the government, forcing a reluctant bureaucracy to comply, or if they are not expeditiously transmitted to the courts in case of criminal proceedings. They are of limited use if the dysfunctions they detect are not redressed through remedial legislative action, for example through corrective legislation, inquiry commissions or impeachment proceedings. The indicator of the degree of enforcement of audit findings (which does not only depend on the AAA) is based on a measure of the legal status and binding nature of audit rulings by the United Nations Development Programme (UNDP 2004). However, this indicator measures whether AAAs are legally empowered to enforce their decisions, not necessarily whether they do so consistently.

Table 3.3 shows how the index is constructed and Figure 3.3 illustrates the index of effectiveness of AAAs in ten Latin American countries. The Brazilian TCU and Chilean CGR perform above the regional average, while the Argentine AGN's performance is significantly worse.

These data highlight three key issues:

- First, the general index and its sub-indices reveal in particular that, while (formal) political independence and enforcement capabilities are not necessarily lacking, the low credibility of audit work and the inadequate timeliness of audit findings are major impediments to the effectiveness of AAAs. As mentioned previously, there is an important gap between formal powers and actual practice, measured by public perceptions of effectiveness. Brazil, Chile, Colombia and Costa Rica possess the most effective external audit institutions amongst our sample; Argentina, Peru, Ecuador, and to a lesser extent Mexico, have weak external auditing agencies.
- Second, the overall performance of an AAA does not appear predetermined by the model of external auditing chosen by a given country. Table 3.4 shows institutional arrangements and organisational performance of

Table 3.3 Index of effectiveness of AAAs in Latin America

Country	*Index of institutional effectiveness*	*Independence*	*Credibility*	*Timeliness*	*Enforcement*
ARG	0.28	0.46	0.22	0.13	0.33
BRA	0.63	0.88	0.42	0.24	1.00
CHI	0.60	0.81	0.40	0.18	1.00
COL	0.61	0.78	0.46	0.21	1.00
CRI	0.50	0.69	0.48	0.16	0.67
ECU	0.28	0.67	0.14	0.00	0.33
SLV	0.41	0.58	0.08	0.00	1.00
MEX	0.36	0.61	0.38	0.12	0.33
NIC	0.43	0.82	0.20	0.03	0.67
PER	0.33	0.82	0.12	0.04	0.33
LAC10	0.44	0.71	0.29	0.11	0.67

Note: Indicators are in a scale from 0 to 1, with lower scores meaning lower performance.
Sub-index of independence of audit agencies: Author compilation based on the constitutions, organic budget laws, financial administration laws and organic laws of fiscal control and government auditing along 12 key variables. Sources include the AAAs' websites; America's Accountability and Anticorruption Project (AAA) (2005) *Banco de Datos Administración Financiera y Auditoría Gubernamental América Latina y el Caribe* (www.respondanet.com; 8 March 2005); Political Database of the Americas (1998) *Comparative Analysis of Audit Institutions* (www.georgetown.edu/pdba; 20 March 2005); as well as Santiso (2006a, 2004c), UNDP (2004), Moreno *et al* (2003:126–7), Payne *et al* (2002:228–31), and Petrei (1998). The normalized value for the sub-index ranges from 0, reflecting limited independence, to 1, signifying strong independence.

Sub-index of credibility of audit findings: Author compilation based on the IBP's indicator of the credibility of external auditing, which is itself a sub-index of the Index of Budget Transparency (Lavielle *et al* 2003). Four statements were taken into consideration to quantify this variable: (i) the external comptroller is trustworthy; (ii) the recommendations of the external comptroller have contributed to combat corruption; (iii) the external comptroller verifies that the executive complies with the physical goals of the budget programmes; (iv) the external comptroller has the capacity to effectively oversee federal spending. The normalised value for the sub-index ranges from 0, reflecting low credibility, to 1, signifying high credibility.

Sub-index of timeliness of audit reports: Author compilation based on the IBP's indicator of the quality and timeliness of fiscal information, which is itself a sub-index of the Index of Budget Transparency (Lavielle et al 2003). The sub-index of timeliness of audit reports measures the perception of timeliness of fiscal and audit information during the control stage of the budget process. This variable measures 'with what degree of timeliness is budget information made public during the control and oversight phase of the budget' (Lavielle *et al* 2003:21). Its normalized value ranges from 0, reflecting low perception of timeliness, to 1, signifying high timeliness.

Sub-index of enforcement powers of audit agencies: Author compilation derived from a proxy indicator measuring their formal enforcement powers of the AAAs, provided by the UNDP (2004, Table 16). It reflects the binding nature of audit decisions and AAAs' capacity to enforce sanctions. It nevertheless measures whether external audit agencies are legally capable of enforcing their decisions, not necessarily whether they do so consistently. As a result, the construction of this dummy variable is not particularly robust. The normalized value for the sub-index of enforcement ranges, from 0, indicating low enforcement capabilities, to 1, reflecting high enforcement capabilities.

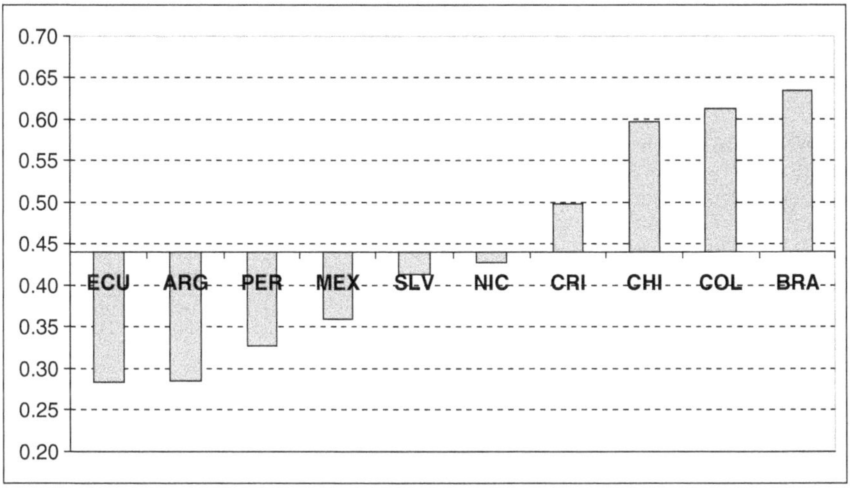

Figure 3.3 Index of institutional effectiveness of AAAs.

different models of AAAs in various country contexts. While Ecuador, Peru, Costa Rica, Mexico, Chile and Colombia follow the monocratic model, they show great variation in organisational performance. Similarly, while Brazil and El Salvador follow the court model with quasi-judicial powers, their relative performance differs substantially.

- Third, specific institutional arrangements vary greatly within the three models of AAAs. In fact, as a result of their unique historical roots and institutional development, each external audit agency is a unique hybrid often combining elements of the three ideal types of AAAs. These findings suggest that other factors linked to the broader governance context and the agencies' institutional trajectories bear greater explanatory power on their organisational performance, across countries and over time.

Assessing impact

Statistical evidence from cross-country correlations suggests a strong link between, on the one hand, the effectiveness of AAAs and, on the other hand, the quality of fiscal governance and budget institutions. This section uses the aggregate index of institutional effectiveness to assess the impact of external auditing systems on budget performance and fiscal governance. It measures the influence of external auditing on both the *quality of the budget* and the *quality of financial governance*:

- The *quality of the budget* is measured by two sets of variables: (i) fiscal outcomes, using the budget deficit as a proxy indicator; and (ii) budget

Table 3.4 Institutional arrangements and organisational performance

Monocratic model	*Court model*	*Collegiate model*
	Brazil (0.63)	
Colombia (0.61)		
Chile (0.59)		
Costa Rica (0.49)		
		Nicaragua (0.42)
	El Salvador (0.40)	
Mexico (0.36)		
Peru (0.32)		
Ecuador (0.28)		
		Argentina (0.28)

Source: Author compilation.

processes, using budget credibility, volatility and transparency as proxy indicators.

- The *quality of governance* is measured by four sets of variables assessing: (i) overall institutional quality; (ii) government effectiveness and bureaucratic quality; (iii) rule of law and corruption control; and (iv) checks, balances and constraints on executive discretion.

We run simple correlations to investigate the relationship between the effectiveness of AAAs and fiscal outcomes and governance quality. There are caveats to this exercise however, linked to the methodological limitations of working with small samples. This limitation is reflected in low levels of statistical significance and, therefore, explanatory power. More fundamentally, cross-country statistical analysis provides a measure of correlation but not of causality. Lastly, while the indicators have been selected and constructed to minimise endogeneity problems, some of these nevertheless remain.

Impact on the quality of the budget

Measuring the impact of external auditing systems on budgetary systems requires defining fiscal outcomes and carefully selecting proxy indicators, both in quantitative (types) and qualitative (measures) terms. In quantitative terms, we use two proxy indicators to assess the soundness of the budget: (i) the *primary budget balance of central government* as percentage of GDP, both for 2002 and as an average for the 1990–2000 period; and (ii) the *annual average growth rate* for the period 1990–2002. The International Country Risk Guide (ICRG) of the Political Risk Services (PRS) provides data for the former indicator and the World Bank's World Development Indicators (WDI) for the latter.

We use three qualitative measures to assess the credibility of the budget: (i) the degree of *budget transparency*; (ii) the degree of *centralisation of the budgetary system* within the executive branch and, in particular, the ministry of finance and the central budget office; and (iii) the extent of the *budgetary powers of the president and the legislature*. Other qualitative measures might have been more adequate, in particular budget out-turn and budget volatility, but most are still unavailable for the ten countries under review. We run simple correlations between the index of effectiveness of AAAs and these indicators of budget credibility to gauge the strength of the relationship between external auditing and public budgeting.

The correlations reveal three key findings regarding the relationship between the effectiveness of AAAs and the quality of the budget captured:

- First, the aggregate index of effectiveness of AAAs is only weakly correlated with *quantitative* measures of economic and budgetary performance. This finding suggests that external auditing has only limited direct influence on fiscal outcomes and the budget deficits. The limited data available even suggest that there might exist a negative relationship between external auditing and the budget balance, which suggests that AAAs, however effective, cannot *alone* prevent fiscal indiscipline.
- Second, the aggregate index of effectiveness of AAAs nevertheless appears to have a greater significance for the credibility of budgetary processes measured in *qualitative* terms, in particular in terms of its impact on transparency (see Figure 3.4) and, to a lesser extent, the budgetary powers of the president.
- Third, and surprisingly, external auditing does not appear to be correlated with the strength of legislative budgetary powers, which suggests an important disjuncture between external auditing and legislative oversight. In fact, there appears to be a stronger association with the budgetary powers of the president and the degree of centralisation of the budgetary system in the executive. It could well be that greater centralisation of the budget system, and therefore greater executive predominance in public budgeting, requires more robust external auditing systems to check executive discretion and compensate for weaknesses in legislative oversight.

Impact on the quality of governance

We proceed with testing the correlation between the effectiveness of external auditing and the quality of financial governance, measured by four proxy indicators: (i) overall institutional quality; (ii) government effectiveness and

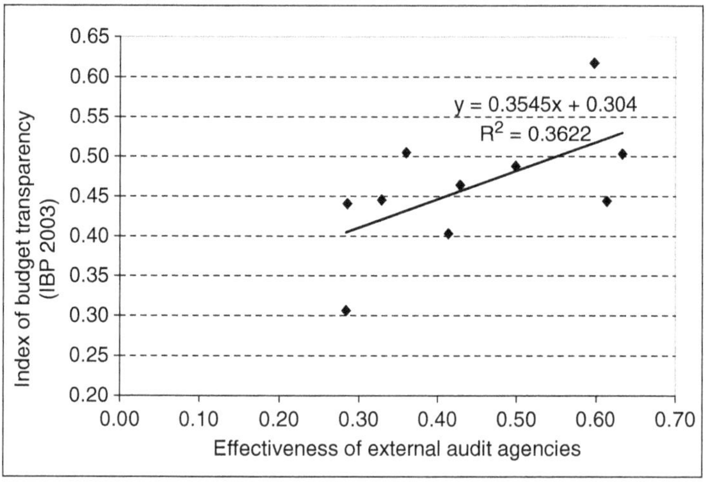

Figure 3.4 External auditing and budget transparency.
Source: Budget transparency is measured by the Latin American Index of Budget Transparency of the International Budget Project (IBP) (Lavielle *et al* 2003). To mitigate endogeneity problems, we use the aggregate perception index of budget transparency, which is constructed differently from the series of disaggregated indicators of transparency of the different phases of the budgetary process.

bureaucratic quality; (iii) rule of law and corruption control; and (iv) constraints on executive discretion, as a measure of the strength of checks and balances.

We run simple correlations between various indicators of institutional and governance quality and the aggregate index of effectiveness of AAAs to gauge the strength of the relationship between these variables.

Statistical evidence from cross-country correlations suggests a strong link between, on the one hand, the effectiveness of external auditing agencies and, on the other hand, the quality of fiscal governance and budget institutions. Two key findings can be extracted from this analysis:

- First, at a macro level, this statistical evidence reveals an important effect of external auditing on the quality of public institutions and government effectiveness. Our statistical analysis highlights in particular the strong correlation with the quality of public institutions and the strength of the rule of law (Figure 3.5), quality of the civil service (Figure 3.6), the transparency of the budget (Figure 3.4), the control of corruption (Figure 3.7), and constraints on the executive (Figure 3.8). While correlation is not causation, it can nevertheless be inferred from these data that AAAs are a core component of the system of fiscal control and government accountability in financial matters.

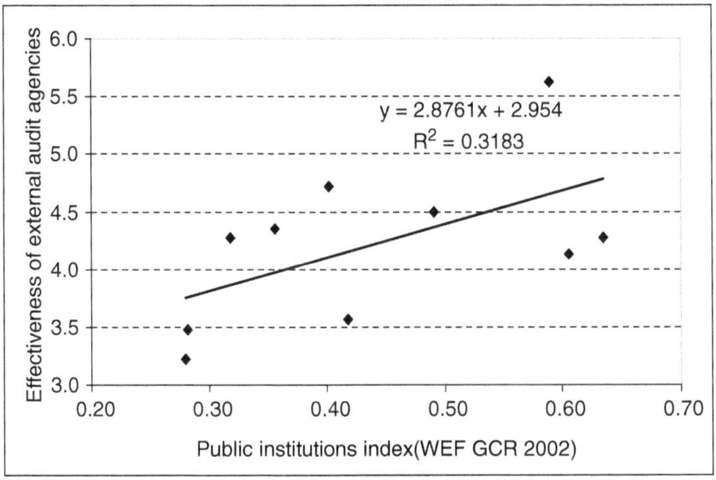

Figure 3.5 External auditing, public institutions and rule of law.

Source: The Political Institutions Index is derived from the World Economic Forum's Growth Competitiveness Index, of which it is one of the three sub-indices (World Economic Forum 2002). It is composed of two equally weighted components, one measuring the reliability of contract enforcement and adherence to the rule of law, and a second one gauging the extent of corruption. The normalized value index is on a scale from 1 to 7, where higher values indicate better institutional quality.

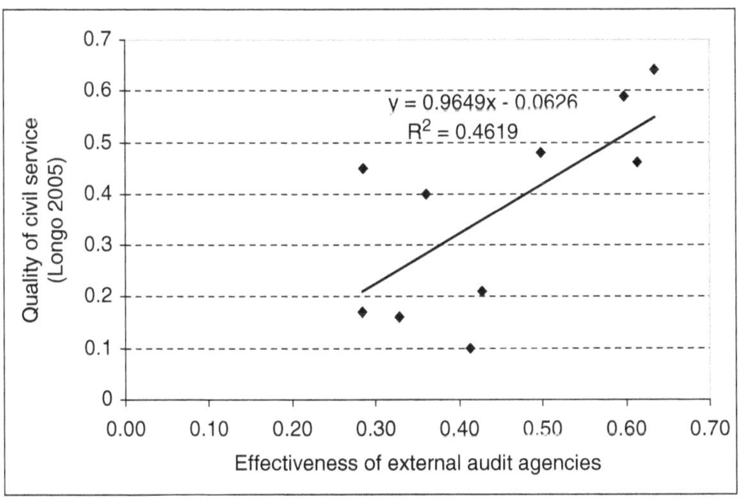

Figure 3.6 External auditing and quality of the civil service.

Source: Government effectiveness and bureaucratic quality are measured using a recently devised indicator of the quality of civil services in the region, on a normalized scale from 0 to 1, with greater values reflecting more effective bureaucracies (Longo 2005, 2003).

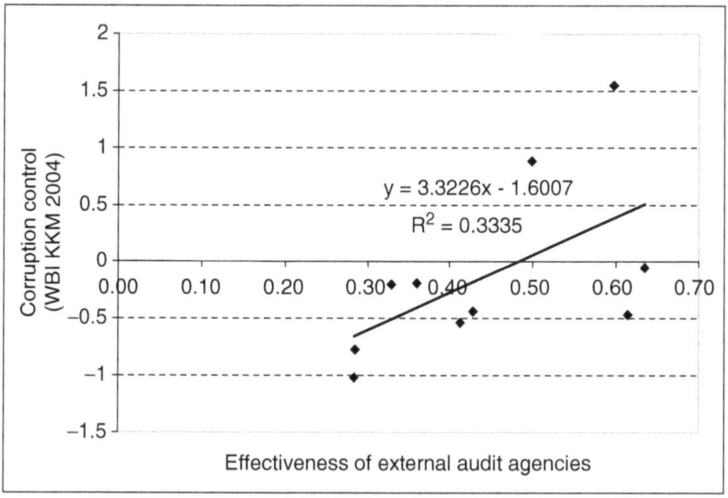

Figure 3.7 External auditing and control of corruption.
Source: Control of corruption is measured by the World Bank's Control of Corruption Indicator (Kaufmann *et al* 2005). Its value ranges from -2.5 to 2.5, with high values meaning greater control of corruption.

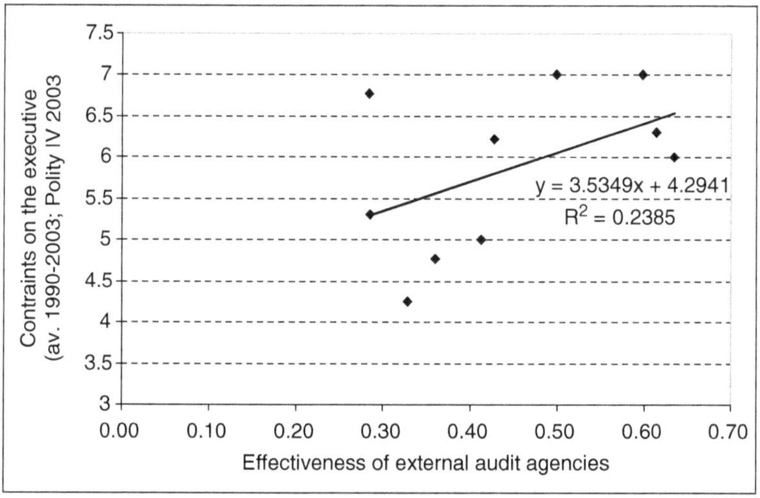

Figure 3.8 External auditing and constraints on the executive.
Source: The indicator for *restraints on executive discretion* provides a commonly used indicator for the strength of the systems of checks and balances and separation of powers. It provides a measure of the number and strength of veto players in public policymaking and the number of independent branches of government with veto power over policy change. We use the normalized value of the average index of executive constraints of Polity IV for the period 1990–2003 (Polity IV 2003), where lower values indicates more executive discretion and higher values more constraints on executive discretion.

- Second, the data reveal a weaker connection between external auditing and adherence to the rule of law and constraints on the executive. This finding might suggest that AAAs only marginally contribute to strengthening checks and balances in financial governance and institutional restraints on executive discretion. It demonstrates that AAAs alone cannot constrain executive discretion; they are themselves often undermined by it. It also confirms the intuition behind the book's main argument, that, while AAAs should play a critical role in strengthening government accountability, they often fail to do so because of structural dysfunctions in the system of fiscal control and the architecture of checks and balances in which they are embedded.

These results suggest that failures are systemic, rather than agency specific or related to the agency's internal governance. As discussed above, available data thus do not confirm the existence of a *direct* impact of AAAs on fiscal outcomes and budget deficits. Nevertheless, considering existing theoretical and empirical evidence on the impact of the quality of governance on fiscal performance, we can infer that AAAs have an *indirect* bearing on fiscal outcomes through their contribution to improving governance. Theoretical and empirical evidence thus suggests that the contribution AAAs make to the management of public finances is primarily through improving fiscal governance and budget transparency, confirming that effective AAAs are a key element in the national systems of financial accountability.

However, as underscored in this chapter, causality chains are more difficult to ascertain. Undoubtedly, further research and new data are required, in particular on budget out-turns as an indicator of budget predictability, to ascertain the causality links between external auditing, fiscal outcomes and budget credibility. There are, furthermore, limitations to comparative analysis based on such a small sample of observations. Moreover, latitudinal analysis provided by cross-country statistical inquiry has necessarily limited explanatory power. It must be complemented by longitudinal analyses of selected case studies, which can only provide the necessary understanding of the trajectory of institutional change of AAAs over time.

To ascertain the influence of the governance context on agency performance, we complement the preceding cross-country statistical analysis with three case studies, following the most-similar method of comparative inquiry. The following three chapters compare and contrast the three main models for organising the external audit function at the national level, as applied to three country cases: Argentina, Brazil and Chile. Each case study analyses the agency's institutional profile, its institutional trajectory and its institutional linkages with the other components of the system of fiscal control, in particular the legislature.

Chapter 4

The board model and the case of Argentina

Somos argentinos y tenemos anomias. Las cosas, a veces, no son como la ley dice que son (We are Argentineans and have our anomies. Things are not always what the law says they are)

Héctor Rodríguez 2002:161.

¡Para preservar las tradiciones, violemos las leyes! (To preserve traditions, violate the laws!)

Carlos Fuentes, *La Silla del Águila*, 2003:322.

Introduction

The Collegiate or Board model of AAA is an institutional hybrid. AAAs under this model are collective decision-making bodies headed by a board of auditors and presided over by a rotating presidency. Under this model, the AAA emits an audit opinion on the reliability and probity of government accounts, usually for the legislature to consider. They are independent from the executive and report to the legislature, to which they are linked to various degrees. Although maintaining a collegial decision-making similar to that found in the courts, they do not possess judicial authority or quasi-judicial powers, nor do they render judgments on the accounts of administrators. Although some AAAs following the collegiate model are called tribunals or courts, they do not, in fact, have judicial functions. This is the case, for example, in Germany's *Bundesrechnungshof,* Sweden's *Riksrevisionen* or the Netherlands' *Algemene Rekenkamer*.

The effectiveness of this model highly depends on the quality of the links AAAs forge with the accountability institutions, in particular the legislature and the judiciary. As in the court model, there can be a great deal of uncertainty as to who the agency's principal is, although, in most cases, the agency is functionally linked to the legislature to which it reports and which nominates its auditors. Under this model, AAAs can more easily shift from *ex ante* compliance control to *ex post* performance auditing. In Latin America, this model is that of Argentina since 1992 and Mexico since 2000.

The Argentine *Auditoría General de la Nación* (AGN) is a collegiate AAA with close institutional links with the legislature. The trajectory of the AGN highlights the limits of institutional design and technical solutions as a strategy to improve organisational effectiveness (Santiso 2008c, 2007a). It functions as the legislature's auxiliary agency in the oversight of government finances. The case of Argentina provides an example of the fiction of control and failure of radical reform.

The case of the AGN is an interesting one in two respects. First, it suggests that AAAs can have only a limited impact when formal fiscal institutions are undermined by informal practices and undercut by adverse political incentives. The AGN ranks among the least performing AAAs in the aggregate index of institutional effectiveness, as seen in Figure 3.3 and Table 3.3. This suggests that performance is deficient across all dimensions and particularly in terms of independence and timeliness. Second, it illustrates the limits of radical reform strategies based on the import of exogenous institutional models. As in the tango, extravagant advance was followed by swift retreat, as the implanted AAA proved not to be fit for purpose in a highly politicised bureaucracy lacking a culture of control and with weak adherence to the rule of law. The nature of the political system, regularly dominated by fused legislative and executive majorities, provides a particularly inauspicious environment for any form of external control and oversight.

Institutional profile

On paper, the AGN is a powerful organisation inserted into a coherent framework for financial governance and fiscal control, with clearly delineated responsibilities.[1] Admittedly, Argentina has made significant advances in rationalising public budgeting and financial administration. However, there exist important dysfunctions that severely limit the AGN's effectiveness and adversely affect government accountability.

The AGN emerged in 1992 as part of sweeping reforms of public budgeting and the adoption of a new financial administration law. However, despite being provided for in the Constitution, the AGN still lacks an organic law cementing its internal governance and procedural rules. It acquired constitutional status in 1994 as a legislative body. Responsibility for the oversight of government finances ultimately rests with the legislature, assisted by the AGN. Legislative budget oversight is exercised through the joint audit and public accounts committee of the bicameral legislature (the *Comisión Parlamentaria Mixta Revisadora de Cuentas*, CPMRC), which is integrated by 12 members (six senators and six deputies), designated on a proportional basis for the duration of the legislature and presided over by a representative of the majority.

The AGN is an autarkic institution with legal persona, functional independence and financial autonomy. Its structure, functions and internal procedures are approved by the legislature by joint resolution of the budget and finance committees of each chamber and the CPMRC (Rodríguez and Bonvecchi 2006). The CPMRC oversees the AGN and is its main institutional anchor in the legislature. The AGN is a collegial organisation with collective decision-making structures. It is governed by a college of seven auditors-general designated for an eight-year, renewable term. The Senate and the Chamber of Deputies designate three auditors each on a proportional basis.

The seventh auditor-general, the president of the college, is designated by a joint resolution of both chambers and, since 1994, by the main opposition party.[2] However, this does not necessarily mean that the majority of the college of auditors belongs to the opposition; quite to the contrary, in fact, and the president of the college of auditors has usually been in the minority. Since decisions are taken either by consensus or majority vote, the representatives of the legislative majority can veto adverse audit rulings. This institutional set-up therefore allows the ruling party to neutralise any initiative that could damage or embarrass the executive. Furthermore, the ruling party can also delay, dilute or veto adverse audit rulings in the legislature and the CPMRC, which it usually dominates.

The AGN has a broad mandate, extending its jurisdiction over the economic, financial, legal and patrimonial management of the federal government, including programmes financed by international financial institutions, debt financing and social spending (AGN 1993). The purpose of external auditing is clearly corrective, rather than punitive, being carried out *ex post* and being non-binding in nature. External auditing includes both performance and compliance auditing. *Ex ante* compliance control was abandoned in 1992 and was devolved to the internal control system, which was also restructured under the supervision of a central internal audit agency, the *Sindicatura General de la Nación* (SIGEN), placed under the authority of the President. The AGN does not possess direct enforcement and sanctioning powers and, therefore, enforcement is indirect through the referral of cases to the competent authorities.

Institutional effectiveness

The independence of the auditors-general and that of the entire staff of the AGN is compromised by the partisan origins of their nomination. Muruzabal Lerga (1999) underscores that audit independence (objectivity and neutrality) has three main dimensions: the political independence of its governing authorities, the impartiality of its staff, and the ability to perform its tasks independently. None of the three dimensions of individual independence are fulfilled in Argentina.

Excessive politicisation constitutes a major hindrance to the agency's credibility as an impartial auditor of government finances (Makón 2002 and 1997). The partisanship mode of designation of external auditors leads to a high degree of politicisation of the college of auditors, which is compounded by the politicisation of the agency itself. The AGN is literally 'sliced up' amongst the two main political parties.[3] Furthermore, political parties in the legislature are able to interfere with the auditing process at several stages, from the definition of the agency's work-plan to the follow-up of audit findings. As a result, as confirmed by several auditors-general, audit findings are often negotiated, rather than evaluated on their own merits. Furthermore, while auditors-general in theory have long tenures, in practice, the constitutional provision according to which the AGN president is to be designated by the opposition effectively means that the college changes every time there is a change in government.

As Ivanega (2004) suggests, while the AGN may be independent from the executive, it nevertheless is not independent from political interference. The controversies surrounding the designation of Rodolfo Barra as president of the AGN between 1999 and 2002 illustrate this point. In 1999, Menem, then in the opposition, nominated Barra, a former justice minister under his government and former Supreme Court judge, as head of the AGN. Barra's designation was interpreted as an attempt to neutralise the AGN and make sure it would not investigate allegations of corruption during the government of Menem (1989–99) of which Barra had been a member (González de Rebella 2001). A Salta Peronist, former Senator Emilio Cantarero, also chaired the legislature's CPMRC.

Originally, the purpose of politicising the decision-making structure of the external audit agency was to ensure that political and technical rationality were adequately combined to inform audit opinions (Fadel 2002; Lamberto 2002).[4] However, the fact that *both* the external audit agency and the joint public accounts committee are politicised organisations increases the likelihood of politically biased audit rulings. As González de Rebella (2001:28, author translation) observes:

> Instead of establishing institutional arrangements capable of impeding that the representatives of the ruling party could influence and compromise the exercise of external control, the decision to put professionals linked to political parties at the helm of the AGN has generated paralysis, scant audacity in oversight, few contacts with the media, except when there exists a clear political motivation of either the opposition or the governing party to bring a scandal to the attention of the public.

Furthermore, the auditing process is riddled with 'veto gates' and 'pressure points' which undermine its independence and effectiveness. The rule has been for the college of auditors to vote on audit reports by unanimity, a procedure that allows representatives of the ruling party to dilute or veto audit findings. Moreover, once the audit report reaches the legislature, it can be delayed further, as the CPMRC can request complementary information and investigations.

Moreover, the CPMRC is able to shape the AGN's work-plan, either directly or indirectly by requesting special studies and ad hoc investigations, and thus restrict its margin of manoeuvre. It can also influence the AGN's budget, not necessarily by curbing it but rather by not endowing the AGN with the necessary resources to fulfil its mission.

Capacity constraints, procedural restrictions and institutional flaws further compromise the credibility of audit findings. External audits are sparse, usually not timely and seldom go beyond legal compliance. The timeliness of audit reports is inadequate to allow them to feed back into the policy process. For example, the AGN presented the audit report for the social programme for pensioners (PAMI) for the year 1994 in 1999. According to Berensztein et al. (2000), audit reports have not been used as an effective tool by the legislature either to oversee the budget and improve budget efficiency, or to prevent corruption and punish those responsible. Social expectations are indeed very low and, until recently, audit reports were neither expected nor considered by the public and the press. The credibility of government auditing is further inhibited by the *ex post* nature of external audits and the absence of robust internal *ex ante* controls. Furthermore, the focus on legal and financial compliance tends to emphasise lower-level details of administrative and financial probity of bureaucrats, tasks that should normally be undertaken by internal administrative controls.

Things have been improving in recent years, however. Leandro Despouy, a renowned human rights lawyer who assumed the presidency of the AGN in 2001, has sought to improve the timeliness of audit reports and move towards concomitant control. Since 2002, audit reports have been made publicly available as soon as the college of auditors has approved them. This apparently minor procedural change is nevertheless significant, as it ends the informal veto power of the CPMRC and its capacity to 'park' adverse audit findings, '*enviándolos al cajón*'. Audits have also been made more politically relevant, targeting sensitive areas such as social spending, trust funds, public concessions, state subsidies and external debt. The AGN has revealed irregularities by public utilities providers, occasionally leading to the suspension or annulment of public contracts.

The current president of the AGN firmly believes that improving the disclosure of and access to audit reports should enhance the effectiveness of the AGN, by making their release mandatory and sanctioning obstruction (Despouy *et al* 2002). In 2003, the government adopted a decree to improve freedom of information, but limited to the federal government and without the binding powers of a law. The fiscal responsibility laws of 1999, and 2004 and the 'federal pact' of 2001 also oblige the government to disclose more fiscal and financial information, an obligation it has not actively complied with (Uña *et al* 2004, 2005). The broadening of fiscal transparency has nevertheless carried political costs, reflected in the recent tensions between the government and the AGN. In 2006, the legislature, dominated by the ruling party, threatened to initiate impeachment proceedings against the president of the AGN on unrelated allegations of impropriety.

Nevertheless, the enforcement of audit recommendations and the imposition of sanctions in case of non-compliance remain deficient. Voluntary implementation of audit recommendations by the bureaucracy is sparse and there are no rigorous mechanisms for following them up and monitoring compliance. In 2000 and 2001, for example, almost one fourth of audit reports were redirected to the public prosecutor's office and to judicial authorities, as there were suspicions of malpractice, fraud or corruption (Fadel 2002). Yet, these have had little effect, except when relayed by the media or the opposition.

The effective separation of powers and the degree of political competition matter greatly to explain the effectiveness of external auditing. In the case of the AGN, the technical quality of audit reports is seldom questioned. The main criticism rests with their being inconsequential in terms of judicial redress or legislative accountability (Fadel 2002; Rodríguez and Bonvecchi 2006).[5] Audit information is seldom used to hold government to account, and is often short-circuited in the legislature, which is usually dominated by the ruling party. During the Menem era, the ruling party dominated all three state powers and, therefore, was able to block adverse audit findings either within the AGN or beyond it.

Enforcement of audit findings has tended to occur indirectly through the peer pressure of societal control and increasingly assertive civil society organisations. The media has proved a particularly effective actor to publicise audit findings and indirectly enforce audit recommendations. Between 1997 and 2001, of all corruption investigations that appeared in the two main journals (*La Nación* and *Clarín*), over half of them resulted from leaked AGN reports that were either not yet approved or had been blocked (González de Rebella 2001). Interviews suggest that frustrated auditors often leaked the information. However, the media's interest in audit work tends to focus on highly visible corruption scandals, rather than more mundane efforts at improving public sector efficiency.

Improving the disclosure of and access to audit reports, making their release mandatory and sanctioning obstruction, could enhance the effectiveness of the external audit agency. The current President of the AGN believes that increased public transparency, greater publicity and proactive dissemination of audit findings is likely to be the most effective reform to strengthen external auditing in Argentina (Despouy *et al* 2002). As former economy minister Ricardo Gutiérrez (1997:48) underscores:

> the proliferation of laws and oversight agencies does not guarantee per se the elimination of corruption. This can only be achieved through greater transparency [...]. For me, transparency is the best way and most effective method to exercise control and fight corruption.

The production and aggregation of more timely financial information within the public sector (Braceli 2002) and the setting and monitoring of performance targets (Makón 2002; Fadel 2002) would undoubtedly help in anchoring a performance culture in public budgeting.

Institutional trajectory

To fully understand the determinants of the effectiveness of the AGN, it is necessary to inquire into its historical origins and institutional trajectory. The AGN emerged in 1992 as part of broader efforts to discipline public finances and rationalise public budgeting (World Bank 2001; Uña *et al* 2005). By the end of the 1980s, the budget process had dramatically deteriorated to the extent that it became irrelevant (Petrei 1998). No budgets were approved in 1990 and 1991.[6]

Under pressure from international financial institutions, the 1992 reform of financial administration was designed to tackle the disarray in public budgeting and government finances. However, the government's original proposal for a new federal AAA was significantly altered during the legislative debate, which lasted for a year and a half, from April 1991 until September 1992 (Makón 2002; Baglini 2002). The main areas of contention centred on the features and functions of the AAA.

The AGN replaced the National Tribunal of Accounts (*Tribunal de Cuentas de la Nación*, TCN), established in 1956 as a court-type AAA modelled after its French and Spanish counterparts. It was made up of five permanent members with life-tenure, tasked with controlling legal and financial compliance of federal public finances. It possessed *ex ante* control authority and was endowed with quasi-judicial enforcement powers. The TCN reviewed *ex ante* the legality of the executive actions, including executive decrees, and was able to suspend or annul them. In addition, the TCN judged the public accounts of public administrators and held accountability proceedings.

Yet, despite having wide powers, the performance of the TCN was uneven. By the end of the 1980s, there was a broad consensus that the TCN needed reform. However, there is evidence to suspect that the decision to abruptly change the audit system, rather than introduce changes to the existing system, was designed to neutralise external constraints on executive discretion. In the first months of the Menem administration, the TCN conflicted with the president's expeditious style of government and his reliance on urgency decrees. Allegations of corruption emerged, especially in the privatisation process and public procurement, including overpricing and favouritism. The TCN questioned several executive decrees and exposed financial improprieties by government officials (Morgenstern and Manzetti 2003).

When it became too much of an irritant, the TCN was eventually dismantled. In March 1990, Menem dismissed the members of the TCN and replaced them with close allies led by his own brother, Eduardo Menem, in flagrant violation of the law according to which auditors-general could only be fired if impeached by the Senate. The courts recognised this abusive dismissal several years later. Not surprisingly, the TCN ceased to create problems for the government. Upon neutralising the TCN's administrative oversight, Menem pushed the new financial administration law through the legislature, which led to the replacement of the TCN by the AGN. Between 1990 and 1993, the AAA was thus effectively neutralised.

Anecdotal evidence suggests that this manoeuvre was intentional, similar to the well-documented packing of the Supreme Court.[7] It represents another example of the strategies deployed by the Menem administration to undermine oversight agencies and defuse 'veto points' in economic policy and 'accountability checks' in financial administration. For most of his two terms in office (1989–95 and 1995–99), Menem could count both on a working majority in the legislature and a docile judiciary, which allowed him to undercut most checks and balances. In retrospect, most experts agree that changes in the existing external auditing system would have been preferable to a radical change of external audit model.

The final proposal stripped the AGN of some of the important prerogatives of its predecessor, including its selective *ex ante* control of legality, its ability to suspend or annul unlawful administrative acts, its direct sanctioning powers in administrative matters, and its powers to initiate judicial proceedings and act as plaintiff. Internal control mechanisms were strengthened. Selective *ex ante* control of major operations (in particular privatisation and procurement) was abandoned and substituted by *ex post* performance auditing. While this shift followed international best practice, the continued weakness of internal bureaucratic control and the rule of law meant that, in practice, *ex ante* compliance control became ineffectual. The most important change to the original proposal, modelled after the US and Canadian AAAs, was the collegiate nature of the AGN and the mode of designation of auditors-general along partisan lines (Guitiérrez 2002).[8] These alterations resulted in the politicisation of the AGN, which was reinforced by the 1994 reform (Fadel 2002).

In sum, these reforms, although in theory compelling, were unfortunate and inopportune in the Argentine context (Baglini 2002; Despouy *et al* 2002). The reforms changed the formal institutions of fiscal control but did not affect the informal institutions and underlying power relationships in which the system of financial scrutiny is embedded. In Argentina, strengthening administrative probity required enhancing *ex ante* controls, not undermining them.

Measures of institutional quality reproduced in Table 4.1 underscore the structural deficiencies in Argentine governance, both in absolute and relative terms. There has been an important deterioration in the quality of governance since 1996 and in 2004 Argentina clearly underperformed compared to the regional average and other countries with similar income levels.

Table 4.1 Argentina governance profile (1996–2004)

	1996	*1998*	*2000*	*2002*	*2004*	*Regional average (2004)*	*Income country average (2004)*
Voice and accountability	66.5	59.7	62.3	52.5	62.1	53.6	64.6
Political stability	65.2	64.2	64.2	23.8	38.3	39.2	67.6
Government effectiveness	72.1	73.8	67.4	37.6	42.3	42.1	62.2
Regulatory quality	81.8	81.0	66.5	19.6	20.2	49.8	63.0
Rule of law	65.7	67.6	61.6	27.8	28.5	39.1	64.4
Control of corruption	54.0	59.6	44.6	27.8	42.9	44.6	63.4

Source: Based on Kaufmann *et al* (2005) and World Bank GRICS: Governance Research Indicator Country Snapshot 1996–2004 (2005) (www.worldbank.org/wbi/governance/bycountry.html).

Note: The figure depicts the percentile rank on each governance indicator over the years 1996–2004. Percentile rank indicates the percentage of countries worldwide that rate below the selected country in each component (subject to margin of error). Higher values thus imply better governance ratings.

Institutional linkages

In Argentina's model of external auditing, the AGN functions as an auxiliary body to the legislature in the oversight of government finances. There are, nevertheless, important dysfunctions in the institutional linkages between the AGN and the legislature, which hinder the effectiveness of the system of fiscal control and, ultimately, government accountability. These are partly rooted in faulty institutional design, but more fundamentally in the nature and functioning of the political system.

The process of certification of public accounts illustrates these dysfunctions. One of the main instruments for the legislature to exercise political control over government is through the *ex post* oversight of the budget. Through the annual review of government accounts, it decides whether or not to discharge government. In theory, the process is coherently organised. However, informal practices and legal controversies have precluded the system of legislative certification and discharge from functioning as intended, impeding the prompt and timely review of government accounts (Lamberto 2005; Baglini 2005; Barra 2002).

The certification process is riddled with technical, procedural and political problems, which cause significant delays in the review of government public accounts in every stage, which has become a 'labyrinth' (Lamberto 2002). For example, the CPMRC posits that the prior opinion of the AGN is required for it to proceed with the review of government accounts. However, the AGN has repeatedly abstained from emitting an audit opinion on the entirety or portions of the government accounts. It has repeatedly argued that government accounts did not provide sufficiently reliable information on the true nature of public accounts and budget execution, thus blaming the executive for the poor quality of the fiscal information it generates (Braceli 2002).

The result has been a breakdown of the entire certification process. Between 1994 and 2006, the legislature failed to either approve or disapprove government accounts. In 2005, the last public accounts to have been approved were those of 1993, which were approved by the CPMRC in June 1997 and by the legislature a year later in June 1998 (Uña *et al* 2005). Nevertheless, in March 2006, the CPMRC approved the public accounts of 1997 and 1998, which were subsequently approved by the legislature in May 2006.

However, the public accounts of 1994, 1995, and 1996 remain imbued in controversy. They were audited by the AGN in 1997, 1998, and 1999, respectively, and reviewed in the CPMRC in late 2002, but resulted in majority and minority opinions. These public accounts are particularly problematic, as the aftermath of the financial crisis in México in late 1994, known as the *Tequila crisis*, had an important impact throughout the region. The crisis made the growth and macroeconomic estimates on which the budgets were built irrelevant and converted the budgets, especially those of 1994 and 1995, into a legal fiction. As a result, the public accounts of 1994 to 1996 cannot be approved. However, there is uncertainty in the legislature of what should happen were government not to be granted discharge and who should be held to account.

Such delays tend to make the whole exercise extraneous, all the more because the review of government accounts tends to restrict itself to a review of compliance with legal and procedural rules, rather than a substantive review of government performance. Moreover, the legislative decision whether or not to discharge government is an ordinary law, which could, in theory, be vetoed by the executive; an absurd situation that has nevertheless not yet occurred (Baglini 2005; Rejtman 2005).

Table 4.2 shows that delays in the certification process originate in the legislative stage, rather than in the audit stage. In 2004, the AGN processed the public accounts of 2002 and, in 2006, those of 2003 and 2004. The AGN has been able to gradually catch up on its backlog. By mid-2007, it was reviewing the accounts of 2005 and considering those of 2006. These findings suggest that dysfunctions in the auditing process do not originate in the AGN's weak technical capacity, but rather in the political filtering of audit findings in the legislature. The result is a lack of enforcement of audit recommendations, ineffectual follow-up of audit findings, and limited publicity of audit reports.

These shortcomings reflect deeper structural flaws in the system of fiscal control. They impede the budget from functioning as an instrument for

Table 4.2 Status of reports on government public accounts in Argentina

Status of the public accounts	*Fiscal year*	*Year processed*
Last report completed by the AGN	2004	2006
Last report approved by the AGN	2004	2006
Last report approved by the CPMRC	1998	2006
Last report approved by the legislature	1998	2006

As of December 2005.

Source: Lamberto (2005) and Uña *et al* (2005:29), based on information provided by Gerardo Uña and Damián Staffa in May 2007. In 2007, the CPMRC was processing the audited public accounts of 1999 and 2000 and the AGN is reviewing the public accounts of 2005. However, the public accounts of 1994, 1995, 1996, which had been audited by the AGN in 1997, 1998 and 1999, respectively, are pending approval or disapproval in the legislature.

strategic planning and a tool for legislative scrutiny. They are partly a result of a lack of interest or incentives of the legislature to use external audits to effectively oversee government finances. This situation is not new, however, but has deep roots in Argentina's history. More fundamentally, it reflects wider dysfunctions in financial governance, in particular legislative oversight and bureaucratic integrity. Excessive polarisation and a general weakness of the rule of law constitute key hindering factors to the independent auditing of government finances (Ducoté 2001).

The fiction of control

A characteristic feature of the Argentine system of fiscal control is not the lack of control, but the fiction of control. A former auditor-general, Hector Rodríguez (2002:161), summarises the Argentine ambivalence towards the law: 'we are Argentineans and have our anomies. Things are not always what the law says they are.' This gives the impression 'that the administration is being controlled or that it is possible to control it, when in reality the system ties the hands of those who are supposed to exercise such control' (Atchabahian 2002:155). While the law is complied with formally, reflecting a formalism of control techniques inherited from the country's legal system, it is not complied with substantially. The absence of evaluation of management performance, both inside and outside the government, precludes substantive government accountability. This façade formalism nevertheless constrains public managers by detecting minor procedural and administrative mistakes, rather than tackling structural dysfunctions and political corruption.

Since the process has been in disarray for so long, the question then becomes why politicians and policymakers have maintained the fiction of control. The root cause of such dysfunctions is not a lack of technical capacities, but rather a lack of political incentives to use existing audit information to hold government to account, both for compliance and performance. In the Argentine institutional set-up, the relations between the AGN and the legislature, mediated by the CPMRC, are essentially political in nature, between the representatives of political parties in the legislature and the professional auditors designated on partisan grounds. The ruling party tends to dominate the CPMRC, which diminishes its incentives for critical oversight. The result is that the AGN has ended up hierarchically depending on those very authorities it is meant to control. As the Argentine writer José Hernandez (1834–86) once wrote, 'the law is like a knife: it does not menace the one who holds it.'

The weakness of the CPMRC is also rooted in the broader institutional weakness of the legislature in the budget process (Rodríguez and Bonvecchi 2006). The partisan mode of designation of external auditors is compounded by the high rate of rotation and limited expertise of the members of the CPMRC who are, to paraphrase Jones *et al* (2000) 'professional politicians, amateur legislators,' with few exceptions. Unlike their counterparts in Brazil and Chile, Argentine legislators have short-term political horizons as a result of electoral rules based on closed-list proportional representation and the overwhelming influence of provincial politics on legislative careers (Jones 2001; Spiller and Tommasi 2000). Legislators' careers do not depend on their standing in the legislature, but rather on their ability to cultivate connections in the provinces or the federal government. They thus have few incentives to specialise and invest in the legislature's oversight capacities. Nevertheless, in recent years, several legislators have proposed to strengthen the legislature's budget capacities through the creation of a legislative budget office.

As a result of these weaknesses, formal budgetary rules are often circumvented, if not blatantly violated. The legislature participates in the fiction of control. For example, while the 1992 law allows the executive to modify the budget during its execution only in exceptional cases, budget reallocations have become the rule rather than the exception since 1997. Annual budget laws have repeatedly lifted restrictions on the executive's ability to modify the budget during the fiscal year (Uña *et al* 2005). The legislature has also failed to establish the committee to oversee executive decrees, as provided for by the 1994 amendment to the Constitution. In August 2006, the executive pushed through a reform of the 1992 law giving it free reign over the budget, a proposal sanctioned by the legislature. The role of the legislature in the budget process is now limited to approve the overall amount of the budget and the level of indebtedness (Díaz Frers 2006). The measure was accompanied by a relaxation of the rules governing the approval of executive decrees, which are now automatically approved unless explicitly objected by the legislature.

In sum, flaws in institutional design are compounded by the broader political context in which the AGN is embedded. Some of the characteristic features of financial governance in Argentina include a broad delegation of budget powers of the legislature to the executive, an ample discretion of the executive in public financial management, a centralisation of the budget process in the executive, and a disproportionate recourse to executive decrees to reallocate budget appropriations during the fiscal year (Santiso 2003, 2001; Bambaci *et al* 2002; Ferreira Rubio 2000). These tendencies are reflected, for example, in the multiplication of off-budget special funds in recent years (Abuelafia *et al* 2005). The concentration of budgetary powers in the executive is the result of the legislative delegation of budgetary powers combined with the concentration of fiscal prerogatives in the executive, including through the use, abuse and misuse of executive decree authority (Uña *et al* 2005; Carey and Shugart 1998; Mainwaring and Shugart 1997). This 'addiction' to decrees, especially in public budgeting, has outlived Menem to become engrained in budgeting practices under his successors.

The failure of institutional transplant

In terms of approaches to reform, an important lesson from the Argentine case is the failure of institutional transplant. The trajectory of the AGN constitutes a clear case of failure of radical reform and institutional engineering based on the import of exogenous models of external auditing. The external audit model imported in the early 1990s prematurely eliminated critical features of the previous model without replacing them with adequate substitutes. Unlike in Chile, the Argentine bureaucracy was simply not ready for *ex post* performance auditing and the abandonment of *ex ante* compliance control.

The *ex post* and corrective nature of external auditing and the lack of effective *ex ante* preventive mechanisms are particularly problematic in the context of a politicised bureaucracy lacking self-control and in which impunity prevails. Financial laws and control systems are either circumvented or lack the necessary supplementary legislation to be effectively enforced. Procedural uncertainties and ambiguities, for instance in the certification of public accounts, allow room for interpretation, delays and dilution. The weakness of the AGN is a reflection of broader dysfunctions in public management, in particular the nature of economic policymaking and the absence of a professional civil service (Rodríguez 2002). Human resource management in the public sector remains a critical hindering factor. The absence of a specialised *corps d'état* in the AAA has precluded the emergence of an *esprit de corps* within the agency, as in Brazil or Chile. Half of the staff of the AGN are under short-term contracts.

The core dysfunction of the system of fiscal control is therefore not to be found in intrinsic flaws in the AGN's institutional design, but rather in its inadequacy to the Argentine public sector (Abuelafia *et al* 2005). The problem does not lie with existing legal provisions, but in their effective application and the incentives of those tasked with enforcing them (Fadel 2002; World Bank 2001). As Berensztein *et al* (2000:2) argue, 'the problem of lack of transparency does not reside in the nature or characteristics of the mechanisms of control theoretically in place, but the fact that they are not used.'

Ultimately, political economy factors explain why, while it was conceptually sound, the model of external auditing introduced in 1992 has failed in practice. It might have been preferable to opt for second-best options of workable systems that could have been gradually improved and fine-tuned. Thus, while technical solutions and organisational reforms can help improve the AGN's performance, the absence of political incentives to make it work hampers its ultimate effectiveness. As Rodríguez and Bonvecchi (2006) note, the main problem is political, residing in the skewed incentives of legislators to effectively exercise control and hold government to account. Consequently, only greater political competition is likely to improve the fate of the AGN's audit work. In fact, the review of public accounts progressed most when the opposition had expectations to gain power (1991–93 and 1997–99).

Chapter 5

The court model and the case of Brazil

Rouba, mas faz (he steals but gets things done).

Slogan of a former mayor of São Paulo during an electoral campaign in the 1950s, cited in Laranjeira 1999.

Introduction

The Court model, often referred to as the Napoleonic model, is a collegiate court of auditors or tribunals of accounts, endowed with quasi-judicial powers in administrative matters, often acting as an administrative tribunal. The quasi-judicial features and functions of the court model privilege legal and financial compliance over performance auditing. The links with the legislature are limited; yet those with the judiciary are also ambiguous. As a result, there is often uncertainty as to who is the agency's principal.

Under this model, the AAA renders judgments on government compliance with budget regulations and can impose administrative sanctions on administrators of public funds, enforcing individual responsibility on bureaucrats. These can nevertheless appeal to the regular courts, which often contest the legal standing of audit rulings. Most such agencies have a collegial structure mirroring that of the courts and the auditing process is often structured in a way that closely follows judicial proceedings. They judge the legality of public accounts and the actions of government chief accountants. They either grant a discharge or impose a penalty. Courts or tribunals of accounts with judicial enforcement powers may establish administrative legal responsibility for the misuse of public funds or the violation of financial administration regulations. The judicial functions of the court model tend to privilege a legal approach to external auditing focusing on compliance with rules and regulations, over performance auditing. It is mainly staffed with lawyers and judges and its independence is usually secured by its relationship with the Supreme Court or its quasi-judicial status.

Thus, in the court model, according to Dye and Stapenhurst (1998:1), 'the institution is an integral part of the judiciary, makes legal judgments on compliance with laws and regulations, and exercises a budget control function to assure that public funds are well spent' and for the purpose intended. This model is used in Roman law European countries, such as France's *Cour des Comptes*, Italy's *Corte dei Conti*, Spain's *Tribunal de Cuentas*, Portugal's *Tribunal de Contas*, and the European Union Court of Auditors.[1] This model was transferred to the former colonies of France, Spain and Portugal. Most of North African countries, such as Morocco and Tunisia, Francophone Sub-Saharan African countries, such as Burkina Faso, Mali, Benin or Cameroun, as well as Lusophone Sub-Saharan African countries, such as Mozambique or Angola, have adopted this model. In Latin America, this model inspired Brazil, the Dominican Republic, El Salvador, Honduras and Uruguay.[2]

The Brazilian *Tribunal de Contas da União* (TCU) follows the court model of external auditing. It illustrates the potential but also the limitations of the court model. The experience of the Brazilian TCU contrasts with that of the Argentine AGN. While Argentina exemplifies the failure of radical reform through a change of audit model, Brazil illustrates the promises of gradual reform through piecemeal adjustments in the audit system. However, as in Argentina, the case of Brazil also shows the limits of fiscal control imposed by the wider political economy in which the system of external auditing is embedded. While the Brazilian TCU enjoys greater independence than the AGN, its relations with the legislature and the judiciary are marked by important dysfunctions that undermine its effectiveness.

Institutional profile

The TCU is an institution deeply anchored in the Brazilian political landscape, with a solid reputation, significant resources and recognised technical capacity. The TCU's effectiveness is reflected in the aggregate index of institutional effectiveness in Figure 3.3 which ranks it as the best performing AAA in our sample across all but one dimension in Table 3.3. The TCU has a long historical trajectory dating back to the first republican constitution of 1891. It was established at the insistence of the executive shortly after Brazil became a republic in 1889 to rein in federal spending and prevent the misuse of public resources (Roque Citadini 1995). Its main architect was former finance minister, Rui Barbosa (Barbosa 1994). Its first organic law which dates back to 1896 sets its internal structures, rules and procedures. These have remained relatively stable until today, with some modifications.

The TCU is a collegiate body modelled as an administrative tribunal of accounts with quasi-judicial powers. A board of nine auditors-general, or 'ministers,' with ample guarantees of individual independence, governs the TCU (Rocha 2003; Brown 2002a, 2002b). Auditors-general are appointed for life and have the same rights, privileges and immunities as members of the Supreme Court of Justice. The Federal President appoints three auditors-general with the approval of the Senate. The legislature appoints the other six auditors-general, three being appointed by the Senate and three by the Chamber of Deputies. Moreover, two of the three ministers nominated by the Federal President must be chosen from the TCU's career personnel, restricting the President's choice. The president of the TCU is selected by his peers and rotates every year but, since 1934, can be re-elected for up to three years. Audit reports are adopted by majority vote (there are some cases which are reviewed by a subset of the nine auditors-general).

The composition of the TCU thus reflects legislative preferences, rather than executive preferences, and auditors-general often are former legislators. As in Argentina, the nomination process is highly politicised, but politicisation is tamed by the life tenure of the Brazilian auditors-general and the professionalism of the agency staff. It is expected that, over time, the political connection of auditors-general will gradually diminish, as government majorities change and auditors-general develop a sense of professional and corporate allegiance. The 1988 Constitution also establishes requirements for candidates as auditors-general in terms of technical capability and professional experience.

Although functionally dependent on the legislature, the TCU is an autarkic agency with ample autonomy. As in Argentina, the oversight of public finances and the evaluation of government performance are constitutionally entrusted to the legislature, which is assisted by the TCU. For example, only the legislature can suspend federal public contracts in case of alleged impropriety. The TCU performs routine oversight of government finances on behalf of the legislature.[3] Its core function is to oversee the accounts of federal entities, primarily through legal and financial compliance auditing, 'the political control of accounting and financial legality *par excellence*' (Lopes Meirelles 1989:602).

The TCU must ensure the integrity of financial administration, the probity of public spending and the lawful execution of the budget. All in all, the TCU has jurisdiction over about 2600 direct and indirect public administration units (compared with 2288 in 1991 and 3275 in 1996), as well as federal funds administered by the 26 states, the federal district and the 5564 municipalities (TCU 2003). It has control and inspection functions (through special inspections and operational audits), consultative and normative functions (through the advice it provides to the legislature), as well as corrective powers (through the imposition of sanctions and correcting administrative acts or omissions). In terms of enforcement capabilities, in addition to reporting alleged irregularities to the judiciary, the TCU has direct sanctioning powers in administrative matters. It judges the accounts of public managers and imposes administrative sanctions in case of impropriety. As such, 'when the TCU gives its final verdict on the correctness of administrators, it is undeniably close to judicial power' (Speck 1999:4). However, while binding,

TCU sanctions are not self-enforcing and require coactive enforcement by the courts.

The 1988 Constitution expanded the scope of the TCU's mandate. The TCU is primarily concerned with compliance with rules and procedures but has gradually expanded its remit to include broader aspects of financial administration and service delivery. The TCU controls the legality, legitimacy and economy of public finances, including both revenues and spending (Pessanha 1999). The TCU's competence now includes a wide array of functions, including the review of the federal government's public accounts; the examination of the accounts of public managers, the control of the legality of public sector hiring, retirement, and pensions; the monitoring of privatisations; and the investigation of allegations of irregularities made by any individual citizen, political party, civic association or trade union. In the area of federal revenues, the TCU has authority over multilateral agreements, oil royalties, and the distribution of the tax-sharing funds allotted to municipalities and states through the calculation of the corresponding coefficients. Moreover, legislation often adds new tasks, for example to verify compliance with laws on public procurement and human resource management.[4] The fiscal responsibility law of 2000 requires the TCU to ensure compliance with caps on civil service recruitment and help enforce fiscal discipline.

In terms of audit techniques, the TCU has traditionally focused on compliance auditing. Until 1967 it had the authority to perform *ex ante* reviews of selected government acts and transactions. Since 1988, it has gradually embraced performance auditing, assessing the economy, efficiency and effectiveness of federal public spending. The TCU has interpreted its mandate flexibly in order to widen its remit and have greater impact on policy. For example, the TCU has been able to influence public policies in the energy and electricity sectors, public procurement and, more recently, social protection. It is nevertheless criticised for not sufficiently focusing on improving public sector results (including its own performance) and for the low level of recovery of resources.

Institutional effectiveness

The TCU enjoys a significant degree of autonomy in the performance of its responsibilities. While its independence is not enshrined in the Constitution, which establishes it as an auxiliary organ to the legislature, it is anchored in practice. The TCU has ample autonomy in the manner in which it structures its organisation, deploys its resources and programmes its activities. Its independence has practical limits, however (Speck 1999). The TCU has to undertake a series of routine oversight activities, which consume most of its resources. These include the registration of administrative acts and the verification of annual accounts, most of which are largely passive forms of control (Gonçalves 1991).[5] The TCU also undertakes special audits and inspections at the request of the legislature. It is constitutionally bound to attend to the legislature's requests, emanating in particular from its numerous ad hoc inquiry commissions.[6]

In terms of budgetary independence, the budget has generally not been used to pressure the TCU. However, nor have budget increases been used to strengthen it. Its budget has tended to decline in relative terms over the past decade, representing 0.05 per cent of the federal budget in 2005, down from 0.10 per cent in 1995. The TCU's budget is set in the same way as any other federal entity, as part of the government's budget proposal approved by the legislature.

Although less pronounced than in Argentina, the politicisation of the TCU's decision-making structure represents an important hindrance to the agency's effectiveness. Alston *et al* (2005:46) argue that, though the TCU 'is endowed with resources and instruments to affect public policy, its lack of independence from other political actors limits its actual impact.' The 1988 Constitution changed the mode of designation of auditors-general in significant ways, taming the influence of the executive and increasing that of the legislature. Until then, the Federal President designated all the auditors-general, with Senate approval. However, partisan influence has remained. The designation of auditors-general follows partisan lines, with final choices subject to political negotiations among political parties within each chamber. For Alston *et al* (2005:49):

> the process of nomination of the nine ministers assures that the majority coalition in Congress will generally have control over the decision-making process in the TCU. Furthermore, the relationship between the President and Congress [...] implies that the majority coalition will generally not have an interest in having the TCU create problems for the President.

Unlike in Chile, few auditors-general devote most of their professional careers to the TCU (Pessanha 2000). Auditors-general enter the TCU at a later stage in their political career and stay less time in office.[7] Not surprisingly, the TCU is often compared to either a 'golden parachute' for political allies in their crepuscule (with sumptuous pension benefits) or a 'reserve bank' after which auditors-general pursue other careers in the public or private sectors. Nevertheless, in a context of frequent changes in political power and fragmented government coalitions, the composition of the TCU could have been much more heterogeneous than it actually is. As certain political parties have remained in power for decades, the composition of the TCU has been relatively stable in political terms (Speck 1999:6). Pessanha (2000) shows that auditors-general come predominantly from Minas Gerais, Rio de Janeiro and Rio Grande do Sul, the powerbases of Brazilian politics.

The TCU's decision-making process, which follows court proceedings, is prone to political capture. Decisions can be voted on, but are generally taken by consensus (Rocha 2003), a practice that endows each auditor-general with a virtual veto power. As a result, as Figueiredo (2003:185) remarks: 'The improvements in the TCU's technical expertise and capacity for auditing government accounts have outpaced its capacity to impose policy changes and sanctions against the misuse of public resources. The recommendations contained in the reports prepared by the TCU's technical personnel are usually not followed by its board of ministers for political reasons.' For example, a Senate inquiry commission recently revealed a corruption scandal in the building of the labour courts in São Paulo. The chief justice of the labour tribunal had embezzled more than US$50 million. The TCU was notified of the case in 1992, after irregularities had been detected. However, only in 1998 did the TCU decide to include that construction in a list of illicit public works.

Nevertheless, the politicisation of the college of auditors-general is partly counterbalanced by a stable, professional and cohesive staff. TCU has approximately 2000 staff and a decentralised structure. Advantageous pay conditions, attractive career prospects and status provide staff with important incentives. They contribute to creating an 'esprit de corps' within the agency, instilling professionalism and providing a sense of purpose to its staff. Since 1988, staff are selected through open competitive recruitment and receive continuous technical training. Many within the agency favour more pro-active interventions seeking to improve public management and influence public policies, beyond simply checking the regularity of public spending. In recent years, it has sought to follow up on audit recommendations more systematically and ensure that audit findings result in concrete changes in administrative practices (TCU 2000a, 2000b). In terms of financial impact, the TCU measures the savings it generates, both through corrective and preventive measures. In 2002, it imposed administrative sanctions for a total of US$350 million, compared with US$166 million in 2001 and US$37 million in 2000. The TCU also calculates the impact of its 'decisions that resulted in potential savings for the treasury' (TCU 2003:25) at R$3.2 billion in 2002.

However, the main benefits from fiscal oversight are the actual improvements in public sector governance, for example by redressing irregularities in public procurement, including overpricing, or correcting deficiencies in the management of external debt. Performance audits have often resulted in significant improvements in service delivery. Auditors do recognise that performance auditing allows for a more productive and, ultimately, effective engagement with the bureaucracy than the inquisitorial approach of *ex post* compliance auditing. The TCU has also contributed to improving control systems in federal programmes, for example in the conditional cash transfer programme *Bolsa Família*.

Incidentally, while inspections and audits are among the most effective and most publicised activities of the TCU, they only absorb a limited portion of its resources, 17 per cent and 5 per cent in 1997 and 1998, respectively. Most resources are devoted to routine activities. The judgment of the accounts of public administrators (*tomadas e prestação de contas*) absorbed over 50 per cent of its resources in 1998 (TCU 2000b). The average time for rendering audit judgments is between 10 and 14 months, which conforms to international standards (TCU 2000c). These routine checks must follow the same rigid court-type procedures as apply to regular court proceedings. However, they detect few irregularities and usually concur with those performed by internal control units. Moreover, the TCU judgements can be appealed in the courts, a strategy which is often adopted by the defendants in case of an adverse ruling by the TCU.

Thus, a more selective approach to external auditing, based on the identification of risk areas and informed by opinions emitted by the internal audit system, might yield important efficiency gains, as the TCU recognised in a recent review (TCU 2000b). The TCU could improve its effectiveness by being more selective, abandoning its tedious routine compliance control, and embracing more actively *ex ante* performance auditing, especially as internal control systems are gradually strengthened under the *Controladoria-Geral da União* (CGU).

Institutional trajectory

The institutional trajectory of the TCU is marked by gradual reforms and successive adjustments *within* the system of financial oversight and fiscal control. These reforms have significantly altered its institutional profile. They have also generated confusion regarding the location and role of the TCU in the architecture of the state and the system of checks and balances. The TCU emerged from the executive's concern with controlling government finances, to become a quasi-administrative court with functional ties to the judiciary, yet constitutionally placed under the purview of the legislature.

There have been three main waves of reform in the TCU, a first wave in the 1930s and 1940s, a second one in the 1960s and a third one in the late 1980s. Reforms in 1934 entrusted the TCU with verifying the legality of public procurement, with a brief interlude during the *Estado Novo* dictatorship (1937–45). Since 1946, public contracts only take effect if they have been previously registered by the TCU. The denial of a registration will suspend the execution of a contract until the legislature has ruled on the matter. The 1946 Constitution introduced the obligation for the TCU to render a prior opinion or judgment on the public accounts that the President submits annually to the legislature.

A second wave of reforms occurred in 1967 under military rule (1964–85). While the TCU was not dismantled, the military revoked its independence and undercut its authority, including in the registration of public contracts (*registro prévio*).[8] Simultaneously, the TCU's authority was expanded to include all three branches of government and sub-national governments, as a means of extending the military government's control over the bureaucracy and the states. The 1967 reforms also strengthened internal controls under what later became the Secretariat of Internal Control (SFC) in the Ministry of Finance, which reports to the President.[9]

Most importantly, the 1967 reforms abandoned *ex ante* control, in place since 1891, in favour of *ex post* auditing. The abandonment of *ex ante* control followed the logic of separation of powers but significantly diminished constraints on the executive. As a result, the TCU's 'veto powers' in public budgeting and financial administration were greatly reduced (Tsebelis 2002, 2000).[10] *Ex ante* control was gradually transferred to the internal control system and tightly attached to executive power. Nevertheless, the culture of *ex ante* compliance control still pervades the organisation (Speck 2000). The abandonment of *ex ante* control paved the way to modern approaches to external control. In that period, the government became convinced of the need to evaluate public sector performance more rigorously (Braga de Figueiredo 1991). The TCU started to pilot performance audits in the early 1980s under criteria of efficiency and effectiveness without the explicit authorisation by the 1967 Constitution.

The return of democracy in 1985 marked another important stepping stone in the development of the TCU. The Constitution of 1988 substantially strengthened the budgetary powers of the legislature, restored the authority of the TCU and strengthened the links between the two. The strengthening of the legislature's budgetary powers was considered as an integral part of the restoration of democracy and of dismantling the authoritarian heritage (OECD 2003). The new Constitution reorganised and modernised the budgetary system, giving the legislature greater oversight powers, although the executive remains the dominant actor in the budget process. These reforms were part of a broader re-equilibration of executive-legislative relations in favour of the latter. As mentioned previously, the mode of designation of auditors-general was radically modified to strengthen the role of the legislature. The logic of external auditing gradually shifted from being an instrument of executive control of the bureaucracy to becoming an instrument of legislative restraint on the executive. The organic law of the TCU was adopted in 1992 and its competence was expanded beyond compliance auditing (legal and financial) to include performance auditing (economic efficiency and legitimacy), endorsing past practice.

Despite recurrent turbulence in financial markets and the incidence of corruption, Brazil has nevertheless been able to strengthen the institutional framework governing the budget process and public financial management (IMF 2001; World Bank 2002). The 2000 fiscal responsibility law disciplined federal finances and, in 2001, the budgetary system was further rationalised. Moreover, since the late 1990s, planning, management and budgeting are becoming more integrated. Budget reform has gradually become the key lever for reforming the state, disciplining public finances and improving public management.

The TCU has benefited from significant improvements in the budgetary and accounting systems. This contrasts with the experience of Argentina where the failings of external auditing are compounded by weaknesses in public budgeting and accounting. The TCU is embedded in a relatively capable and competent bureaucracy that has matured over time, in particular with the modernisation of the state bureaucracy introduced during the *Estado Novo* of the government of Getúlio Vargas (1937–45) (Bresser Pereira and Spink 1999).[11] As a result of successive reforms that have progressively strengthened public administration, the state apparatus is relatively strong and autonomous (Geddes 1990).

Measures of the quality of governance reproduced in Table 5.1 reflect the relative robustness of the formal institutions underpinning fiscal governance, in relative as well as absolute terms, in particular in terms of bureaucratic effectiveness and regulatory quality. These indicators suggest the relative reliability and predictability of economic policymaking.

Institutional linkages

Despite important improvements in the institutional environment, effective changes in the quality of the scrutiny and oversight of federal accounts have been slow (Pessanha 1999). The effectiveness of external auditing remains inhibited by important dysfunctions in the institutional linkages between

Table 5.1 Brazil governance profile (1996–2004)

	1996	*1998*	*2000*	*2002*	*2004*	*Regional average (2004)*	*Income country average (2004)*
Voice and accountability	59.7	64.4	63.9	58.1	55.8	53.6	39.9
Political stability	48.2	30.9	56.4	48.1	43.7	39.2	36.5
Government effectiveness	52.5	48.1	48.4	50	58.2	42.1	40.2
Regulatory quality	60.2	57.6	63.8	63.4	58.1	49.8	38.5
Rule of law	46.4	56.8	55.1	50	46.9	39.1	37.4
Control of corruption	55.3	68.9	59.8	56.7	53.2	44.6	38.6

Source: Kaufmann *et al* (2005) and World Bank GRICS: Governance Research Indicator Country Snapshot 1996–2004 (2005) (www.worldbank.org/wbi/governance/bycountry.html).

Note: The figure depicts the percentile rank on each governance indicator over the years 1996–2004. Percentile rank indicates the percentage of countries worldwide that rate below the selected country in each component (subject to margin of error). Higher values thus imply better governance ratings the TCU and the other components of the system of fiscal control. Although the TCU follows the court model and has quasi-judicial powers, its insertion into the judicial system is questioned and contested. At the same time, its relations with the legislature, its ultimate principal, exhibit important shortcomings as a result of skewed political incentives. As a result, proposals to reform the TCU continue to abound.

In terms of the relations between the TCU and the judiciary, there is controversy over the judicial nature of the TCU, the legal status of its decisions, and the enforceability of its audit rulings. While TCU follows the court model, its status as a quasi-judicial administrative court is contested. While its decision-making process mirrors a judicial process, its linkages with the judiciary are ambiguous. As a result, the enforcement of audit recommendations and the imposition of sanctions for non-compliance suffer serious shortcomings.

TCU considers itself a quasi-judicial organ as an administrative court. As Speck (2000:210) argues, the 'procedural structure of the TCU is currently guided by the logic of procedural legitimacy, which is a characteristic trait of the judicial process.' However, the quasi-judicial powers of the TCU have been contested from the onset by the courts, which consider the TCU as an administrative rather than a judicial body. A key unresolved controversy is whether audit rulings are subject to judicial review (Rocha 2003). The courts question the judicial nature of audit rulings based on the legal principle that there cannot exist administrative acts shielded from judicial review. Furthermore, the Brazilian judicial system does not establish the legal principle of *stare decisis* (stand by things decided) and each case is therefore evaluated on its own merits. This allows the courts to re-examine each TCU ruling independently of any legal precedent, preventing the gradual emergence of a body of audit jurisprudence. Moreover, the TCU does not have the right to coactive execution, which is enforced by the public prosecutor's office.

The Supreme Court has ruled on repeated occasions to circumscribe the competences of the TCU, for example excluding the state oil company Petrobras from its purview in 2002 or contesting its oversight of regulatory agencies and public companies. It has also challenged the judicial nature of audit rulings, reducing them to simple recommendations to administrative authorities (Silvera e Silva 2002). In response to the courts' challenge, the TCU has staunchly defended the judicial nature of audit rulings as '*coisa julgada administrativa*' that can only be appealed in the courts in case of procedural irregularities (Guimarães Souto 2002:228; Affonso 1997, 1996), but to no avail. As Rocha (2003:15) remarks:

> the more the TCU insists on the jurisdictional nature of its decisions, the more it is exposed to the criticism of the judiciary, which, attentive to defending its own prerogatives, has imposed restrictions on the TCU's competence.

The bottom line for the courts is that the TCU is a tribunal, not a court, and therefore its decisions can be appealed in the courts including in administrative matters (Zanella di Pietro 1996). Furthermore, the courts usually do not accept audit findings as evidence. Hence, while final and binding, TCU decisions are not directly enforceable. As a result of thorny appeals processes, the actual collection rate of fines and other administrative penalties is extremely low, less than one per cent (Speck 1999). For example, there is controversy concerning the judiciary's right to try a politician whose accounts have been cleared by the TCU. Public administrators accused of corruption cite the approval of their accounts by the TCU as evidence of their innocence. However, the judiciary reserves the right to try such cases and review the TCU's rulings.

Similarly, the TCU's relations with the legislature are also dysfunctional, which undermines its ability to hold government to account. However, as in Argentina, the major dysfunctions occur in the legislative stage of the budget process, rather than in the auditing stage. As mentioned previously, the TCU provides technical assistance to the legislature in the oversight of government public accounts; but it is the legislature that is ultimately responsible for enforcing accountability on government. Detailed legislative scrutiny of the budget takes place in the Joint Committee on Plans, Public Budgets and Auditing of the bicameral parliament (*Comissão Mista de Planos, Orçamentos Públicos e Fiscalização*, CMO).

The annual review and judgment of the president's accounts constitute the main instrument through which the legislature holds government to account (Gonçalves 1984).[12] Since 1934, Brazilian presidents are required to render accounts to the legislature every year, through the CMO (Machado *et al* 1996). The TCU prepares a report on the public accounts of the federation within 60 days of receipt from the legislature. It issues a 'preliminary opinion' or 'prior judgment' (*parecer prévio às contas*) to guide the discussions in the legislature on whether to approve the government's statements or not. Based on the TCU's opinion, the CMO emits its own recommendation to the legislature by unanimity vote. The process then follows normal legislative procedures, being examined and voted on by both chambers successively. However, the TCU's preliminary opinion is not a formal audit ruling and seldom includes any reference to corrective measures or a follow-up of the irregularities detected in previous years.

While the legislature 'makes the final judgment on the discharge of government, the analysis of the TCU is conclusive and carries its own weight' (Speck 1999:3). The formal judgment of the public accounts generally takes place during an extraordinary session of the TCU and receives significant media coverage, as it often includes criticism of specific government programmes. Nevertheless, the TCU has usually recommended approval, though it typically includes reservations, recommendations and warnings. Between 1946 and 2002, the preliminary opinion of the TCU was always positive, recommending the legislature to approve government accounts, except on three occasions when it was inconclusive (1946, 1950 and 1953) (Pessanha 2003).[13] Only in 1992 did the TCU give a negative opinion on the accounts of President Collor de Mello for 1991. The impact of this verdict was minor, however, compared with the process of parliamentary inquiry that resulted in Collor's impeachment. Alston *et al* (2005:48) therefore argue that:

> these reports are to a large extent innocuous as the politicized nature of the decision-making process acts as a barrier that filters decisions that may be troublesome for congress and for the president.

As in Argentina, the certification and discharge processes are marked by greater hurdles in the legislative stage than in the auditing stage of the budget process, which brings their ultimate usefulness into question. As the same political forces tend to dominate the executive, the legislature and the TCU, incentives for enforcing accountability on government are limited, leading a federal deputy to conclude that the certification process is an '*acto entre irmãos*'.[14] The legislature has generally approved the public accounts, with few reservations, concurring with the TCU's preliminary opinion (Pessanha 2000; Pontes and Pederiva 2004).

Furthermore, the legislature's discharge of government has occurred with significant delays, at times reaching almost a decade. For example, the 1959 public accounts, although approved by the TCU on time in 1960, were only certified by the legislature 12 years later, in 1972. Approval of the government's accounting after the end of the president's term has not been unusual. On several occasions, to clear the backlog, the legislature approved the public accounts of several years simultaneously, often in the same day, as in 1972 and 2002. The public accounts of 1993 and of 1995 through 2001 were all approved in December 2002.[15] The public accounts of 1990 through 1992 have yet to be reviewed. There have also been important procedural problems. The legislature approved the public accounts of 1995, 2000 and 2001, without the preliminary approval of the CMO, as required by law. Moreover, there have been cases, such as in 1996 and 1997, where the reporting officer failed to complete his review.

The dysfunctions in the certification process reflect systematic failures in legislative oversight, which undercut the effectiveness of the TCU. As in Argentina, the process of certification is hindered by the legislators' lack of interest and incentives to use it effectively.[16] A better interaction between the legislature and the TCU is warranted. 'On rare occasions', note Pontes and Pederiva (2004:23), 'has the analysis of public accounts by the legislature generated substantial debate or positive results, or led the legislature to take corrective action.' However, as the World Bank (2002:47) remarks:

> this process [...] needs to be seen in its political context. Any debate on approval or disapproval, involving a detailed discussion of the President's

annual report provides an opportunity for opposition parties to attack the fiscal policies and record of the President. Approval or disapproval thus does not relate to the quality of the financial statements. But there also appears to be some lack of interest by Congress in reviewing past events, and a correspondingly greater interest in issues of budget construction. TCU reports generally appear to attract little Congressional or public interest.

The next stage of reform

This review demonstrates the potential of gradual reforms and adjustments in the system of external auditing. Improving not only the probity of public management but the efficacy of public spending is a priority for Brazil which must come to grips with a state that is overgrown, but is neither efficient nor effective. The TCU has an important role to play, which would nevertheless require further reforms and in particular clarifying its relations with the legislature and the judiciary.

As a result of successive reforms, the location of the TCU in the state apparatus and its insertion into the system of fiscal control has become ambiguous, reflected in a confusion of roles (as a quasi-judicial body or a legislative institution) and tensions in approaches (between compliance and performance auditing). Britto (2001) argues that the TCU is neither an auxiliary institution to the legislature (in the sense of being hierarchically subordinated to the legislature), nor an administrative court *per se* (in the sense of rendering self-binding judgments as the court of last instance in administrative matters).

In terms of its relations with the legislature, former auditor-general Guimarães Souto (2002) recognises that a more efficient relationship with the legislature would improve the TCU's effectiveness, in particular in risk areas such as public procurement. This review suggests that a hindering factor resides in the lack of political incentives of legislators to exercise responsible oversight, rather than the lack of technical capacities of the TCU to audit public finances. Ultimately, the analysis demonstrates that the means (technical capacities) and motives (political incentives) for legislative oversight are intrinsically linked.

In terms of the TCU's relations with the judiciary, the combination of quasi-judicial functions (through the judgment of accounts) and managerial functions (through operational auditing) in the same oversight agency is tricky. These two functions require cultures of control that are radically different, if not contradictory. Thus, the TCU finds itself facing a critical choice: either its judicial functions are transferred to the judiciary, ending the conflict of competence and the duplication of processes, or it becomes an administrative court in its own right. The TCU has thus far pursued the latter strategy, with limited results, however.

In terms of the TCU's relations with the bureaucracy, this analysis suggests that the gradual transition from a prosecutorial approach to a managerial approach to external auditing could yield important results. As the role of the TCU gradually shifts from that of a judge to that of an advisor, its impact on bureaucratic behaviour increases. Indeed, the bureaucracy tends to respond more positively to performance auditing than compliance control.

These limitations notwithstanding, the case of the TCU illustrates the benefits of a gradual approach to reform. Such adjustments can significantly alter the model of external auditing, such as with the abandonment of *ex ante* controls in 1967 or the rapprochement with the legislature in 1988. As Speck (2000:53) observes, 'the model of AAAs is influenced more by historical traditions than legal purism.' Reform initiatives continue to abound, from both within and outside the TCU. In 2001–02, President Fernando Henrique Cardoso sought, unsuccessfully, to modify the mode of designation of auditors-general to give the executive greater leverage.[17] At the end of 2002, there were no less than 46 different proposals to reform the system of fiscal control, at both the federal and state levels (Rocha 2003). In 2003, there were 23 proposals for constitutional amendments and 25 other legislative reform proposals related to the TCU, on issues such as changing the nomination process, increasing the court's jurisdiction, and revisiting its institutional links with the legislature's CMO.

These attempts reflect both a general dissatisfaction with current arrangements, and the difficulty of pushing through reform from outside of the TCU. They also reveal that, while challenging to achieve, reforms do occur and tend to stick once adopted. Following a series of corruption scandals in the federal government, the internal control system was revamped in 2001, leading to the creation, in 2002, of the CGU whose role is to assist the presidency in the prevention and prosecution of irregular acts or omissions in the federal administration.[18]

The institutional trajectory of the TCU illustrates the need for a more nuanced approach to agency autonomy. It is often believed, within the TCU in particular, that independence ought to be preserved at all cost, often as an end in itself.[19] However, as this review suggests, the ultimate effectiveness of the TCU depends both on its autonomy as well as the fluidity of its relations with the other components of the systems of fiscal control. The main question therefore is not whether AAAs should be independent, but how much independence is enough and how much independence is too much. The case of Chile further illustrates this point.

Chapter 6

The monocratic model and the case of Chile

El que vive fuera del presupuesto, vive en el error (he who lives outside the budget lives in error).

Carlos Fuentes, *La Silla del Águila*, 2003.

Chile is a country that governs itself by the law.

Gustavo Sciolla Avendaño.[1]

Introduction

The Monocratic model, often referred to as the Westminster model, consists of a uninominal AAA headed by a single auditor-general, at times an officer of parliament as in the UK, and generally acting as an auxiliary institution to the legislature, albeit with ample autonomy. This model is prevalent in most Commonwealth countries where the AAA is an autonomous body, independent from the executive and reporting to the legislature (McGee 2002). It is an integral part of the system of legislative accountability and has no jurisdictional powers, although its findings may be passed to judicial authorities for further action in criminal or civil matters. The Constitution generally guarantees its independence. The AAA's principal is the legislature, although, in some cases, such as in Chile and other Andean countries, the links between the AAA and the legislature are weak.

AAAs under this model tend to focus on *ex post* auditing, rather than *ex ante* control, and emphasise financial and performance auditing over compliance control. Their staff is predominantly made up of accountants and auditors. Although recommendations and findings made in their reports are not binding *per se*, these agencies use follow-up mechanisms that can prove relatively effective corrective and deterrent devices. In these cases, 'the controls seek to correct rather than penalize' (Payne *et al* 2002:227). This model is closest to the ideal model advocated by the International Organization of Supreme Audit Institutions (INTOSAI), which emphasises the importance of the agency's independence from the executive. It corresponds to the US Government Accountability Office, Canada's Office of the Auditor General, the UK's National Audit Office,[2] and Australia's National Audit Office. In the UK and the US the auditor-general has a controllership role as well, in that he countersigns releases of budget funds to spending agencies.

This model was transferred to the former colonies of the UK in particular, such as, in Anglophone Sub-Saharan Africa: Uganda, South Africa, Tanzania and Malawi. In Latin America, this is the model adopted by most Andean countries in the early twentieth century as part of the budget reforms promoted by the US and the technical advice of the Kemmerer missions. It is the model adopted by Bolivia, Chile, Colombia, Costa Rica, Ecuador, Guatemala, Nicaragua, Panama, Paraguay, Peru and Venezuela.

The Chilean *Contraloría General de la República* (CGR) illustrates the monocratic model. Under this model, AAAs tend to focus on *ex post* auditing rather than *ex ante* control, and emphasise financial and performance auditing over compliance control. The Chilean CGR, as this chapter will discuss, nevertheless represents an exception in the context of this model.

The CGR also illustrates a third path to reform, or, rather, the lack thereof. The CGR is anchored in a highly centralised budgetary process and in a public administration highly respectful of the rule of law. Its relative effectiveness is reflected in its performance against the four criteria in Table 3.3 and the aggregate index in Figure 3.3. It has decisively contributed to anchoring probity and integrity in the public sector; it has also greatly benefited from it (Faundez 2007). There exists a strong correlation between the quality and rule-abidance of the civil service and the effectiveness of the CGR, but causality is difficult to ascertain.

The case of the CGR is interesting for two main reasons. First, its effectiveness is hampered not by a lack of political independence, but rather by its excessive independence and insulation in the system of political accountability. Ironically, while the effectiveness of the Argentine AGN and the Brazilian TCU is hindered by political and partisan interference, that of the Chilean CGR is hampered by its excessive independence in the architecture of financial governance and fiscal control. In many ways, the CGR is an agent without a 'principal' to which to report and which can enforce its recommendations. The oversight it exercises, essentially legalistic and procedural in nature, fails to translate into effective accountability of government. Failures in the system of fiscal control originate in dysfunctions in the transmission mechanisms between the oversight agency and accountability institutions. Relations with the legislature, the judiciary and the executive are characterised by mutual suspicion and benign neglect. The legislature has developed its own capacity for fiscal oversight and the executive has strengthened its own capacities for performance evaluation. The bipartisan political system would have predicted a more active role of the opposition in using the CGR to check government.

Second, the institutional trajectory of the CGR is marked by a failure to reform and, consequently, the threat of anachronism. Its high degree of independence has allowed it to resist repeated attempts at reform. It has few incentives to reform itself from within because of its pyramidal structure and gerontocracy ethos. Institutional insulation has also prevented the CGR from adapting to new trends in public sector management and financial governance, especially performance auditing. The CGR has largely been left out of the reform movement and has failed to keep up with the rest of the public sector, rendering it an 'island of un-reform'. It is something of an anomaly in the Chilean state, which has otherwise been able to modernise. As a result, it is increasingly exposed to the threat of anachronism, if not irrelevance. Thus, in Chile, the main question is not whether CGR ought to be reformed, but rather how.

Institutional profile

The CGR is a highly respected state institution with a long historical trajectory. It is embedded in a relatively strong state founded on the respect of the rule of law. It was established in 1927 to oversee public spending. It is an autarkic organisation independent from all state powers, which acquired constitutional rank in 1943. It follows the monocratic model of AAA, but unlike similar organisations in the US, the UK or Canada, it is not linked to the legislature. Moreover, unlike its counterparts in Argentina and Brazil, it is neither part of the system of legislative oversight of government finances, nor of the judicial system of fiscal control. It is often referred to as the 'fourth power of the state' (Aylwyn Azócar 2002; Sciolla Avendaño 2002, 2003).

CGR's primary task is to preserve and promote the principles of legality and probity in public administration and government finances. As Siavelis (2000:80) notes, 'both the executive and congress were willing to grant [the CGR] increasing power because of its scrupulous insistence on legality and propriety.' The CGR is inserted in a robust budgetary system regulated by laws dating back to the military regime of Augusto Pinochet (1973–90).[3] The 1975 financial administration law was subsequently incorporated into the 1980 Constitution. The CGR is itself governed by an organic law of 1952, substantially reformed in 1964 and last amended in 2002. The 1980 Constitution provided for the adoption of a new organic law, but controversies surrounding the CGR's core functions have prevented this from happening.[4] Nevertheless, in 2000 the CGR adopted an institutional doctrine clarifying its core mission and values.

As a result of its origins, the scope of CGR's mandate is very broad, encompassing a *smörgåsbord* of functions, some of which are unusual for an AAA and conflicting with one another.[5] It verifies the legality of the administration's transactions, inspects fiscal revenues, public expenditure and government investment, as well as municipal resources. Its core responsibilities include: (i) judicial review functions through the *ex ante* control of constitutionality, legality and regularity of administrative acts through the legality review procedure of the '*toma de razón*' (Faundez 2007), (ii) jurisprudential functions through the legal interpretation of financial administration legislation via '*dictamenes*', contributing to reduce bureaucratic discretion in the interpretation of legal norms; (iii) audit functions through selective *ex post* audit and inspections of administrative agencies, systems and processes, including controlling the reliability of internal control mechanisms and the compliance with statutory obligations of civil servants;[6] and (iv) quasi-administrative functions through the supervision of the state accounting system, the oversight of internal control systems and standards, and the control of compliance with statutory provisions related to the management of human resources in the public sector.[7] In particular, and somewhat unusually for an AAA, the CGR oversees the government accounting system, including the setting of accounting standards.

A constant criticism of the CGR centres on its conservative stance and authoritarian legacy. The CGR adopts a legalistic approach to external auditing, exercising control over the legality of the administration's actions. The oversight it exercises is essentially of a judicial nature 'to ensure adherence to the legal order, the protection and appropriate use of public funds, the preservation and strengthening of administrative probity, and the reliability and transparency of financial information' (CGR 2003:1). The CGR is indeed permeated with the liberal concern for checking and restraining executive discretion, rather than with the managerial concern for improving public sector management. It privileges preventive control through *ex ante* compliance control, over corrective control through *ex post* performance auditing (Llanos González and García Yerkovis 2002).

The CGR exercises *ex ante* control of constitutionality and legality through the mechanism of '*toma de razón*', a function deeply embedded in Chilean administrative law and constitutional order. In political terms, *ex ante* authorisation of administrative actions endows the CGR with veto powers over policy implementation (Animat *el al* 2006; Tsebelis 2002). *Ex ante* control does not rectify an irregular administrative act; rather, it impedes it (Larraín 1995:61).[8] While this procedure predates the military dictatorship, its preservation illustrates the efforts deployed by the outgoing military regime to constrain democratic governments, a strategy which Boylan (2001) describes as 'defusing democracy'. The function of *ex ante* control has often been compared to an 'authoritarian enclave' or a 'gate keeper' (Orrellana Vargas 2003; Garretón 1989).

Historically, the CGR inherited this function because the Chilean judicial system had no effective judicial review of administrative actions by administrative tribunals (Faundez 2007). *Ex ante* control has proven particularly effective in some areas, such as privatisation and public procurement, contributing to ensure probity and transparency. The CGR progressively adopted an expansive approach to the interpretation of its *ex ante* legality review powers, partly at the insistence of the legislature. Successive governments generally complied with the CGR's rulings and seldom abused their powers to override them by issuing '*decretos de insistencia*'.[9] However, it is often criticised for being cumbersome and formalistic, intruding in administrative prerogatives, interfering in policymaking, and resulting in 'co-administration' (Lillo Valenzuela 2002).

The CGR also has quasi-judicial powers in administrative matters, entrusted in a tribunal of accounts located within itself (the *Tribunal de Cuentas*, TC), through the judgment of accounts (*juicio de cuentas*) of current and former public servants (CGR 2000). Since 2002, the deputy comptroller-general acts as the first instance judge and a collegiate tribunal of accounts composed of the comptroller-general and two prominent lawyers designated by the President acts as the second instance court. The TC can impose binding administrative sanctions ordering the reimbursement of the damages caused through salary retentions, career demotion or dismissal.

Institutional effectiveness

The constitution of 1980, the CGR organic law of 1964 and the financial administration law of 1975 guarantee the institutional independence of the CGR as a constitutional body. The agency's independence is statutory (guaranteed by the constitution), personal (guarantee of immovability once nominated, until 75 years of age), functional (the CGR is not hierarchically dependent on any other state power and its decisions are not submitted to revision or approval by other organs of the state) and normative (power to emit binding norms in its areas of responsibility).

The organisation's autonomy is enhanced by the political independence of the comptroller-general and the privileges and immunities from arbitrary removal he or she enjoys. A single comptroller and auditor-general with ample powers heads the CGR, assisted by a deputy comptroller-general. The comptroller-general is nominated by the President and confirmed by the Senate and his or her term of office is for life, until the statutory retirement age of 75. While formal nomination procedures are clearly politically motivated, as in Brazil, permanence in office and life-tenure are designed to reduce, over time, the political origins of the comptroller-general.[10] Furthermore, the comptroller-general can only be removed through impeachment.[11] The impeachment procedure is a radical form of control, however, and is unlikely to be effective in cases of lesser misconduct or arbitrary actions. It also requires a degree of political consensus that is difficult to muster.

The individual independence of the comptroller-general is reinforced by an unwritten rule according to which the deputy comptroller-general succeeds the comptroller-general. As the comptroller-general nominates his deputy usually from within the ranks of the agency, he or she largely determines his or her succession. This tradition has only been broken twice: in 1977 by Augusto Pinochet and in 2002 by Ricardo Lagos, generating intense controversy. Lagos' decision was part of a broader strategy of the ruling *Concertación* coalition to tame the influence of the political right in the CGR and unroot what it considered one of the last bastions of the military regime.[12] In 2006, President Michelle Bachelet attempted to nominate her own candidate, but her attempt ultimately failed.

The comptroller-general also has complete discretion over the management of the CGR and its staff. He or she sets the agency's budget, level of staff and salary scales within the financial constraints of the state budget and in consultation with the President and the Senate. Agency staff benefits from an advantageous pay regime and permanent tenure. These factors, coupled with rigorous recruitment procedures, a predominance of law and accounting professionals, and the existence of career prospects within the organisation, contribute to creating a strong *esprit de corps* and sense of mission. Officials pursue most of their careers within the CGR and often within the department they first joined. For example, Sciolla Avendaño had 48 years of public service when appointed as comptroller-general, 43 of which were spent in the CGR. These factors nevertheless lead staff to develop personal allegiance to the comptroller-general and reverence to hierarchy, which tends to generate a 'bastion' mentality, institutional inertia and aversion to change.[13] Deference to authority and stringent adherence to rules and procedures permeate the internal organisation of the CGR, reflecting its pyramidal structure.

The budgetary independence of the CGR is not guaranteed by law, but by practice. The CGR drafts its own budget and submits it to the finance ministry for consideration. Despite this legal limitation, empirical evidence suggests the CGR's budget has not been used to pressure it. The CGR's budget has nevertheless decreased over time, from 0.32 per cent of the state budget in 1977 to 0.13 per cent in 2000 (Larraín 1995:68). In 2000 political parties agreed to strengthen the CGR and contract a loan from the Inter-American Development Bank. In 2005, the CGR's budget increased to 0.20 per cent of the state budget. Larraín (1995) argues that what the CGR needs is not more resources but greater financial independence, returning to the system that existed between 1959 and 1977 when the CGR was assigned a fixed percentage of the state budget (0.32 per cent).

A central controversy surrounding the CGR concerns *ex ante* compliance control. *Ex ante* control is generally considered to delay administrative action, dilute administrative responsibilities and lessen the legitimacy of *ex post* external auditing. The CGR is both judge and party as it controls administrative acts in which it participated by authorising them. The CGR has relaxed some of its *ex ante* controls, increasing the number of exemptions, delegating the authorisation to approve small expenditures, and reducing the time for review (from 30 to 15 days in 2002). Nevertheless, its quasi-administrative functions absorb a great deal of its resources, representing over 175,000 processes in

2000 (CGR 2001). They also prevent it from fully exploiting its *ex post* auditing functions. It is hoped that the consolidation of the internal control system within government will allow the CGR to concentrate on external auditing and progressively abandon *ex ante* control. Nevertheless, internal control has traditionally been deficient, partly because it was considered unnecessary and partly because the CGR assumed core internal control functions.

A related controversy centres on the nature of external control. Agreement on this issue is even more elusive than on the timing of external control. The CGR's control is essentially one of control of legal and financial compliance. Reforming it would entail for the CGR to abandon its traditional formalist and legalistic approach and embrace modern *ex post* audit techniques focusing on performance and results. The CGR's legalistic culture is also reflected in the confidentiality surrounding audit work, considered as '*información privilegiada*'. Such a prudent approach to disclosure is partly rooted in the CGR's understanding of its role and the importance of its privileged relations with the bureaucracy. It is also understandable considering the exposure of external auditors to political threats during successive military regimes. The culture of secrecy nevertheless adversely affects the publicity of audit findings and, ultimately, their effectiveness.

The CGR adopted an institutional doctrine in 2000, partly to compensate for the lack of an updated organic law (CGR 2003). The doctrine, promoted by former comptroller-general Aylwyn Azócar, counselled gradually moving away from the strict application of the principle of legality to embrace a form of performance auditing based on the '*interpretación finalista de la ley*' (Llanos Campos 2003). However, this doctrinal shift was resisted not only within the CGR, but also by the executive, especially the finance ministry's central budget office (which has developed sophisticated systems to evaluate performance in the public sector), and by the legislature (which was wary of an expansion of the CGR powers). Performance auditing by the CGR would thus not only require a change of corporate culture, but also a redistribution of budgetary roles within the state.

Another hindering factor concerns the legal standing of audit rulings (Diez Urza 1995). The CGR possesses only limited direct enforcement and sanctioning powers in administrative matters (notion of '*imperio*'). Successive comptrollers-general have requested more enforcement and sanctioning powers (Sciolla Avendaño 2002; Aylwyn Azócar 2002, 1995). However, the presence of *ex ante* control tends to render sanctioning powers redundant. The CGR makes recommendations to senior managers who decide on the corrective actions required. When administrative impropriety is suspected, the CGR's tribunal of accounts (TC) initiates a judgment of accounts to determine civil servants' administrative responsibility. However, the TC rulings are only partly self-enforcing, as in the case of salary retentions or other administrative sanctions, and can be challenged in the courts. Coercive enforcement is pursued in ordinary courts by the public prosecutor's office in the CGR.

The CGR also performs administrative functions that conflict with its role as auditor of government accounts (World Bank 2004; OECD 2004; IMF 2003). In particular, it supervises the state accounting system. As a result, it does not audit government financial statements in accordance with international audit standards, simply because it prepares them. It nevertheless prepares monthly, quarterly and yearly accounting reports on the state of public finances and presents an annual report on budget execution to the President and the legislature. The CGR also prepares two other annual reports, the *Cuenta pública del Controlador* and the *Memoria anual*, which provide an annual account of the CGR's activities and a review of government finances, including the follow-up given to previous audit recommendations. Both reports have limited impact on political debates.

Institutional trajectory

Recent corruption scandals have shaken the country's confidence in its fiscal control institutions. In 2002, scandals erupted concerning the procurement practices in public works, as well as the questionable gratifications of high-ranking officials financed from the government's discretionary 'reserved funds' (*gastos reservados*). For Orrellana Vargas (2003), these scandals revealed 'complacency with limited corruption' and flaws in internal and external control systems. The CGR was particularly exposed to public criticism, as it is tasked with controlling, *ex ante*, the regularity of public procurement and public sector remunerations. According to Orrellana Vargas (ibid), it appeared 'totally surprised by actions that it is supposed to oversee.'

Many of the dysfunctions of external auditing in Chile today have their origins in history. The CGR performs tasks that, in other countries, are carried out by three or more organisations, including the quasi-administrative functions of a general accounting office and the quasi-judicial functions of a tribunal of accounts (Llanos González and García Yerkovis 2002). This is partly the result of the CGR's origins. The CGR combined the functions of the four state agencies that were merged in 1927 in an effort to rationalise government financial management. These included the comptroller-general's office, the tribunal of accounts, the bureau of statistics and the inspectorate-general of national assets (Llanos Campos 2003).

Both internal and external factors have shaped the configuration of the CGR's powers, the scope of its authority and its approach to fiscal control. In 1925, US financial advisor Edwin Kemmerer made a series of recommendations to strengthen financial administration and fiscal control based on the experience of the US, following the establishment of the US Government Accountability Office (previously known as the General Accounting Office) in 1921.

Nevertheless, the features and functions of the CGR were also shaped by domestic political considerations and the country's legal traditions. Its creation participated in the modernisation of the budgetary system and the re-equilibration of budgetary powers between the executive and the legislature in the 1920s (Animat *et al* 2006; Marcel and Tokeman 2002; Vial 2001; Santiso 2006c, 2006d, 2005a, 2005b, 2004d). A committee presided over by a prominent Chilean lawyer, Julio Philippi, amended the Kemmerer proposals in significant ways, giving the CGR authority to rule on the constitutionality and legality of government decrees through mandatory *ex ante* controls. More fundamentally, the CGR's formalistic approach to fiscal control reflected the legalistic character of Chilean administrative law, in the absence of administrative tribunals responsible for the judicial review of administrative acts.

The reputation of the CGR grew from its insistence on the respect for the law and its ability to restrain executive discretion, laying the foundations for a rule-abiding bureaucracy. Faundez (2007:7) shows that the CGR 'has had a major influence on administrative practices and the quality of governance.' The institution of *ex ante* review of legality and constitutionality of government decrees has been pivotal to anchor the rule of law in the public sector. In fact, the legislature impeached the comptroller-general in 1945 because it felt that he showed too much deference to the executive. The impeachment thus strengthened the authority of the CGR and 'sent a strong message to the executive that the congress was keen to ensure that the president exercise his powers within the limits of the law' (ibid). By the mid-1950s, governments began to show considerable respect for the CGR.

Another tense episode occurred in 1970 when Salvador Allende took office and sought to push through an ambitious programme of reforms. As his left-wing coalition did not have a majority of seats in the legislature, Allende relied heavily on government decrees. Conflict with the CGR rapidly escalated, as the CGR increasingly questioned the legal foundations of government policy initiatives through legality review rulings. In the end, in April 1973, the government issued a '*decreto de insistencia*' to override some 40 legality review rulings, As Faundez (2007:11) highlights, 'this decree brought a strident reaction from the opposition, which depicted it as further evidence of the government's disregard for the rule of law.'

The CGR earned the respect of many Chileans by opposing the military dictatorship's encroachment of the law during the military regime (1973–90). Initially, Pinochet undermined the CGR in subtle ways, ending the mandatory allocation of a fixed percentage of the budget in 1975 and changing the staff salary regime in 1981, which led to the departure of over 500 officials. Pinochet did not dismantle the CGR, as he needed it to ensure that the bureaucracy complied with the junta's decisions. However, when former comptroller-general Héctor Humeres confronted the military regime, he neutralised the CGR by capturing it.

In 1977, Humeres questioned the constitutionality of the plebiscite the junta was planning for early 1978 and threatened to veto it through *ex ante* control. Pinochet expedited the retirement of Humeres, who was due to retire in 1977, and nominated one of his lieutenants, Sergio Fernández, in his stead. Fernández swiftly approved the legality of the plebiscite just two days before it was to be held. He resigned in April 1978 to become the interior minister, a pivotal position in Pinochet's government. Fernández handpicked his successor, Osvaldo Iturriaga, who remained in office until 1997, well into the democratic transition. These events are often cited as grounds for justifying the criticism of the CGR as an 'authoritarian enclave'.

The credibility of the CGR is enhanced by the effectiveness of the state in which it is embedded. The CGR inserts itself into an effective state with an efficient public administration, reliable regulations and adherence to the rule of law, as seen in Table 6.1. Chile's legalistic approach to public administration and financial administration is reflected in its culture of legal and financial compliance control. As Siavelis (2000:80) notes, 'analysts who underscore the importance of the Contraloría [...] often fail to acknowledge the overall social and party context in which it is embedded', in particular the highly institutionalised Chilean party system and the rule-based bureaucracy'.

A prominent member of the tribunal of accounts between 1891 and 1918, Valentín Letelier, contributed to shape administrative jurisprudence and anchor the principles of legality and probity in the Chilean public administration. The CGR greatly benefits from disciplined public finances achieved through the progressive centralisation of the budget process over the past

Table 6.1 Chile governance profile (1996–2004)

	1996	*1998*	*2000*	*2002*	*2004*	*Regional average (2004)*	*Income country average (2004)*
Voice and accountability	74.9	67.0	64.9	84.3	83.0	53.6	64.6
Political stability	76.2	72.1	79.4	85.9	76.7	39.2	67.6
Government effectiveness	84.4	87.4	88.6	86.6	87.0	42.1	62.2
Regulatory quality	93.9	92.4	90.3	90.2	94.1	49.8	63.0
Rule of law	86.7	85.4	87.0	87.1	85.5	39.1	64.4
Control of corruption	86.0	85.8	90.2	90.7	88.7	44.6	63.4

Source: Based on Kaufmann *et al* (2005) and World Bank GRICS: Governance Research Indicator Country Snapshot 1996–2004 (2005) (www.worldbank.org/wbi/governance/bycountry.html).

Note: The figure depicts the percentile rank on each governance indicator over the years 1996–2004. Percentile rank indicates the percentage of countries worldwide that rate below the selected country in each component (subject to margin of error). Higher values thus imply better governance ratings.

century initiated under the first presidency of Arturo Alessandri in the early 1920s (Animat *et al* 2006). Today, Chile has a budget system in which the executive branch is clearly pre-eminent, in the context of a highly presidential system of government. According to Animat *et al* (2006:27–8):

> the Chilean political system is one of the strongest presidential systems in Latin America. The executive has exclusive legislative initiative on several policy areas, has a highly hierarchical control of the budget process, and has an array of urgency and veto options, which makes it a *de facto* agenda-setter [. . .]. Within matters of law, the executive has the sole legislative initiative over legislation concerning the political and administrative divisions of the state, its financial administration, the budget process and the selling of state assets.

The central budget office (DIPRES) of the ministry of finance has a predominant role in the management of the budget and the oversight of public finances.[14] Its role is grounded in a political consensus favouring a central steering role for the executive (Marcel and Tokeman 2002:110). The Chilean budgetary process is also characterised by stable and predictable rules governing the budget process. The stability in the rules regulating the process is further enhanced by the expectations of the actors on the reliability of these rules.

The existence of a strong social consensus on the need to preserve probity and legality in public administration further anchors the credibility of the CGR in the Chilean political and social landscape. Furthermore, there is also a strong cross-partisan consensus favouring a central steering role for the executive and supporting fiscal discipline. As Marcel and Tokeman (2002:112) note, 'the memory of past fiscal instability made Chilean politicians quite supportive of fiscal restraint.' There is a remarkable degree of acceptance of the current policy framework, the de-politicisation of economic policy and the centralisation of the budget process (Animat and Vial 2004). According to Montecinos (2003:1), 'for over a century, budgetary politics in Chile contained protracted efforts to depoliticize economic management and insulate policy decisions from congressional interference.'

As a result, the Chilean budget process is governed by stable and predictable rules. The return of democracy did not question the prevailing consensus favouring executive pre-eminence in public budgeting and, as a consequence, limited legislative oversight of public finances. The nature of the political system also explains the stability of the budget system. Based on uninominal electoral districts, electoral rules lead to a bipartisan system and prompt parties to form coalitions. They require grounding structural reforms in bipartisan consensus.

The broader environment of public budgeting, in fact, makes Chile ripe for *ex post* performance auditing. Chile possesses 'adequate rules and procedures and codes of conduct that accept these rules and procedures as legitimate' (World Bank 2004:3; Iturriaga Ruiz 1995). However, public finance management has remained fairly conventional, privileging adherence to rules and procedures over attainment of results. Furthermore, as Marcel and Tokeman (2002:113) underscore:

> the lack of institutional checks and balances generate uncertainty over the future behaviour of the authorities and prevent the country from fully reaping the benefits of fiscal discipline. In other words, since hierarchical budget institutions were not accompanied by accountability mechanisms over the authorities' management of public finances, the benefits of such arrangements will remain limited.

Institutional linkages

The CGR's institutional linkages with the other components of the system of financial governance and fiscal control represent a major hindrance to its effectiveness. Relations with the bureaucracy are marred by tension and suspicion. Relations with DIPRES are difficult, partly because of the overlap of responsibilities, and partly because of differences in corporate cultures. Tensions between the executive and the CGR escalated with the multiplication of special investigations and *ex ante* controls contesting the legality of government initiatives. Examples include the Plan AUGE, in 2000, in which the CGR contested the legality of the plan's publicity campaign, and, in 2002, concerning procurement irregularities in the Ministry of Public Works (MOP).

Controversies between the CGR and DIPRES centre on performance auditing and government accounting. The role of the CGR in government accounting is particularly problematic, as it prevents the CGR from auditing government accounts. It generates duplications, as both DIPRES and the CGR maintained, until 2001, their parallel financial information systems. The CGR's formalistic approach to fiscal control conflicts with DIPRES' emphasis on performance evaluation. While the CGR is primarily driven by liberal concerns for restraining executive discretion, DIPRES is primarily driven by managerial concerns for improving public management through greater managerial accountability.[15]

In the course of the 1990s, the Chilean authorities introduced important reforms in public management and financial governance. As Animat and Vial (2004:20) note:

> since the restoration of democracy there has been a constant effort to improve the budget process, with special emphasis on budget discipline, execution, and control. Together with the *ex ante* spending limits established by the structural fiscal surplus rule, the most significant reforms to the budget process have been at the control stage.

Progressively, as in Brazil, the modernisation of the budget system became the driver of state reform, under the stewardship of the central budget office (World Bank 2005; Guzmán 2005). There have been important improvements in terms of fiscal transparency and public access to financial information. The executive must now provide more information on government finances, reporting on budget execution to the legislature on a monthly and quarterly basis. These reports are public since 2000. As Marcel and Tokeman (2002:108) note:

> budgets are now seen not only as a tool of macroeconomic policy, but also as having a managerial and political role [...]. The key to successful public finance management is to balance the economic, managerial and political roles of public finances. It is, therefore, a matter of governance.

Nevertheless, the sophistication of performance evaluation undertaken by DIPRES begs the question of whether performance auditing by the CGR would add any value. While there might be a conflict of interest in having DIPRES evaluate the performance of the budget system it supervises, the executive opposes the extension of the CGR's prerogatives to *ex post* performance auditing or '*auditoria de gestión*'. It argues that the CGR's legalistic approach to fiscal control would hinder, rather than improve public management. It also fears that the CGR would concentrate too much power and would not be sufficiently accountable. Interviews with legislators confirm that this is also the view held in the legislature. The challenge of performance auditing is thus dual: changing the CGR's corporate culture and overcoming DIPRES resistance.

Relations with the legislature are also deficient. The CGR is not an auxiliary institution to the legislature and it has not actively sought to develop the legislative connection. Interactions between the CGR and the legislature are not strategic, reflected, for example, in the ad hoc nature of the legislature's requests for special audits. The weakness of the links between the CGR and the legislature must nevertheless be placed in the broader context of a weak legislature in budgetary terms. Senator and former Minister of Finance, Alejandro Foxley, acknowledges that:

> the follow-up of audit findings is particularly problematic, as the CGR does not possess enforcement powers and the legislature is neither designed nor equipped to do so [...]. There is a legal vacuum here.[16]

As the CGR supervises the accounting system, there is no independent auditing of government financial statements and no annual certification of government public accounts. Moreover, there is no public accounts committee within the legislature to review government accounts and follow up on audit findings. Thus, the Chilean external auditing system deviates from international best practice, as 'the absence of any external audit opinion on the financial statements of the government does not correspond with a modern approach to external auditing of the public sector' (World Bank 2004:9). However, for the CGR to emit an audit opinion on government financial statements, this would require abandoning its role in government accounting and ceasing to participate in administrative decision-making through *ex ante* control. Both these reforms would require amending the constitution.

As a result, the CGR provides little advice or support to the legislature in the oversight of government finances. The weakness of the links between the CGR and the legislature must nevertheless be placed in the broader context of a weak legislature in budgetary terms. As Siavelis (2002) underscores, legislative budget oversight, whether through routine 'police patrols' such as those provided by the CGR or through inquisitorial 'fire alarms' of legislative inquiry commissions, is deficient, as reflected in recent corruption scandals.

Presidents Eduardo Frei and Ricardo Lagos have made improved accountability to the legislature a political priority. The legislature has enhanced its own capacities for government financial oversight and is taking a more active role in public budgeting, requesting more fiscal information from the government. In 2003, the legislature's joint budget committee became a permanent structure, assisted by an embryonic budget research office established in 1997. Until then, this committee was only activated for the review of the government's budget proposal.

The legislature has also sought to enhance government accountability and legislative oversight through political agreements, often formalised in (non-binding) protocols annexed to the budget. These protocols, introduced in 1997, are agreed between political parties and signed by the legislature and the finance ministry. While they are not yet fully institutionalised, they have proven to be an effective mechanism for inter-branch cooperation and increasing the influence of the legislature in budgetary matters (Animat and Vial 2004). Examples of such political agreements include the informal rule of structural fiscal surplus of one percent of GDP. Similarly, the political response to the 'salary supplements' corruption scandal in 2002 resulted in an all-party anti-corruption pact in 2003. This pact included 50 separate initiatives including the reform of the CGR.

The expertise of individual legislators sitting in the budget and finance committees partially compensate for the lack of institutionalised capacity for budget oversight in the legislature. These legislators have ample experience and expertise in fiscal policy and public finances, often acquired in the executive branch as finance minister or director of the central budget office. Both chambers also show high re-election rates and committee membership is relatively stable, rotating every four years. Legislative coherence is reinforced by party discipline in what is essentially a bipartisan political system. Nevertheless, the high rate of re-election in the legislature only partially translates individual expertise into institutional expertise.

Reforming external auditing

The consensus view in Chile is that the CGR does not need strengthening; it needs reforming. The challenge is how to make it happen without jeopardising the budgetary system and fiscal discipline. Many fear that reforming the CGR would open a Pandora's box that would make the entire system of public budgeting and fiscal control crumble like a house of cards. The paradox of the CGR is that of an increasingly anachronistic agency in what is otherwise a relatively efficacious state bureaucracy. While it is widely respected for its contribution to strengthening public financial management and anchoring integrity in the public sector, it is also criticised for its institutional inertia and its inability to accompany the modernisation of public management. A defining challenge of the reform of external auditing is:

> to surpass the country's legalistic culture embedding the Chilean public administration, [...] an administrative ritualism, that expresses itself in a persistent culture of procedures emphasizing compliance with rules over achievement of results (Ramírez Aluja 2002:182).

Unlike in Argentina, the weakness of formal oversight institutions is compensated by the probity of the Chilean public administration and its adherence to the rule of law, which the CGR has contributed to anchoring. Chile's tradition of legality was supported 'by a series of state institutions with independent decision-making authority that were considered above party politics', most notably the CGR which was a 'feared institution, infamous among bureaucrats for ensuring relative efficiency in Chilean state institutions' (Siavelis 2002:72). The CGR does constrain behaviour and deters unlawful actions through its *ex ante* control function. However, it has failed to reform and keep pace with broader reforms in public management.

Structural reform has proved elusive, stumbling on the controversies surrounding *ex ante* compliance control. The few reform proposals that were advanced during the military government in 1982 and the democratic government in 1992 resulted only in partial reforms and the rationalisation of existing functions. The CGR rightfully underscores that its organic law ought to be revisited, as provided for in the 1980 Constitution. Its current organic law dates back to 1952 and was reformulated in 1964. In 2000, a cross-party agreement recognised the need to strengthen external auditing and reform the CGR. In 2002, the CGR articulated a modernisation programme, which nevertheless focused on improving its internal functioning (CGR 2002).

The challenge for Chilean authorities is to redefine the role of the CGR in the oversight of government finances, as part of a broader structural reform of financial governance. As Waissbluth (2001) argues, what is required is 'an entirely renovated institution, with greater constitutional powers and streamlined competences, and with different approaches to the external control of public sector management.' Clearly, as an evaluation of fiscal governance in Chile highlights, 'some of the current functions of the CGR are incompatible with its ultimate responsibility as external auditor of the system', in particular the supervision of the government accounting system (World Bank 2004:2; OECD 2004).

Any reform of the control functions of the CGR would involve systemic changes in the overall system of financial governance and fiscal control. Six interrelated reforms should be considered. First, were the CGR to abandon its *ex ante* compliance control functions, the government would have to substantially upgrade its internal control system, which ought to be undertaken *ex ante*, and strengthen the General Council of Internal Government Auditing (CAIGG). Similarly, the review of legality and constitutionality of government decrees should be transferred to the judiciary with the creation of administrative tribunals and the instauration of judicial review, undertaken *ex post*.

Second, were the CGR to abandon its supervision of government accounting, these functions should be assumed by an executive agency, possibly through the creation of a general accounting office within the finance ministry. Third, as government accounting responsibilities are transferred to the executive, the CGR should develop its *ex post* auditing functions and audit government financial statements, including annual public accounts. Enforcing *ex post* controls would, in turn, require the agency to be endowed with greater sanctioning powers. Fourth, the greater focus on *ex post* performance auditing that the abandonment of *ex ante* compliance control would allow would require substantial changes in the CGR's corporate culture and a widening of the panoply of *ex post* audit instruments.

Fifth, the auditing of government financial statements by the CGR, including annual government accounts, would also require strengthening the role of the legislature in the oversight of government finances and an improvement in the functional relations between the legislature and the CGR. A major challenge for the CGR is 'how to develop more effective mechanisms to ensure that the legislature duly considers its findings and recommendations and uses them in an appropriate and apolitical manner to scrutinize the activities of government' (World Bank 2004:48). The CGR necessarily inserts itself in the politics of executive-legislative relations and, in fact, the legislature has been critical to strengthen the authority of the CGR, granting it constitutional status in 1943 and impeaching the comptroller-general in 1945 for failing to provide effective restraints on government. As Faundez (2007:11) notes:

> by the mid-1940s, as congress began to express an interest in effectively controlling the powers of the executive, the Contraloría was identified as the institution with the potential and capacity to perform this task.

Sixth, the CGR also should develop its linkages with the wider society through a more proactive approach to the publicity of its audits. In recent years, the political momentum for reform has quickened, as corruption scandals have affected the public trust in the system of fiscal control. Upon assuming office in 2006, *Concertación* President Michelle Bachelet launched a series of initiatives to restore confidence and increase transparency in the public sector. She commissioned a report from a group of independent experts, which submitted its conclusions in November 2006. The following month, President Bachelet outlined her reform plan based on the commission's recommendations, including a radical reform of the CGR through the adoption of a new organic law.

The proposed reforms seek to modernise external auditing and recast the CGR by increasing the focus on *ex post* compliance control and financial auditing, limiting *ex ante* control functions further, disclosing audit reports, and broadening the scope of the CGR. The commission also advised that the CGR abandon its quasi-judicial functions as a tribunal of accounts and recommended the creation of a specialised court of accounts. In terms of government accounting, it suggested separating government accounting and external auditing functions, thus paving the way for the CGR to audit government accounts. It proposed establishing an autonomous accounting agency.

The commission also recommended creating an autonomous agency to evaluate the performance of public agencies and programmes. This agency should be linked to the legislature and would be independent of the central budget, thus ending the conflict of interest whereby DIPRES evaluates the performance of the public budgeting system it supervises. The government put forward a legislative proposal to establish a National Agency for the Quality of Public Policies in December 2006. The commission also recommended strengthening the internal control system and its supervisory body, the CAIGG, and enhancing the legal framework for freedom of information. The government responded by beefing up the 1999 legislation on access to public information and proposing the creation of an Institute for the Promotion of Transparency, following the Mexican model.

The new organic law for the CGR will be based on the CGR's own proposals and an independent review of the CGR to be carried out in 2007. However, current proposals do not envisage enhancing the role of the legislature in the oversight of public finances, or strengthening the linkages between the legislature and the CGR. The reform process has nevertheless become imbued with controversy in the context of the selection of a successor to the comptroller-general, Sciolla Avendaño, who had reached the age limit. As in 2002, when Lagos sought to nominate a candidate from outside the CGR, Bachelet initially proposed an outsider to the CGR, Pablo Ruiz-Tagle, instead of the former deputy comptroller-general and acting comptroller-general since

June 2006, Noemí Rojas Llanos. This was interpreted as another attempt to diminish the influence of the right on the CGR.

The opposition in the Senate rejected the president's candidate in November 2006, paving the way for a consensus candidate.[17] In April 2007, the Senate finally endorsed President Bachelet's second nominee, a renowned lawyer and academic, Ramiro Mendoza Zúñiga, for an eight-year mandate. The Senate's approval was accompanied by a cross-party agreement to reform the CGR. Mendoza Zúñiga represents a unique chance to reform and modernise the external auditing function. He is relatively young (47 years of age), is an outsider to the CGR, and his mandate is now backed by a political consensus on the need for reform.

Chapter 7

Government auditing in transition

Introduction

The budget process is a key policy process reflecting countries' political priorities and spending arbitrages. The independent scrutiny of government finances that AAAs perform is intrinsically a political process embedded in the broader context of the shifting balance of political powers, the evolving executive-legislative budget relations, and, more fundamentally, the strength of the system of checks and balances. This book underscores the importance of the political context shaping the politics of budget reform. As such, understanding of the politics of the budget process is critical to strengthen it and anchor the rule of law in the budget process.

This chapter draws general lessons and policy implications intended for policymakers, practitioners and scholars seeking better to understand the logics of accountability in the budget process, enhance the rule of law in the management of public finances, and strengthen the independent auditing of government finances. These lessons have more general applicability beyond Latin America, in particular for developing countries seeking to establish or strengthen their external audit functions and agencies, in particular in Sub-Saharan Africa.

Key findings from comparative analysis

The research for this book gleans important lessons and reveals what does and does not work, and why. As such, it provides an important contribution to our understanding of the reform of public sector governance and the strengthening of government financial management.

First, effective autonomous audit agencies improve the credibility of the budget and the quality of governance

As emerging economies and developing countries embark on the second stage of reform seeking to improve governance, this book confirms mounting evidence of the influence of political institutions on financial governance. AAAs have the potential to contribute more actively to the credibility of the budget, the prevention of corruption and the accountability of government, thereby increasing the public's trust in the state's management of public funds.

At a conceptual level, this research has revealed that there exists a positive correlation between the credibility of external auditing and the quality of financial governance. This positive effect is reflected in the influence of external auditing on the quality of public sector governance, in terms of enhanced rule of law, greater transparency of the budget, improved efficiency of the bureaucracy and more effective prevention of corruption. In particular, AAAs are instrumental in redressing information asymmetries between the executive and the legislature, occupying a critical juncture in executive-legislative budget relations. More fundamentally, by improving transparency in the budget process and accountability in the management of government finances, they have an important role in increasing public trust in the state.

However, the research does not find a direct correlation between the *model* of external audit agency and the *effectiveness* of external auditing. Institutional arrangements only partially explain the effectiveness of AAAs, be it the monocratic model, the quasi-judicial model or the collegial model. This finding, based on a cross-country statistical analysis of ten Latin American countries and empirical evidence from Argentina, Brazil and Chile, confirms our hypothesis according to which institutional arrangements have only a limited influence on agency performance. For example, evidence from the three case studies suggests that there is no direct and unambiguous relationship between the probity of public administration and the existence of *ex ante* controls performed by the AAA.

Causality relations remain uncertain. The research does not find the *direct impact* of external auditing on fiscal performance to be statistically significant. This finding suggests that expectations of the role of AAAs in government financial management ought not to be exaggerated but kept realistic. However, it confirms that AAAs do have an *indirect influence* on fiscal performance through their contribution to improving financial governance. As Premchand (1999:186) underscores, 'a paradoxical feature of the current situation is that expectations and demands of the public are growing faster than the existing machinery for accountability can handle.'

Second, external audit agencies are part of the broader system of checks and balances in government financial management

The persistence of endemic corruption in many developing countries and emerging economies underscores the need for strong preventive and corrective control mechanisms. Ultimately, however, the effectiveness of AAAs depends on the quality of their insertion into the system of financial governance, as well as the efficacy of the overall system of fiscal control. In other words, the dysfunctions that can be observed in the functioning of AAAs are systemic rather than agency-specific. The fluidity of inter-institutional cooperation between the various components of the system is therefore critical. Dye and Stapenhurst (1998) develop the notion of 'national integrity systems' to capture the importance of systems, rather than agencies.

Forward and backward linkages between AAAs and legislatures are critical determinants of the system's overall efficacy. AAAs are effective only to the extent that they are allowed to conduct their work independently and to the degree to which their audit findings are effectively followed up by those institutions with enforcement powers. Often, accounting systems are dysfunctional and public accounts are poorly maintained, failing to provide the financial information on which audits can be based. Similarly, audit recommendations are not always implemented by government agencies and audit reports are often blocked in the legislature's public accounts committees. Reluctant courts often do not prosecute flagrant abuses identified by the AAAs. The reports and recommendations of AAAs are largely ineffective if they are not acted on by other institutions within the system of control, in particular the public administration itself (administrative accountability), the judiciary (criminal accountability) and parliament (political accountability).

Increasing the sanctioning powers of AAAs is often cited as a means to improve enforcement of audit findings. Nevertheless, based on the empirical evidence gathered in the course of this research, we take a different view. What matters most is that accountability is effectively enforced by those state institutions with the powers to enforce accountability and sanction government. Therefore, it is critical to improve the effectiveness of the overall system of budget oversight and financial accountability and the links between its various components. In other words, AAAs should be conceptualised as *oversight agencies* with indirect enforcement powers, rather than *accountability institutions* with direct sanctioning powers. Their contribution to fiscal governance and corruption control resides in the support they provide, as auxiliary institutions, to those state powers tasked with enforcing accountability on government as part of the system of checks and balances and the separation of powers, namely the legislature (for political accountability) and the judiciary (for penal and criminal accountability). The enforcement capabilities of AAAs are mainly *indirect*, through the information they provide to the legislature, the judiciary and the public.

There are four important dimensions to the functional linkages hypothesis advanced herein. First, if we accept that the key variable is the functionality of the system, rather than the powers of its elements, the enforcement capabilities and sanctioning prerogatives of AAAs are secondary issues. The accountability literature may indeed overemphasise the importance of direct sanctioning powers as a key attribute of 'horizontal accountability' agencies (Mainwaring and Welna 2003). What matters is that enforcement does occur, as a result of the effective functioning of the system of control and the coordination between its various components. Accountability often fails, not because of failures in individual organisations, such as AAAs or anti-corruption commissions, but because of dysfunctions in the overall system. For example, the case of Argentina illustrates that while the AGN is technically competent, it fails to have a deterrent impact because audit findings are not effectively acted upon by the legislature. Similarly, in the case of Brazil, dysfunctions in the links between the TCU and the judicial system, reflected in the controversy over the legal status of audit rulings, hamper the effective enforcement of audit recommendations, including sanctions.

Second, the functional linkages hypothesis draws attention to the balance between technical capacities and political incentives to improve the effectiveness of the system of fiscal control. Technical improvements in auditing techniques can certainly help enhance agency performance. However, political incentives tend to have even greater influence, as they determine the extent to which political actors effectively use the powers and the capacities they possess to enforce accountability on government.

Third, the functional linkages hypothesis is also critical to understanding the sustainability of oversight agencies and the strategies they deploy to anchor their independence. AAAs often have to perform a delicate balancing act between independence as a means to anchor their credibility and engagement as a means to ensure their relevance. The kinds of relationships that autonomous agencies develop with their institutional environment to preserve and reinforce their autonomy are key (Manning and Matsuda 2000). The choice of strategy is between 'insulation' and 'engagement', or between 'buffering' and 'bridging' (Matsuda 1997). Looking at the experience of Bolivia, Dove (2002:223) argues that 'agencies are more likely to sustain their autonomy if they minimise dependence on their task environments and close themselves off as much as possible to contacts that could lead to interference' (Dove 2002:223). According to Matsuda (1997:14–15):

> the insulation strategy is based on the premise that the best way to protect the agency autonomy is to stay away from partisan politics, trying [...] to maintain political neutrality and giving political actors few reasons for intervention. The engagement strategy follows from the view that the potential vulnerability of agency autonomy necessitates the agency to develop its own autonomy-enhancing capabilities.

Fourth, the functional linkages hypothesis poses great challenges to both policy and research. It underscores the contribution of political economy to decipher the influence of political variables such as party politics and electoral rules on the efficacy of budget-oversight institutions. It also underlines the need to understand the interaction between the mechanisms of vertical accountability and the institutions of horizontal accountability (Persson and Tabellini 2000, 2001). There thus exists unexplored potential to improve government accountability by tackling the dysfunctions in political systems and incentives, beyond the narrow focus on technical improvements and institutional adjustments.

Third, independence is critical to guarantee impartiality, but should not be an end in itself

The research finds that securing the political independence of AAAs is a critical determinant of their credibility and effectiveness as agencies of restraint. If AAAs are not sufficiently independent from political powers, they are likely to be neutralised or even captured by the ruling majority. The case of Argentina confirms that the credibility of the AGN is undermined by the 'political filtering' of its audit rulings through the process of auditing (Ducoté 2001). Audits are first filtered within the agency by a politicised college of auditors and then outside the agency by the ruling majority in the legislature. The result of these successive political filters is a fiction of control and a real risk of political capture. Political independence is not only about independence from the government, but more generally from political interference and partisan interests. Brazil shows that while the TCU is independent from political interference by the executive, its credibility is hindered by the influence of partisan politics, reflected in the composition and motivations of its college of auditors.

This finding reveals the *paradox of independence*: while AAAs ought to be sufficiently independent to adequately perform their tasks, they largely depend on other state institutions to have a meaningful impact and need to develop effective functional relations with those institutions tasked with enforcing government accountability. The challenge, therefore, is to determine how much independence is enough and how much is too much. Independence should be approached as a continuous variable rather than a dichotomous one. AAAs should be sufficiently independent from government influence and partisan interest to be credible; but, at the same time, they should not be too insulated from the broader system of fiscal control to remain relevant. Independence should not be an end in itself, but a means for achieving greater impact.

There are therefore limitations to the literature on agency autonomy (Manning and Matsuda 2000). These theories tend to approach autonomy as an end in itself, a central survival strategy and core organisational objective, rather than as a means to improve the agency's political impartiality and technical credibility. Second, it fails to acknowledge that excessive autonomy may undermine agency effectiveness. Indeed, autonomy through insulation might well guarantee survival but can lead to irrelevance. As Dove argues (2002:224):

> an agency strategy based on cautious engagement tends to win an oversight agency more real autonomy, while one based on insulation tends to result in the oversight agency becoming irrelevant and thus less technically autonomous.

The case of the Chilean CGR illustrates this intuition. The CGR is a highly independent institution, often compared to a fourth power. However, its independence is decried by many as excessive, putting it at risk of becoming irrelevant. Interestingly, the Chilean legislature has developed its own instruments to evaluate public sector performance independently of the information provided by the CGR, by requesting more financial information from the executive. The executive has also developed its own systems for monitoring budget performance. Excessive independence not only undermines its effectiveness, it also hinders its ability to reform, paralysed by 'institutional sclerosis' and unable to adjust itself to new trends in public management. By insulating and isolating itself in the architecture of fiscal governance, it has largely failed to develop synergies with the other elements of the system of fiscal control, which severely hinders its impact.

Fourth, shortcomings in government financial accountability reflect deeper dysfunctions in the relations between external audit agencies and legislatures

The fluidity of the functional relationship between AAAs and legislatures is critical to the overall effectiveness of the system of fiscal control and financial accountability. As this book has shown, external auditing is not as effective as it could be partly because of the inadequate follow-up of audit findings and enforcement of audit recommendations by legislatures. Accountability failures in financial governance tend to originate not in faulty external auditing, but rather in the lack of effective oversight by the legislature.

The research reveals structural dysfunctions in the principal-agent relations between the legislature (as the principal) and the AAA (as the agent) in the oversight of government finances. At the same time, these relationships insert themselves in multilayered principal-agent relationships, between the legislature and the executive, and between the executive and the bureaucracy. These dysfunctions find their origins in the principal's inability or unwillingness to oversee its agent (government) using the information its oversight agent (the AAA) provides it with. Through greater publicity, AAAs can circumvent the legislature to directly serve their ultimate principal, the public, in particular by developing more effective relations with the media and civil society.

This book confirms that 'agents cannot hold other agents accountable, only their principals can' (Moreno *et al* 2003:117). In other words, only the legislature (or the public) can enforce accountability on the executive, not the AAA. As oversight agencies, AAAs are merely auxiliary organisations to the legislature in the oversight of government finances. They provide advisory services to the legislatures in the exercise of their oversight responsibilities. In Argentina and Brazil, for example, the AAA is a legislative body and constitutional clauses state that only the legislature can hold the government to account, with the assistance of the AAA.

This finding relates to the evolving role of legislatures in public budgeting and economic policy, which is subject to increasing controversy (Santiso 2008a, 2008b, 2006c, 2005a, 2005b). Experience from developed countries confirms that the connection between the AAAs and the legislature is crucial to explaining the effectiveness of the former. For example, in the UK, which has one of the most effective AAAs, the National Audit Office (NAO) became a legislative organisation in 1983, developing closer links with the legislature's public accounts committee. Similarly, the reform of the budgetary system in France in 2001 and the constitutional reform of 2008 gave greater prerogatives to the legislature in the oversight of public finances. There is now a debate on the role of the French *Cour des Comptes* and its links with the legislature (Carcassone *et al* 2005).

Looking at the certification of government's annual public accounts and legislative discharge of government, the qualitative analysis of this book's case studies reveal that the most critical problems are found in the legislative phase of the certification process, rather than its auditing phase. This finding confirms that the accountability gaps in the oversight of the budget originate more in the lack of political incentives of the legislature to oversee government finances, than in the capacity constraints facing the AAA. It is the legislature that most often fails to exercise its oversight responsibilities and hold government to account for the manner in which it administers public funds. The challenge is not only to hold government to account *ex post facto* for its management of public finances, which is crucial for democratic accountability, but also to ensure that this evaluation feeds back into the budget process to improve the performance of the public sector. This process is largely incipient in Latin America and many other developing countries.

Fifth, external audit systems are in transition, seeking to redefine their role in fiscal control and their contribution to public management

AAAs are in transition not only in developing countries, but also in developed countries. As one examines the performance and reform of AAAs in developing countries, it is important to recall that the much-acclaimed model of external auditing in the UK has only been in place since 1983. Similarly, Sweden undertook a profound reform of its external auditing system in 2003 (Hjalmarsson and Jonsson 2003) and France is currently reassessing the adequacy of its model (Carcassone 2005).[1]

In many emerging economies, 'external control institutions seem to lack clarity about what their role actually is, should be or could be' (Speck 1999:3). Our research finds that, to be fully effective, AAAs should clearly define the role they want to perform in the oversight of government finances, the architecture of financial governance and the system of checks and balances. In particular, they should decide whether their main mission is to *restrain government* or *improve management*. Furthermore, they encounter difficulties in adjusting themselves to new developments in public sector governance and shifting executive-legislative budget relations, partly because they are, per se, conservative institutions tasked with preserving the established legal order.

AAAs often find themselves torn between a *liberal concern* for restraining the state and controlling government, mainly through *ex ante* control and compliance auditing and a *managerial concern* for improving government performance and ensuring value-for-money, achieved through *ex post* performance auditing (Speck 2000). The liberal approach to fiscal control is concerned with ensuring predictable, rules-based governance and ensuring legality and probity in administrative behaviour. It is about the limitation of power. It emphasises the separation and balance of powers and the role of legal rules and formal procedures for constraining executive discretion. As Speck (1999:3) underscores:

> liberal concern is about the abuse of power and the non-compliance with all these rules. Allocation of financial resources plays a major role for the exercise of political power. Therefore control of compliance with norms is essential not only to guarantee an efficient use of public funds but also to keep power holders within a near bandwidth of norms and make them responsible for their acts.

The *managerial concern* provides a second source of legitimacy to the institutions of fiscal control. It emphasises the quality of public spending, the results achieved in the delivery of public services, and the performance of public managers in achieving those; it privileges the principles of economy, efficiency and effectiveness in the public sector. The liberal approach is primarily punitive and preventive, based on the legal compliance with formal rules and regulations (and the imposition of sanctions in case of non-compliance), while the managerial approach is primarily corrective, focused on improving the use of public finances and based on the establishment of incentive systems that would induce public managers to perform better in a framework of delegated responsibilities.

AAAs may have preventive, corrective or repressive functions. The key question, however, is which of these functions ought to take precedence: to punish and prevent illicit and irregular behaviour or provide incentives to improve public management. While compliance auditing may prevent and deter irregularities (punitive and preventive functions), only performance auditing can contribute to improving public management (corrective and advisory functions). Admittedly, both functions are equally critical for the efficient functioning of a modern state. However, their relevance in specific country contexts depends on various factors, including the quality of the bureaucracy, the strength of internal controls and adherence to the rule of law. It should be underlined that administrative incompetence, unlike corruption, is not a felony. Hence, the punitive approach to fiscal control focused on compliance control is unlikely to tackle incompetence in the public sector.

The international trend is clearly from *ex ante* compliance control to *ex post* performance auditing, informed by the experience of Anglo-Saxon countries, in particular the UK, the US and Canada. However, according to Speck (1999), this transition generates tensions in the organisations' redefinition of their mission.[2] Furthermore, as external audit systems gradually shift from compliance control to performance auditing, there is increasing pressure to strengthen internal control systems within the bureaucracy to ensure compliance with rules and regulations. However, in practice, internal control systems fail to catch up.

There exist important complementarities between the two approaches to external auditing and fiscal control. The managerial approach is based on the assumption that a sufficiently reliable, rules-based public administration already exists, guaranteeing adherence to administrative rules and financial regulations. This assumption, however, does not necessarily hold in most emerging economies, as the case of Argentina shows. There also exist 'fundamental tensions between managerial efficacy and administrative control,' as Jorge Danós, chief of staff of the Peruvian prime minister, remarks.[3] Excessive administrative control and invasive financial oversight, rigidly applied may suffocate managerial flexibility and innovation, as the case of Chile suggests.

Standard typologies of AAAs do not fully capture this distinction in approaches to fiscal control, diminishing the explanatory power of such typologies. The liberal concern is predominant in the court model of tribunal of accounts (such as Brazil) and in those that emphasise *ex ante* compliance control (such as Chile). The managerial concern is reflected in auditing techniques privileging *ex post* performance control (such as in Argentina and increasingly in Brazil). The case of Brazil nevertheless shows that these two functions are not necessarily compatible within the same organisational model and that the institutional arrangements for assuming these may differ significantly. In Chile there is strong resistance, within the CGR but also within the ministry of finance, to the introduction of performance auditing or *auditoria de gestión* in the mandate of the CGR.

The tragedy of many developing countries and emerging economies, such as those of Latin America, is that they have been unable to achieve either restraint (controls and oversight) or delegation of managerial autonomy (focus on performance). As a former head of the Argentine central budget office and key proponent of budgetary reform remarks, Latin American bureaucracies continue 'to suffer from a severe lack of control and oversight that, in the case of Argentina for example, renders performance-management a premature task.'[4] AAAs anchor themselves in the countries' bureaucratic culture and traditions of control, which might or might not be ready for performance-based approaches to public management.

Argentina's public administration was clearly not ready for such an approach in the early 1990s when its model of external auditing abruptly shifted from *ex ante* compliance control to *ex post* performance auditing. By changing models radically in a highly politicised context, the public sector lost both forms of fiscal control, which suited Menem's discretionary style of government. In Chile, the public sector is in a better position for undergoing such a transition towards *ex post* performance auditing and performance-based budgeting, partly because of the relative efficacy of its bureaucracy and its adherence to the rule of law. Chile's central budget office (DIPRES) has been championing new methods of government focused on performance and results since the mid-1990s (Guzmán 2005). However, the paradox is that the CGR's deep-seated legalistic culture of control on formal compliance with rules and regulations, combined with its institutional independence, prevent it from adjusting its model of external control.[5]

AAAs are embedded in specific cultures of control and traditions of public administration. This is reflected in the correlation between external auditing, the rule of law and bureaucratic efficiency. The poor quality of the bureaucracy in many Latin American countries partly explains why institutional arrangements for external auditing may appear perfect on paper, but dysfunctional in practice. The critical lesson from the Latin American experience is, as Schick (1998) advises, to 'get the basics right first:' have effective financial auditing before adopting performance auditing; operate a reliable accounting system before installing an integrated financial management system; establish external controls which will reinforce internal controls; have reliable internal controls before devolving managerial responsibility; and maintain a high performance civil service before entrusting civil servants with broad discretion.

Policy implications: What does and does not work, and why

The research findings discussed above have important implications for policymakers seeking to strengthen and reform external auditing. They also bring important lessons to international financial institutions and donor governments providing technical and financial assistance to strengthen financial governance in developing countries.

First, politics matter to explain the effectiveness of budget oversight and external auditing of public finances

Institutional arrangements do matter to a certain degree to explain AAAs' effectiveness (or lack thereof), but the empirical evidence gathered from statistical analyses and case studies shows that political and governance factors are critical. As a result, no definite conclusion can be drawn regarding the superiority of any one model based solely on its institutional design and organisational attributes.

In Argentina, the failing of the AAA is a failure of politics. While institutional arrangements for government auditing are perfect in theory, they fail to function in practice because of the political dynamics framing executive-legislative relations in the budget process (Santiso 2008c, 2007a). Conversely, while the Chilean model of external auditing is largely antiquated and anachronistic, it does nevertheless contribute to guaranteeing probity and integrity in public administration. A characteristic feature of the Argentine formal system of fiscal control is not the lack of control, but rather the fiction of control, which gives the impression that the administration is being controlled when, in reality, the system ties the hands of those who are supposed to exercise such control (Atchabahian 2002).

Politics not only explains how AAAs can be neutralised, it also explains regression in the reform of AAAs. In Nicaragua, for example, state reform suffered a major setback in the wake of the constitutional reforms of 2000, which resulted in the division of key state institutions along party lines. A five-member council divided along partisan lines was appointed to head the Nicaraguan AAA, the *Contraloría General de la República* (CGR). Capacity constraints and organisational dysfunctions were compounded by the politicisation of the agency. The fiscal control system is characterised by poor government accounting, weak *ex ante* controls, ineffective internal audit systems and inconsequential external audits. The political capture of the Nicaraguan AAA mirrors that of the Peruvian *Contraloría General de la República* (CGR) during the administration of Alberto Fujimori who, in 1992, dismissed the legislature and fired the auditor-general to appoint a political ally, Víctor Caso Lay, between 1993 and 2000.

Ultimately, the effectiveness of budget-oversight institutions depends on the broader political economy of executive-legislative budget relations, the quality of their insertion into the system of checks and balances and the strength of the separation of powers. It is therefore critical to adequately consider the institutional context in which AAAs are embedded when devising reform strategies. Context is critical to: (i) decipher the framework of incentives in which actors operate; (ii) gauge the political feasibility of alternative reforms; (iii) assess the likely adoption or neutralisation of reforms; and (iv) weigh the benefits of gradualism and the centrality of time, timing and sequencing.

Second, politics are often the catalyst for fundamental reform in the arrangements for external auditing, for better or worse

External auditing in Mexico has experimented with important reforms which have strengthened oversight of government. The Mexican AAA, the *Auditoría Superior de la Federación* (ASF), was substantially reformed in 1999 (Solares Mendiola 2004).[6] In 2000, the legislature approved a new law on external control and financial accountability at the federal level, the *Ley Superior de Fiscalización de la Federación*. The ASF replaced the *Contaduría Mayor de Hacienda* of the lower chamber of parliament and was endowed with greater powers to control the public accounts of the Mexican federation. The new law on fiscal control thus brought the external audit agency closer to the legislature to better assist the lower chamber in the scrutiny of federal public finances and the review of federal public accounts. The ASF acts as an auxiliary institution to the legislature, being itself overseen by a special legislative committee. The law has also improved the timely availability of fiscal audit information by substantially reducing the time for examining public accounts, from 24 months to no more than 15 months. The ASF now has nine months to audit the public accounts and submit its opinion to the legislature. Access to fiscal information is further facilitated by the legislation on transparency and access to public information adopted in 2002 and rigorously enforced by an autonomous agency, the *Instituto Federal de Acceso a la Información Pública* (IFAI).

The case of Mexico is particularly interesting in several respects. The reconfiguration of political power following the electoral defeats of the long-time ruling party in 1997 and 2000 has led to a surge in budget activism in the legislature (Weldon 2002; Gutiérrez *et al* 2001). The emergence of an effective opposition in the Chamber of Deputies (the chamber dealing with budgetary issues) since 1997 has provided strong incentives for enhancing the oversight of the budget exercised by the legislature and for increasing its capacities for independent budget review. Opposition legislators recognised that significant steps ought to be taken to allow the legislature to fully exercise its constitutional powers in the budgetary process (Sour *et al* 2003). Among those steps were ensuring that the legislature had adequate access to independent information in fiscal and budgetary matters. This recognition led to the establishment of a legislative budget office in 1998, the *Centro de Estudios en Finanzas Públicas* (CEFP).

The emergence of an effective opposition has also revealed the flaws of the formal budget process. Between 1928 and 1999, the formal institutional framework regulating the budget process was largely ignored, neutralised by the 'meta-constitutional' powers of the president (Weldon 2002). In Mexico, the budgetary powers of the legislature are determined not only by its own constitutional and legal prerogatives, but more fundamentally by the partisan powers of the president. Unified government, party discipline and the recognition of the president as the party leader gave the latter unusual *de facto* budget powers. Under this institutional arrangement, which lasted over seven decades, the president had been *de facto* delegated enormous discretion over public expenditure. The legislature used to rubber-stamp the budget sent by the president without major amendments. As Weldon (2002:119) remarks, a striking feature of legislative politics in Mexico has been 'the disuse of Congress' power to oversee the executive budget'. Clarification of the 'rules of the game' of executive-legislative budget relations is now warranted under divided government.

Third, to build effective external audit agencies, mobilising political power is often more important than increasing technical capacity[7]

In many developing countries, the proposed solutions to the lack of effectiveness of AAAs often rely on increasing technical capacity. Admittedly, lack of technical capacity and basic infrastructure is often a major hindering factor in poor countries; however, it is not necessarily the only one, or the predominant one.

The means (technical capacities) and motives (political incentives) for financial accountability and legislative oversight are intrinsically linked (Santiso 2006a, 2005a). In other words, the efficacy of horizontal accountability mechanisms such as AAAs largely depends on the strength of vertical accountability mechanisms, the degree of political contestation and the extent of electoral competition. The political economy literature indeed shows that variation in institutional differences in electoral rules and political systems is an important determinant of the variation in corruption levels across countries (Lederman *et al* 2001; Adsera *et al* 2003; Persson *et al* 2002). External auditing inserts itself into the relations between the executive and the legislature in the budget process, and therefore is dependent on the intensity of the role of the legislature in policymaking in general and in public budgeting in particular.

The degree to which legislatures use audit findings to bring the government to account is likely to depend on the configuration of political power and the scope of political competition (Santiso 2006c, 2005a; Morgenstern and Manzetti 2003). For example, legislatures are more likely to develop technical capacity to oversee government finances if the opposition is numerically important and develops a proactive role. Legislatures generate technical knowledge either directly through public accounts committees or legislative budget offices or indirectly through auxiliary institutions such as AAAs. In situations of fused government, where executive and legislative majorities coincide, legislatures have few incentives to develop oversight capacities.

The case of Argentina shows that legislators do not necessarily lack technical capacity, but rather political incentives to use this capacity effectively, exercise the oversight powers they have and invest in the legislature's oversight functions. Moreover, existing political incentives, excessive executive discretion and expeditious modes of government conspire to circumvent or neutralise fiscal control and external oversight. Low re-election rates, electoral rules and party dynamics partly explain these skewed incentives. By contrast, the case of Mexico since 1997 illustrates that when political incentives are right, the degree of political competition adequate and the weight of the opposition sufficient, legislatures are more likely to exercise oversight and develop technical capacities to do so. Similarly, in Chile, electoral rules for legislative elections, based on single-member districts, tend to generate bipolar political configurations, which provide stronger incentives for legislative oversight of government. Recent research on Brazil shows that electoral rules and the party system mediate executive-legislative relations in public budgeting (Pereira and Mueller 2004; Figueiredo and Limongi 2002).

The balance between technical capacities and political incentives provides a potent explanation for institutional performance. While capacity constraints explain why oversight agencies do not exercise their budgetary powers effectively, governance constraints tend to explain why they sometimes do not exercise them responsibly. The nature of the political system and the degree of political competition therefore critically influence the political incentives of policymakers, and legislators in particular, to effectively use the technical information AAAs provide. Moreover, strengthening technical capacity *per se* does not necessarily, nor automatically, improve the effectiveness of AAAs, nor has it prevented them from being captured.

Referring to those programmes by the international donor community seeking to strengthen governance in developing countries, the Inter-American Development Bank underscores that (IDB 2003:8–9):

> projects that are limited to changing instrumental elements or simply strengthen technical organizational capacities, without altering the structure of incentives that affect the political will to apply them are likely in general to have a negligible impact. Thus institutional changes that condition the effectiveness of instrumental and organizational reforms need to be addressed at the same time [...]. It does little good to establish a financial management system without the development of a budgetary authority with the professional independence, power, and capacity to enforce it.

Fourth, external audit agencies cannot be strengthened or reformed in isolation

This policy recommendation reflects the core finding of this book, namely that the effectiveness of AAAs primarily depends on the efficacy of the overall system of fiscal control. As Diamond (1999:1) aptly notes:

> endemic corruption is a systemic disease that can only be controlled with a systemic cure: a single institution, such as an anticorruption commission, will not do. Effective and durable corruption control requires multiple, reinforcing and overlapping institutions of accountability.

It is thus important to enhance the institutional and functional linkages between AAAs and the other components of the system of fiscal control to enforce government accountability in public finances, in particular the legislature, the judiciary and civil society. Too often, reformers approach organisations in isolation, overlooking the broader governance and institutional context in which they are embedded. By failing to explore reforms in the linkages between organisations, they often fail to bring about systemic improvements and lasting change.

There indeed exists unexplored potential to improve government accountability in public expenditure management by improving the quality of the linkages between external auditing and legislative oversight (Santiso 2006a, 2004a). Referring to the role of legislatures in the policy process, Stein *et al* (2005:258) underscore:

> it is difficult to produce institutional change by addressing an institution in isolation. To intervene effectively, it is important to understand the complex interdependencies that exist among institutions [...]. Trying to strengthen the legislature to improve its technical contribution to the design and implementation of policies requires changing the incentives for legislators to invest in such capacities, which in turn may require changing the electoral system or the party system.

Furthermore, this research confirms North's theories on institutional change. Budget institutions are costly to reform and exhibit a high degree of inertia, both of which characteristics result in a strong status quo bias. They change in significant ways only when performance is highly unsatisfactory. This is particularly the case of AAAs, which are, by nature, conservative institutions. Hommes (1996) offers examples of the 'stickiness' of budgetary rules and institutions in the case of Colombia. While in a few cases reform followed a severe crisis (for example, in 1892), in most cases budget reform was implemented by reformist officials motivated by good management principles, and in some cases, imposed from outside. Veto-player theory partly explains the inertia inherent in budgetary systems and the persistence of budget deficits. Tsebelis and Chang (2004:449) show that 'countries with many veto players [...] will have difficulty in altering budget structures.'

Fifth, stages of institutional development cannot be bypassed

This finding has critical implications for the design of reform strategies and the choice between radical and gradual reforms. The research underscores that political institutions in general and AAAs in particular are rooted in specific trajectories of state building. Their effectiveness is highly dependent on the administrative traditions and the shape of the state in which they are embedded.

In particular, the efficacy of AAAs critically depends on the prevalence of the rule of law in the public sector. The comparison between Argentina and Chile is particularly instructive. In sharp contrast with Chile where practice precedes legislation, in Argentina legislation is a pale substitute for the absence of practice. The radical reforms introduced in Argentina in 1992 were based on the erroneous assumption of a rule-based bureaucracy in which effective managerial controls existed. It was also based on the assumption of the existence of 'professional legislators' (Jones 2001) with the technical capacities and political incentives to oversee government financial management. These assumptions clearly did not hold in Argentina, neither in the 1990s nor today. These factors explain why, while the model of external auditing introduced in 1992 was conceptually sound, it has failed in practice.

Therefore, as Stein *et al* (2005:258) note, it is critical to conceive reforms as a matter 'not of achieving an ideal model, but improving the existing model on the basis of available resources and existing restrictions.' This finding suggests that gradual reforms within existing external auditing systems are more likely to be successful than radical changes of external audit systems. Nevertheless, while a strong correlation exists between bureaucratic efficiency and audit effectiveness, the causality links are harder to decipher.

The contrast between Argentina and Brazil is particularly instructive in that regard. In the early 1990s, when it reformed its financial administration system, Argentina was considered as a 'stellar-performer' of first-generation economic reforms. By contrast, Brazil was considered as an irremediable 'reform-laggard,' unable or unwilling to reform. The comparison, a decade later, illustrates the dangers of radical reform in Argentina and the benefits of gradual reform in Brazil. In other words, it reveals the dangers of excessive executive discretion and unchecked policy decisiveness in Argentina and the benefits of the piecemeal reform in Brazil, where the political system imposes gradualism and 'muddling-through,' but generates, over time, resoluteness in policymaking (Haggard and McCubbins 2001).

Colombia provides an example of reform failure and the inability to rationalise a fragmented and overly complex system. The modernisation of fiscal control was among the constitutional reforms put to referendum by President Alvaro Uribe in 2003 and which were ultimately rejected. Under the terms of the 1991 Constitution, the *Contraloría General de la República* (CGR) exercises selective *ex post* control and audit. In 2001, the CGR had a staff of 4057, 31 departmental offices and a budget of US$131 million. However, there also exist external audit agencies at the level of the departments (32) and municipalities (35), which function largely independently from the CGR. The *Auditoría General de la República* (AGR) oversees the CGR. In recent years, there have been proposals to suppress the AGR and the departmental and municipal AAAs, but these ultimately failed. Colombia provides a case of too many layers of fiscal control and the deficient coordination between them (Naranjo Gálvez 2002).

Sixth, radical reform strategies based on the institutional transplant of exogenous models are likely to fail

The key challenge is not how to change systems, but rather how to make existing systems and institutions work. The analysis reveals the limits of radical reforms based on institutional transplant and technical approaches to the reform of AAAs. Reform strategies that seek to mechanically import institutional audit models from abroad without taking into account the underlying conditions that make them work are likely to fail (Dove 2002). Institutional arrangements for external auditing are path-dependent and country specific, and therefore difficult to replicate or transpose. Hence, rather than seeking to transplant 'best practices' from abroad, reformers should privilege 'best fit' approaches to achieve 'good enough' governance reforms and gradual improvements.

Reforms must be adapted to and assimilated by the culture of public administration in the recipient country. They must take into account the trajectory of change of its audit system over time. The example of the radical change of the external audit model in Argentina in 1992, which changed from the court model to the collegiate model almost overnight, constitutes an example of reform failure resulting in the weakening of the oversight agency and the neutralisation of external control of government. The reforms changed the formal institutions of fiscal control but did not affect the informal institutions and underlying power relationships in which the system of financial scrutiny and government accountability is embedded. Conversely, gradual approaches based on incremental adjustments, such as those privileged by the Brazilian TCU since its creation in 1891, are likely to bear greater results. These findings underscore the limits of institutional design and 'institutional import' (Dove 2002) as effective reform strategies. At the same time, failure to reform, as in Chile, threatens the AAA with becoming antiquated and irrelevant.

The case of Bolivia illustrates the limits of 'institutional modelling' and the implantation of exogenous models (Dove 2002). Prior to 1985 the Office of the Comptroller General (*Contraloría General de la República*, CGR) exercised *ex ante* control of government contracts, undertook *ex post* audits and imposed sanctions (Sánchez de Lozada 1999; World Bank 2000). The dysfunctional effects of these rules resulted in a paralysis of government actions, serious conflicts of interests and corruption, lack of internal controls, and political manipulation. Beginning in the mid-80s, Bolivia began to reform the legal framework for external auditing. In 1982, newly appointed comptroller-general Antonio Sánchez de Lozada embarked on a reform of the external audit agency, which intensified between 1985 and 1992.

However, Victor Paz Estensoro, who was elected president in 1985, soon watered down the initial reforms, as 'he did not support structural reforms that would give the agency more power and independence from the executive' (Dove 2002:193). Dove (2002) convincingly argues that the reforms failed because they were imposed from the outside and adopted under pressure from the US in the context of a fiscal crisis. The Bolivian CGR was reformed with the passage of a new financial management and fiscal control law in 1990 and the CGR organic law adopted by executive decree in 1992. These laws increased the CGR's operational and technical autonomy and narrowed its mandate. However, under current arrangements, the Bolivian CGR depends directly on the President, who designates the comptroller-general for a 10-year term from a list proposed by the Senate. It nevertheless drafts its own budget proposal, which the ministry of finance incorporates in the executive's budget proposal without modifications.

Chapter 8

Conclusions: auditing, accountability and anti-corruption

We might hope to see the finances of the Union as clear and intelligible as a merchant's book, so that every member of Congress, and every man of any mind in the Union, should be able to comprehend them, to investigate abuses, and consequently to control them.

President Thomas Jefferson writing to his Secretary of the Treasury in 1802, cited in Walker 2004:10.

Undoubtedly, AAAs have a critical contribution to make to improve fiscal transparency and financial accountability, acting as 'auxiliary precautions' of parliaments in the scrutiny of government finances. However, they are not as effective as they could or should be. Over two centuries ago, former US president Thomas Jefferson expressed his hope to see government finances as transparent as a 'merchant's book.' In many developing countries, this remains an elusive wish.

In many emerging economies, AAAs remain unconsolidated institutions of governance, constrained by inadequate technical capacities, limited financial resources and unfavourable political environments. In many countries, AAAs are criticised because their audit reports are inconsequential. They are contested and their relevance dismissed because of a perceived lack of political independence to credibly control government. This perceived lack of independence may be due to AAAs being captured by the very political forces they are meant to control or because those political forces are able to neutralise their audit work at various stages in the audit process. AAAs must also lead by example and be models of integrity in the manner in which they operate and are managed.

Anchoring integrity and accountability in the management of public finances is indeed a daunting task for emerging democracies struggling to consolidate the rule of law, control corruption and strengthen governance. This book has shed light on the role and relevance of AAAs in the architecture of checks and balances and has delved into what determines the effectiveness of AAAs as 'pillars of integrity' and agencies of 'horizontal accountability' within the state. It has shown that the effectiveness of AAAs is only partially explained by the choice of institutional model for organising the external audit function. It underscores in particular the decisive influence of the political economy environment in which AAAs operate and the critical importance of the politics of the budget process. The budget and its oversight are political processes reflecting delicate arbitrages between competing policy priorities and evolving partisan politics. Ultimately, politics matter.

As the case studies have shown, a critical fault line in the independent oversight of government finances lies in the dysfunctional links between the AAAs and their principal, the legislature and, more generally, the public. Based on the experience of Latin America, we have shown that the ultimate effectiveness of AAAs is determined by the quality of their insertion into the systems of fiscal control and the efficacy of their links with the other components of the system, in particular the legislature. There exists a wide gap between formal rule and informal practices, which undermines the effectiveness of formal political institutions.

Furthermore, the reform and strengthening of AAAs are also inherently political processes, constrained by the political space for reform and the political incentives of reformers. Institutional reform does occur, but inserts itself into the trajectory of state building and the culture of public administration. There are many pathways to reform but the case of Brazil shows that gradual reform has greater chance of succeeding. Conversely, the examples of Argentina or Bolivia suggest that reform strategies seeking to transplant exogenous models are likely to fail.

One should not underestimate the potential role of AAAs in curbing corruption and improving governance, but expectations with regard to the role of AAAs in the oversight of public finances should be realistic. AAAs cannot have a meaningful impact in isolation. AAAs participate in the cycle of legislative accountability, scrutinising the manner in which governments manage public resources and implement the budget voted by the legislature on behalf of the public. As such, their impact also depends on the capacities and incentives of legislatures to oversee government and hold it to account. In many developing countries, such capacities and incentives are often missing, especially in presidential systems with fused government and legislative majorities or predominant ruling parties. As predicted by the general theory of the separation of powers, enforcing accountability on government requires the intervention of those institutions with the power and authority to sanction it, namely the legislature and the judiciary. Therefore, adequately understanding the functioning of AAAs necessarily requires delving into the governance of public finances and the politics of the budget.

The main contribution of AAAs to the fight against corruption is through the information they provide to the public on the manner in which government manages the public purse and whether it delivers services effectively and efficiently. AAAs contribute to enhancing transparency in government financial information and accountability in the governance of the budget.

The effectiveness of AAAs ultimately depends on their capacity to generate behaviour within the public sector, establish credible incentives shaping the behaviour of both individual bureaucrats and public organisations. They do so providing reasonable reassurances on the reliability of government financial information to the legislature and the public, to inform budgetary decisions and enforce government accountability. This research also underscores the potential of freedom of information and the critical role of civil society and the media in increasing transparency in public budgeting and fiscal policy. As such, AAAs must be cast in the broader system of checks and balances in financial governance and the separation of powers in public finance management. This, in turn, opens avenues for further inquiry into the capacities and incentives of legislatures to effectively hold governments to account.

The lessons from this research have broader implications for practitioners and policymakers seeking to reform and strengthen the independent auditing of government finances in emerging economies and developing countries. First, further research is required to understand the dynamics of government auditing and the politics of budget oversight in other parts of the world in order to draw more general lessons. However, scant comparative analysis exists on the functioning of AAAs in other parts of the world, such as in Sub-Saharan Africa.

Second, this research must also be broadened to contrast the performance of AAAs in parliamentary systems of government with that in presidential systems. Does the nature of the political system – presidential or parliamentary – have a structural influence on the effectiveness of AAAs? In Sub-Saharan Africa, for example, this would entail comparing the performance of Francophone and Anglophone systems of external auditing. This book proposes a general framework and benchmark indicators to gauge the effectiveness of external auditing and the performance of AAAs. Further research is undoubtedly required to develop indicators able to track progress over time.

Third, the book also provides important lessons for international financial institutions and donor governments supporting the efforts of developing countries and emerging economies at reforming their audit arrangements. In the past decade or so, a substantial amount of foreign aid has been devoted to strengthening AAAs in developing countries, with mixed results and little evidence of impact. The strengthening of independent oversight and auditing of public finances in developing countries also matters to foreign aid organisations because of the reassurances AAAs ought to provide to ensure that the resources given by aid donors are effectively used for the purposes intended. In addition, donors provide increasing amounts of foreign aid directly through the recipient countries' own budget. This new mode of aid delivery makes it all the more important to strengthen audit systems in developing countries.

Notes

1 Introduction: budget institutions and financial governance

1 Those autonomous state organisations tasked with independently auditing government finances are hereafter referred to as autonomous audit agencies (AAAs). This terminology is used to underscore the autonomy of these organisations within the structure of the state, as part of the checks and balances on government, like oversight agencies and accountability institutions. The International Organization of Supreme Audit Institutions (INTOSAI) officially refers to them as supreme audit institutions to underline their position at the helm of the government auditing systems. They are also called state audit institutions, auditor-general's offices, comptroller-general's offices, national audit offices, courts of accounts, or tribunal of accounts, reflecting different institutional traditions for organising the external auditing function in modern states.

2 The phrase 'checks and balances' was additionally coined by Montesquieu in *The Spirit of the Laws* (1748). As such, when employing a system of checks and balances for governmental action to be processed, it must pass through a so-called Montesquieuian gauntlet. Montesquieuian gauntlet is a term that refers to the delay of governmental action by forcing it to pass through a system of checks and balances to ensure the legitimacy of the action and to ensure a proper separation of powers. In a system of government with competing sovereigns (such as a multi-branch government or a federal system), 'checks' refers to the ability, right and responsibility of each power to monitor the activities of the other(s); 'balances' refers to the ability of each entity to use its authority to limit the powers of the others, whether in general scope or in particular cases.

3 Kautilya (c.350–275 BC), also known as Chanakya, minister to the Indian king Chandragupta Maurya, founder of the Mauryan Empire (c.321–180 BC), was a Hindu statesman and political philosopher who wrote a classic treatise on government, *Arthasastra* (c.250 BC).

4 According to O'Donnell (1999), fundamentally, the weakness of horizontal accountability stems from the feebleness of the liberal and republican components of new democracies, in particular the rule of law, in other words dysfunctions in the realisation and protection of citizen rights, on the one hand, and the fulfillment of state obligations and responsibilities, on the other hand (O'Donnell, 1999).

5 Horizontal accountability deals exclusively with those actions that 'are undertaken by a state agency with the explicit purpose of preventing, cancelling, redressing,

and/or punishing actions (or non-actions) by other state agencies that are deemed unlawful, whether on the grounds of encroachment or of corruption' (O'Donnell 2003:35).

6 Executive discretion creates opportunities for abuse and corruption. As Robert Klitgaard (1988) aptly remarks, corruption equals monopoly plus discretion minus accountability.

7 According to the specialised literature, there exist three main models for organising the external audit function in modern states, the *monocratic model* of an audit agency linked to the legislature and headed by a sole auditor-general; the *court model* of an audit agency with quasi-judicial powers to enforce its decisions; and the *collegiate* or *board model* of a collective decision-making structure without judicial prerogatives. For a review of typologies of AAAs, see: Allen and Tommasi 2001; Stapenhurst and Titsworth 2001; Schiavo-Campo and Tommasi 1999; Dye and Stapenhurst 1998.

8 The emergence of direct budget support in recent years places further onus on the need to strengthen financial accountability, reduce fiduciary risk and curb corruption in developing countries' finances.

2 Political economy of budget oversight and external auditing

1 See Evans 1995, 1992; Evans *et al* 1985; Deutch 1981.

2 The Washington consensus holds that sound economic policy is based on ten policy reforms deemed crucial for economic adjustment in the late 1980s. These market-oriented prescriptions incorporated both macroeconomic (fiscal overhaul, tax reform, interest and exchange-rate reforms) and microeconomic remedies (privatisation, deregulation, trade liberalisation) (Williamson 1993).

3 For useful reviews of this debate, see: Santiso 2004a, 2003, 2001.

4 The new public management separates 'steering from rowing', steering being the core function of central government while the rowing, the actual execution of government policy, is decentralised to executing agencies and private contractors (Kettl 1999). It further proposes to centralise policymaking in the core executive agencies (president, cabinet, finance ministry, central bank), while decentralising the delivery of policy to a number of agencies that operate within limits set by the centre (executing agencies, private contractors, regulatory agencies) (Aucoin 1990).

5 In the US, performance-based management and budgeting at the federal level has been reintroduced in the state reform agenda in the early 1990s with the Chief Financial Officers Act of 1990 and the Government Performance and Results Act of 1993. The reinventing government movement became enshrined in Vice-President Gore's National Performance Review initiative of 1993. The GPRA has always envisioned the complete integration of the performance measurement into the budget process. This integration is perhaps the single most powerful tool for implementing comprehensive performance management within government agencies.

6 For a useful review of Latin American experiments with administrative reform, see Spink 1998.

7 Author interview with Roberto Martinere, former head of the central budget office of the Ministry of Economy and Finance of Argentina, Buenos Aires, Argentina, 13 April 2005.

8 Keefer (2004:13) makes a useful distinction between two broad sets of governance concepts: 'those related to government performance of its core functions and those related to the incentives of government officials to perform those functions.'

9 See in particular Kaufmann et al 2005; Kaufmann and Kraay 2003, 2002; Knack 2002; Knack and Keefer 1997; and Chong and Calderón 2000.

10 A rich body of data has emerged over the last decade to measure institutional strength, governance quality and government performance, enabling us to inquire into the causality links between governance and development (Besançon 2003). Kaufmann *et al* (1999) have deconstructed the concept into clusters of indicators capturing six key dimensions of governance, which include: (i) voice and accountability; (ii) political stability; (iii) government effectiveness; (iv) regulatory quality; (v) rule of law; and (vi) control of corruption. Kaufmann *et al* (1999:2–4; 2005:130–1) provide the definition and components of the six governance clusters.

11 See, in particular, Rodrik *et al* 2002; Knack and Keefer 1995.

12 For example, Persson and Tabellini (2000, 2001) emphasise the role of electoral rules and political regimes on the political incentives shaping fiscal policy. They predict that financing of public goods relative to more targeted goods is higher in parliamentary democracies. Looking at how political institutions shape economic policy, Persson (2001:i) finds that electoral rules (district magnitude and the electoral formula) and political regimes have a systematic effect on the size and composition of government spending: 'presidential regimes have smaller governments and countries with majoritarian elections have smaller welfare-state programs and less corruption'.

13 See, in particular the seminal work by Aaron Wildavsky (Wildavsky 1964, 1992; Wildavsky and Caiden 2000) and Allen Schick (2002) on the politics of the budget in developed countries.

14 A distinction should be made between the budget, the budget system and the budget process. Whereas the budget refers to the document within which financial proposals are contained, the budget system refers to the relationship between the actors intervening in the different phases of the budget process and endowed with different budgetary powers and prerogatives.

15 The literature on political budget cycles studies cycles in fiscal policies generated by the electoral process. These cycles may be in the composition of public spending, in the size of the total budget, and in the choice of taxes or debt to finance the budget.

16 Von Hagen and Harden (1995) have studied the 'tragedy of commons' in public budgeting within the executive, specifically between the ministry of finance, spending agencies and interest groups, and Weingast *et al* (1981) have investigated it at the level of the legislature, where individual legislators have strong incentives to attend to the demands of their constituencies in order to secure re-election.

17 However, heads of internal control units are progressively being transferred under the authority of the comptroller-general while the rest of these units remain part of the executing agencies.

18 From the US GAO website: www.gao.gov (accessed 20 September, 2006).

19 The international financial institutions and donor governments, in particular the US, have supported these efforts through regional initiatives such as

SIMAFAL (*Sistema Integrado Modelo de Administración Financiera para América Latina*). Launched in the early 1990s, SIMAFAL's objective is to integrate financial management systems, joining together the budgetary, treasury, accounting, internal control and external auditing systems.

20 The so-called Kemmerer missions visited Mexico in 1917, Colombia in 1923, Chile in 1925, Ecuador in 1925, Bolivia in 1927 and Peru in 1930. They had a decisive influence on the reform of government and the shape of budget institutions in the region, in particular the choice of institutional models for AAAs.

21 Kemmerer was concerned with the corrupting influence of political parties in administrative affairs and believed that insulating key agencies of economic and financial governance from undue political interference would improve fiscal governance and economic performance. This belief was anchored in the experience of the US at the turn of the century, when the federal administration was riddled with corruption and mismanagement (Morgenstern and Manzetti 2003). Efforts at controlling the executive originated in a growing exasperation with corruption in politics in the 1870s, increasing ineptness in the bureaucracy embodied in the spoils system, and a public outcry for reform after the assassination of President Garfield in 1882 by a spoils-seeker. The US Congress swiftly passed the Pendleton Act thereafter, inaugurating the merit-based bureaucracy in the public sector. At the beginning of the twentieth century, further anti-corruption legislation was passed, with the creation of independent regulatory agencies to oversee public utilities, an independent central bank to steer monetary policy and a strong external audit agency to improve legislative oversight of government finances, the General Accounting Office (GAO).

22 Budget institutions are defined as 'the set of rules, procedures and practices according to which budgets are drafted, approved and implemented' (Alesina and Perotti 1996:3).

23 Alesina *et al* (1999) identify three main institutional arrangements conducive to fiscal discipline: numerical rules that establish *ex ante* fiscal constraints on government spending and budget deficits; top-down or 'hierarchical' procedural rules that concentrate budgetary powers in the executive vis à vis the legislature, and, within the executive, in the finance ministry vis à vis spending ministries; and transparency requirements that ensure the comprehensiveness of the budget and the integrity of the budget process.

3 Institutional arrangements for external auditing

1 Author interview with Enrique Paixão, former President of the Argentine AGN's college of auditors between 1994 and 1999, Buenos Aires, Argentina, 13 August 2003.

2 For a review of typologies of external audit agencies, see: Allen and Tommasi 2001; Stapenhurst and Titsworth 2001; Dye and Stapenhurst 1998; UKNAO 2001.

3 According to Dye and Stapenhurst (1998:1), 'the institution is an integral part of the judiciary, makes legal judgments on compliance with laws and regulations, and exercises a budget control function to assure that public funds are well spent' and for the purpose intended.

4 In Chile, there exists a tribunal of accounts within the CGR, which itself follows the monocratic model.

5 According to Allen and Tommasi (2001:314–42), the functions of an AAA are to: 'detect irregularities involving the misuse of public funds and identify related weaknesses in management controls that may imperil the integrity of the organization and the effective implementation of budgetary and other policy decisions; determine the reliability of reports on budget execution and other financial data; identify instances and patterns of waste and inefficiency that, if corrected, will permit more economical use of available budget resources; and provide reliable data about program results as a basis for future adjustments in laws, policies and budget allocations.'

6 INTOSAI, Lima Declaration of Guidelines on Auditing Precepts, Section 4, 1, October 1977.

7 According to Mainwaring (2003:13), 'Accountability cannot exists with *no* sanctioning power; some capacity to redress wrongdoing by referring the case to other venues (especially the justice system) is critical to systems of accountability [... However], accountability does not require direct, legally ascribed sanctioning power. Agencies of oversight are expected to refer possible wrongdoings to actors that can impose sanctions; this indirect sanctioning power suffices to characterize a relationship of accountability.'

8 This theory holds that political accountability for corruption and mismanagement should be enforced by the legislature on the executive, while managerial accountability for waste and underperformance ought to be enforced by the executive on the bureaucracy. In criminal and penal cases, including cases of corruption, the judiciary is responsible for enforcing judicial accountability.

9 Another important distinction is between managerial accountability and political accountability: 'political accountability involves holding those in public office responsible for performance and decisions, while managerial accountability involves the more technical aspects of fiscal and administrative responsibility' (Newell and Bellour 2002:6). While managerial accountability is part of the process of bureaucratic delegation, political accountability is embedded in the process of legislative delegation. However, managerial accountability is often inoperative in the absence of political accountability.

10 For example, the US GAO gave 217 legislative testimonies and made 2700 audit recommendations during 2004, and claims that 83 percent of these have been implemented. See US GAO 2005.

11 The degree of AAAs' structural independence is captured along three main dimensions: institutional (constitutional guarantees, statutory provisions, formal supervision arrangements, scope of mandate, autonomy in defining work-plan, unfettered access to financial information, scope of authority), individual (rules governing selection, nomination and removal of agency head, length of tenure, individual privileges and immunities of auditors-general, legally-defined procedures for recruiting, promoting and dismissing staff, degree of control of agency head over personnel management, professional standards and technical competence), and financial independence (level and determination of the agency's budget). Dove (2002:83) defines autonomy 'as an agency's ability to carry out its legal mandate without interference from other actors in its environment.' In particular, in terms of the agency's budget, while absolute financial independence is unrealistic and unadvisable, several institutional devices exist for securing adequate funding, such as numerical and procedural rules. The AAA's budget

can be a fixed percentage of the budget, as in Ecuador or Guatemala. The AAA can also have the ability to draft its budget and submit it to the legislature, as in Argentina or Mexico. In Bolivia, Colombia and Venezuela, the executive must incorporate the agency's draft budget in the government's budget proposal without modifications. In Nicaragua, the AAA drafts its budget proposal and submits it for review to the executive as part of the normal procedures of the budget process.

12 This indicator is measured along four main dimensions, including whether the auditor-general is trustworthy; whether the agency's recommendations have contributed to combat corruption; whether the agency verifies that the executive complies with the physical goals of the budget programmes; and whether it has the capacity to effectively oversee federal spending.

4 The board model and the case of Argentina

1 The legal framework of the AGN is provided by the 1853 Constitution revised in 1994 (article 85) and the 1992 financial administration and fiscal control law (Law 24156), which replaced the antiquated 1956 accounting law (Law 23354). The 1992 financial administration law, the 1997 organic budget law (Law 11672) and the annual budget laws regulate the budgetary system.

2 The current institutional arrangements are the result of the 1994 amendment to the Constitution, which sought to strengthen external oversight of government. The 1993 *Pacto de los Olivos* between the ruling Peronist party and the opposition Radical party agreed to the principle of presidential re-election sought by President Carlos Menem in exchange for greater control over the executive and reduced concentration of powers in the presidency.

3 Politicisation also permeates the AGN itself. Each auditor-general is given a specific area of responsibility and has discretion over the designation of directors and deputy directors of internal directorates.

4 According to the current president of the joint public accounts committee, Oscar Lamberto (2002:32, author's translation), 'if the act of control is purely a technical exercise, the conclusions that are reached are not necessarily rational from a political point of view; if it is politically motivated, it can become an instrument of political prosecution with motivations far removed from concerns over the quality of public management.' The challenge is finding the right balance, a balance, which, according to key decision-makers, was not found. Author interview with Oscar Lamberto, Chairman of the joint public accounts committee, Buenos Aires, Argentina, 12 April 2005.

5 It is important to underscore that the AGN emits decisions (*dictámenes*) that are processed through the legislative process. Audit recommendations are transmitted for consideration to the legislature's joint public accounts committee. This committee does not have sanctioning powers either, and, in fact, is not obliged nor has the faculty to press judicial charges. It can nevertheless delay audit reports or abstain from emitting an opinion on audit findings, which 'kills' audit findings. The destiny of the audit reports is, at best, uncertain, lessening their effectiveness and usefulness.

6 The last budget submitted to the legislature within the statutory deadline was in 1966 and the last budget formally approved by the legislature within the required time was in 1954 (Makón 1997).

7 Other administrative oversight institutions neutralised in the first years of the Menem administration included the *Fiscalía Nacional de Investigaciones Administrativas* and *Sindicatura General de Empresas Públicas* (SIGEP).
8 Author interview with a former president of the AGN, Buenos Aires, Argentina, 13 August 2003.

5 The court model and the case of Brazil

1 The European Court of Auditors was established in 1977 in order to strengthen the powers of financial scrutiny of the legislature following the considerable increase in European Community resources during the 1970s. The 1975 Treaty of Brussels extended the powers of the European Parliament in budgetary control. The 1993 Maastricht Treaty enhanced the authority and independence of the European Court of Auditors, making it a full EU institution.
2 In Chile, there exists a tribunal of accounts within the external audit agency, which itself follows the monocratic model.
3 The special ad hoc inquiry commissions of the legislature, the *Comissões Parlamentares de Inquérito*, are more intrusive forms of 'fire alarm' oversight established to investigate allegations of corruption.
4 Specific tasks in the management of human resources in the federal state include reviewing the legality of civil service retirement, severance and pension payments, the recruitment and dismissal of civil servants.
5 During the decade between 1990 and 1999, the TCU examined almost 172,000 cases, more than half of which (about 108,000) related to the registration of civil servants and admissions of pensions, 48,770 review and judgment of accounts (*tomadas e prestações de contas*) and only slightly over 4300 inspections and audits, almost 900 (866) allegations and charges of irregularities and 1513 requests of investigation (TCU 2000d).
6 For example, during the period 1994–99, 47 public auditors and financial analysts collaborated with 16 standing or ad hoc legislative committees and special inquiry commissions (TCU 2000b:4).
7 Life-tenure has not precluded high turnover (about 1.2 rotations a year), shorter tenures (from about 10 years to about 5 years since 1988) and an increase in the average age of auditors-general (from an average of 50 to an average of 60 at entry) (Speck 2000:202; Brown 2002b:76).
8 The military introduced procedural rules that undermined the authority of the TCU and undercut the powers of the legislature. In the area of public procurement in particular, if the TCU detected irregularities it had to transmit the case to the legislature that had 30 days to rule on the matter, after which the contract was deemed approved. According to the principle of '*decisão por decurso de prazo*' or 'positive administrative silence', decisions were considered adopted once a period of time had lapsed without the legislature or the TCU emitting an adverse opinion. This rule introduced by the military regime was designed to neutralise the possible obstruction or veto in policymaking and budget execution, while keeping the façade of democratic procedures.
9 The Secretariat for Internal Control grew from the Office of the Inspector General of Finance, which was in operation from 1975 to 1986.

10 In Brazil, the institution of *ex ante* control caused conflicts as soon as 1893, when the TCU refused to authorise pension payments to a civil servant contracted irregularly (Cotias e Silva 1999). The incident became famous because the civil servant in question was the brother of a former President, Deodora da Fonseca. He had been appointed as a civil servant by the then-president Floriano Peixoto. The case soon degenerated into an open conflict between the President and the TCU, with the then-minister of finance Serzedello Corrêa taking the side of the TCU. Corrêa refused to countersign executive decrees designed to undermine the TCU's independence or suppressing *ex ante* control. This conflict is considered as a defining moment in the history of the TCU, reflecting its struggle for genuine independence in the architecture of the state.

11 Author interviews with Luiz Carlos Bresser Pereira, former Minister of Finance and State Modernization, Barcelona, Spain, 15 January 2001; and Carlos Pereira Department of Political Science, Michigan State University, Brasilia, Brazil, 5 October 2003. In particular, in 1938 Vargas created an administrative department tasked with supervising civil service reform and the modernisation of the bureaucracy, the Administrative Department of the Public Service (*Departamento Administrativo do Serviço Público*, DASP), succeeding in strengthening both the capacity and autonomy of the Brazilian state. DASP marked the beginning of the professionalisation of civil servants in Brazil.

12 Since 1993, the TCU also devotes a chapter of its annual report to the analysis of policy issues, such as administrative reform, privatisation, social security, poverty reduction, and debt management.

13 In fact, between 1952 and 1989, the President whose financial statements were being evaluated had traditionally appointed the TCU's reporting minister selected by the TCU President (Pessanha 2000). Procedural reforms in 1993 corrected this deficiency and, since then, the TCU reporting minister is chosen randomly among the auditors-general.

14 Author interview with a federal deputy, Brasilia, Brazil, 2 October 2003.

15 Interestingly, the accounts of Fernando Henrique Cardoso (1995–2002) were approved after the results of the general elections were known (18 and 19 December 2002).

16 The controversies that surrounded the nominations of two auditors-general in 2005 illustrate the legislature's disinvested attitude. In May 2005, to fill two positions left vacant since 2003, the Chamber of Deputies selected Augusto Nardes (PP/RS) as its preferred candidate. The Senate's choice, Luiz Otávio, generated controversy, as he was accused of misappropriation of public funds in BNDES.

17 These included proposals for fixed, non-renewable mandates of six years for the ministers, with nominations of three ministers occurring every two years, a revision of the nomination criteria and procedures, and a strengthening of social control and transparency mechanisms.

18 The CGU fused the *Secretaria Federal de Controle Interno* (SFC) and the *Comissão de Coordenação de Controle Interno* (CCCI). In 2003, it was renamed the *Controladoria-Geral da União* (CGU) and its head was upgraded to Minister for Control and Transparency (*Ministro de Estado do Controle e da Transparência*).

19 Barbosa originally favored a TCU with wide autonomy from all powers, an intermediary body at equidistance from the executive and the legislature, acting

as an 'independent mediator and assisting both powers' in order for the TCU not to become an 'ornamental and useless institution' (Barbosa 1994:181).

6 The monocratic model and the case of Chile

1 Author interview with Gustavo Sciolla Avendaño, former Comptroller-General, Santiago, Chile, 4 August 2004.
2 In 1983, the National Audit Act made the comptroller and auditor-general an officer of the House of Commons to address legislative concerns over the influence that the executive, in particular the Treasury, retained over public audit. It created a 750-strong staff National Audit Office (NAO) to support him in the performance of his duties. Legislative oversight of public finances has a long tradition in the UK, dating back to the creation of the Committee of Public Accounts in 1861 by the House of Commons on a motion of the then Chancellor of the Exchequer, William Gladstone. The 1866 Exchequer and Audit Act required all government departments to produce appropriation accounts for independent audit and created the position of comptroller and auditor-general. See UK NAO (2001):231–49.
3 Following the 1973 coup, the military junta undertook an important re-ordering of public administration, drafting legislation regulating the public administration (*Ley de Bases de la Administración del Estado*, 1974; *Ley de Procedimientos Administrativos*, 1974), financial management (*Ley de Administración Financiera del Estado*, LAFE, 1975) and government accounting (1976).
4 Two failed attempts were made in 1982 and in 1992.
5 The CGR controls fiscal revenues and public investment and its authority extends to 190 central government agencies, 24 public enterprises, eight mixed enterprises, 340 municipalities, public universities, and public concessions. Nevertheless, the CGR does not audit the central bank, the state bank, or the national copper company. It also audits the projects financed by international lending institutions.
6 Special investigations consume a great deal of the agency's resources, affecting routine oversight and planned audits. The results of special investigations are first transmitted to the audited agencies and then to the corresponding specialised committee in the legislature.
7 Personnel management functions include keeping the register of all public servants, of contracted personnel, and of persons condemned by the courts and therefore prohibited to assume public functions. It also includes the custody of asset declarations of senior civil servants following the adoption of the administrative probity law in 1999.
8 The President, with the backing of the cabinet, can insist on his or her decision through a '*decreto de insistencia*', in which case the CGR's veto is overridden. This override prerogative of the executive does not apply to decrees with force of law, to the promulgation of decrees or to decrees amending the constitution.
9 Initially, between 1932 and 1942, the CGR adopted a minimalist approach to the interpretation of its review powers, showing deference to the executive. The executive also showed little respect for the *ex ante* control functions of the CGR. It adopted the practice of issuing '*decretos de insistencia*' before forwarding its decrees to the legislature. As Faundez (2007:7) notes, 'this practice effectively made

the legality review procedure redundant and revealed little or no respect for the Contraloría.'

10 Some comptrollers-general had extraordinarily long tenures, such as Osvaldo Iturriaga, from 1978 until 1997. However, comptrollers-general are typically appointed at an advanced age, which shortens their tenure. For example, Arturo Aylwyn Azócar was nominated in 1997 but had to retire in 2002, after five years in office.

11 This procedure has seldom been used. In 1945, in the context of increasingly tense relations between the executive and the legislature, Comptroller-General Augustín Vigorena was impeached by the legislature for failing adequately to control the executive.

12 In 2002, Lagos nominated Sciolla Avendaño, the CGR's third highest-ranking official but trusted by the ruling Christian Democrats, rather than the long-serving deputy comptroller-general, Jorge Reyes, considered close to the opposition and who made most of his career in the CGR since he joined in 1959. The Senate confirmed Sciolla Avendaño by a narrow vote of 27 against 21. Media reports have revealed the existence of an unwritten quid pro quo between Sciolla Avendaño and Mario Fernández, then Secretary-General of the Presidency, according to which Sciolla Avendaño promised to cleanse the CGR of remnants of the *ancient régime*. However, upon assuming office, Sciolla Avendaño did not accede to Lagos' demands and even promoted some of the individuals in question, including his deputy. Sciolla Avendaño had to assume a corporate position to assert his authority not only vis à vis the executive, but also within the CGR.

13 Longevity and allegiance to the hierarchy determine career advancement. The 75-year age limit does not apply to staff. As a result, managers seldom retire and there is little renovation or rotation of staff.

14 The centralisation of budget authority is the result of a long process that started as early as the civil war of 1891, which erupted partly as a result of a conflict between the executive and the legislature over the budget. It culminated with the adoption of the 1975 financial administration law and the 1980 constitution, which gave Chile one of the most centralised budget systems in the region. The legislature was closed during most of the military dictatorship between 1978 and 1990.

15 Chilean administrative traditions clearly distinguish fiscal control from performance evaluation. Article 52 of the 1975 law of financial administration (LAFE) underscores that the CGR exercises the 'financial control of the state and the adequate compliance with legal and regulatory provisions', while the 'control and evaluation of the attainment of objectives and the achievement of pre-set targets are tasks that correspond to the administration of the state and which are exercised by the executive' (DIPRES 2004:339).

16 Author interview with Senator Alejandro Foxley, Minister of Foreign Affairs and former Minister of Finance, Santiago, Chile, 12 August 2004.

17 For the first time, the Senate debate and vote were public. The deliberations of the Senate were previously made behind closed doors in a special session and through secret vote.

7 Government auditing in transition

1 Author interview with Emma Öståker and Magnus Gimdal, Auditors at the Swedish *Riksrevisionen*, Stockholm, Sweden, 19 May 2004; and Anne Mondoloni, Auditor at the French *Cours des Comptes*, Paris, France, 24 March 2005.

2 Author interview with Bruno Speck, Senior Adviser for Latin America based in Brazil, Transparency International, Lima, Peru, 11 October 2004. See also Speck 1999 and 2000.

3 Author interview with Jorge Danós, former chief of staff of the Peruvian Prime Minister, Lima, Peru, 31 May 2005.

4 Author interview with Roberto Martinere, former head of the central budget office of the Ministry of Economy and Finance of Argentina, Buenos Aires, Argentina, 13 April 2005.

5 Author interviews with Senator Alejandro Foxley, Minister of Foreign Affairs and former Minister of Finance, Santiago, Chile, 12 August 2004; Mario Marcel, former Director of DIPRES (2000–06), Santiago, Chile, 12 August 2004; and with Joaquín Vial, former Director of DIPRES (1997–2000), Santiago, Chile, 4 August 2004.

6 However, external auditing at the sub-national level remains particularly weak, as in other federal countries such as Argentina and Brazil. Figueroa Neri (2005) negatively evaluates the performance of sub-national AAAs at the state level in terms of political independence and technical capabilities, gaps in constitutional provisions, inconsistency of legal frameworks, and a variety in operational focuses. About half of the 31 states and the federal district do not have an AAA. Like internal control systems, sub-national auditing is amongst the weakest links in the accountability regime of emerging economies.

7 This policy implication draws from Carothers' findings on the determinants of legislative reform. Carothers (1999:181) aptly remarks that, 'to build effective legislatures, mobilizing political power is more important than increasing technical skill.'

References

Abuelafia, E, Berensztein, S, Braun, M and Di Grescia, L (2005) *Who Decides on Public Expenditures? A Political Economy Analysis of the Budget Process: The Case of Argentina*, Buenos Aires: CIPPEC.

Adsera, A, Boix, C and Payne, M (2003) 'Are You Being Served? Political Accountability and the Quality of Government', *Journal of Law, Economics, and Organization* 19(2): 445–90.

Affonso, SB (1997) 'Tribunais de Contas no contexto do poder Judiciário', *Revista do Tribunal de Contas da União* 28(74): 109–19.

________ (1996) 'Eficácia das decisões do Tribunal de Contas', *Revista do Tribunal de Contas da União* 27(68): 113–20.

AGN (1993) *Normas de Auditoría Externa*, Buenos Aires: AGN.

Alesina, A and Perotti, R (1996) *Budget Institutions and Budget Deficits*, Cambridge: NBER Working Paper 5556.

Alesina, A, Hausmann, R, Hommes, R and Stein, E (1999) *Budget Institutions and Fiscal Performance in Latin America*, Washington, DC: IDB OCE Working Paper 394.

________ (1996) *Budget Institutions and Fiscal Performance in Latin America*, Cambridge, MA: NBER Working Paper 5586.

Allen, R, and Tommasi, D (eds) (2001) *Managing Public Expenditure*, Paris: OECD.

Alston, L, Mello, M, Mueller, B and Pereira, C (2005) *Who Decides on Public Expenditures? A Political Economy Analysis of the Budget Process: The Case of Brazil*, Washington, DC: IDB, unpublished mimeo.

Animat, C and Vial, J (2004) *Who decides on Public Expenditures? A Political Economy Analysis of the Budget Process in Chile*, Washington, DC: IDB, unpublished mimeo.

Animat, C, Londregan, J, Navia, P and Vial, J (2006) *Political Institutions, Policymaking Processes and Policy Outcomes in Chile*, Washington, DC: IDB Research Network Working Paper R-521.

Asselin, L (1999) *Integrated Financial Management in Latin America as of 1995*, Washington, DC: World Bank, LATPS Occasional Paper Series 18.

Atchabahian, A (2002) 'Comentarios', *Revista ASAP* 29: 153–8.

Aucoin, P (1998) *Auditing for Accountability: The Role of the Auditor General*, Ottawa, Canada: Institute on Governance Occasional Paper Series.

________ (1990) 'Administrative Reform in Public Management: Paradigms, Principles, Paradoxes and Pendulums', *Governance* 3(1): 115–37.

Aylwyn Azócar, A (2002) 'Entrevista: El prestigio de la institución se debe a la calidad, dedicación y probidad de su personal', *Revista Chilena de Administración Pública* 1(2): 3–10.

________ (1995) 'Discurso en el acto de clausura', in CGR, *Proceedings of the Seminar: ¿Qué Contraloría General de la República Necesita el Chile de hoy y del futuro? Santiago, Chile, 13–14 November 1995*, Santiago: CGR: 123–36.

Baglini, R (2005) 'La Cuenta de Inversión', in O Lamberto (ed) *La Cuenta de inversión*, Buenos Aires: CPMRC: 53–62.

________ (2002) 'La gestación parlamentaria de la Ley no.24156', in L Despouy *et al* (eds) *El control público en la Argentina*, Buenos Aires: AGN: 27–30.

Bambaci, J (1999) 'From Decisionism to Consensus? The Politics of Second Generation Reform in Argentina', *Democratization* 6(3): 118–45.

Bambaci, J, Saront, T and Tommasi, M (2002) 'The Political Economy of Economic Reforms in Argentina', *Journal of Policy Reform* 5(2): 75–88.

Barbosa, R (1994) 'Exposição de Motivos sobre a criação to Tribunal de Contas da União, 7 de novembro de 1890', *Revista do Tribunal de Contas da União* 25(62): 180–90.

Barra, RC (2002) 'El papel de los institutos centrales de control en los ordenamientos jurídicos: el modelo argentino', in Universidad Austral, *Control de la administración pública*, Buenos Aires: Ediciones RAP: 289–306.

Barro, R (2000) 'Inequality and Growth in a Panel of Countries', *Journal of Economic Growth* 5(1): 5–32.

Berensztein, S, Ortíz, HL and Peña, M (2000) *Transparencia, instituciones y reforma: la economía política del proceso de ejecución y ajuste presupuestario*, unpublished mimeo.

Besançon, M (2003) *Good Governance Rankings: The Art of Measurement*, Cambridge, MA: World Peace Foundation Report 36.

Bourdin, J (2001) *De la démocratie budgétaire en Amérique – L'information économique aux Etats-Unis: quels enseignements pour la France*, Paris: French Senate, Report 326.

Boylan, D (2001) *Defusing Democracy: Central Bank Independence and the Transition from Authoritarian Rule*, Ann Arbor, MI: University of Michigan Press.

Braceli, O (2002) 'Incidencia de la Ley 24156 en la reforma del estado nacional y la situación fiscal argentina', in L Despouy *et al* (eds) *El control público en la Argentina*, Buenos Aires: AGN: 55–88.

Braga de Figueiredo, LC (1991) 'Auditoria operacional e avaliação de desempenho', *Revista do Tribunal de Contas da União* 49: 39–55.

Bresser Pereira, LC and Spink, P (eds) (1999) *Reforming the State: Managerial Public Administration in Latin America*, Boulder, CO: Lynne Rienner.

Bresser Pereira, LC, Cunill Grau, N, Garnier, L, Oszlak, O and Przeworski, A (2004) *Política y gestión pública*, Buenos Aires: Fondo de Cultura Económica.

Britto, CA (2001) 'O Régimen Constitucional dos Tribunais de Contas', *Revista Diálogo Jurídico* 1(9): 1–11.

Brown, RJ (2002a) *O Controle Externo Federal no Brasil*, Rio de Janeiro: Fundação Getúlio Vargas.

________ (2002b) *Controle Externo da Administração Pública Federal no Brasil: O TCU – Uma Análise Jurídico-administrativa*, Rio de Janeiro: América Jurídica.

Caiden, G (1994) 'Administrative Reform', in R Baker (ed) *Comparative Public Management: Putting US Public Policy and Implementation in Context*, Westport, CT: Praeger: 107–17.

Campos, E, Lien, D and Pradhan, S (1999) 'The Impact of Corruption on Investment: Predictability Matters', *World Development* 27(6): 1059–67.

Carcassone, G (2005) *Un controleur général pour les finances publiques*, Paris: Institut Montaigne.

Carey, J and Shugart, MS (eds) (1998) *Executive Decree Authority: Calling out the Tanks or Just Filling out the Forms*, Cambridge: Cambridge University Press.

Carothers, T (1999) *Aiding Democracy Abroad: The Learning Curve*, Washington, DC: Carnegie Endowment for International Peace.

CGR (2003) *Doctrina institucional – Versión actualizada*, Santiago: CGR.

________ (2002) *Proyecto de modernización de la Contraloría General de la República, 2002–2005*, Santiago: CGR.

________ (2001) *Cuenta pública del Contralor General correspondiente al año 2000*, Santiago: CGR.

________ (2000) *La función jurisdiccional del juzgado de cuentas*, Santiago: CGR, unpublished mimeo.

Chong, A and Calderón, C (2000) 'Empirical Tests on the Causality and Feedback Between Institutional Measures and Economic Growth', *Economics and Politics* 12(1): 69–81.

Cotias e Silva, A (1999) 'O Tribunal de Contas da União na história do Brasil: Evolução histórica, política e administrative (1890–1998)', in TCU, *Monografias vencedoras do Prêmio Serzedello Corrêa 1998*, Brasilia: TCU: 19–141.

Cukierman, A., Webb, S. and Neyapti, B. (1992) 'Measuring the Independence of Central Banks and its Effects on Policy Outcomes', *World Bank Economic Review* 9 (3): 397-423.

Day, P and Klein, R (1987) *Accountabilities: Five public services*, London: Tavistock.

Despouy, L *et al* (eds) (2002) *El control público en la Argentina*, Buenos Aires: AGN.

Deutch, K (1981) 'The Crisis of the State', *Government and Opposition* 16(3): 331–43.

Diamond, J (2003) *Performance Budgeting: Managing the Reform Process*, Washington, DC: IMF Working Paper WP/03/03.

________ (2002a) *The Role of Internal Audit in Government Financial Management: An International Perspective*, Washington, DC: IMF Working Paper 02/1994.

________ (2002b) 'The Strategy of Budget System Reform in Emerging Economies', *Public Finance and Management* 2(3): 358–86.

Diamond, L (1999) *Fostering Institutions to Contain Corruption*, Washington, DC: World Bank Public Sector PREM Note 24.

Díaz Frers, L (2006) *El debate sobre los superpoderes*, Buenos Aires: CIPPEC Análisis 29.

Diez Urza, S (1995) 'Intervención', in CGR, *Proceedings of the Seminar: ¿Qué Contraloría General de la República Necesita el Chile de hoy y del futuro? Santiago, Chile, 13–14 November 1995*, Santiago: CGR: 35–43.

DIPRES (2004) *Instrucciones para la ejecución de la ley de presupuesto 2004*, Santiago: DIPRES.

Dorotinsky, B and Floyd, R (2004) 'Public Expenditure Accountability in Africa: Progress, Lessons and Challenges', in B Levy and S Kpundeh (eds) *Building State Capacity in Africa: New Approaches, Emerging Lessons*, Washington, DC: WBI: 179–210.

Dorotinsky, W and Matsuda, Y (2002) 'Reforma de la gestión financiera en América Latina: Una perspectiva institucional', *Reforma y Democracia* 23: 141–66.

Dove, S (2002) *Fragile Miracles: The Creation and Sustainability of Autonomous Oversight Agencies in a Politicized Bureaucracy: The Case of Bolivia*, Barcelona, Spain: Universidad Autónoma de Barcelona, unpublished doctoral dissertation.

Drake, P (1989) *The Money Doctor in the Andes: The Kemmerer Missions, 1923–1933*, Durham, NC: Duke University Press.

Ducoté, N (2001) *Sistemas nacionales de integridad: Informe sobre Argentina para Transparency International*, Buenos Aires, Argentina: CIPPEC.

Dye, K and Stapenhurst, R (1998) *Pillars of Integrity: The Importance of Supreme Audit Institutions in Curbing Corruption*, Washington, DC: WBI.

Echeberría, K (2004) 'Objetivar la gobernanza: funciones y metodología. Una aproximación a la objetivación del análisis institucional a través de indicadores de gobernabilidad', paper presented at the IX CLAD Congress, Madrid, Spain, 2–5 November.

Echeberría, K, Subirats, J, Longo, F, Zapico, E, Babino, L, Dequino, D, Hintze, J, Pacheco, R, Oszlak, O, Roberto Motta, P and Lima Bandeira, M (2005) *Responsabilización y evaluación de la gestión pública*, Caracas, Venezuela: CLAD.

Elster, J (1999) 'Accountability in Athenian Politics', in A Przeworski, S Stokes and B Manin (eds) *Democracy, Accountability and Representation*, Cambridge: Cambridge University Press: 253–78.

Evans, P (1995) *Embedded Autonomy: States and Industrial Transformation*, Princeton, NJ: Princeton University Press.

________ (1992) 'The State as Problem and Solution: Embedded Autonomy and Adjustment,' in S Haggard and R Kaufman (eds) *The Politics of Economic Adjustment*, Princeton, NJ: Princeton University Press: 139–91.

Evans, P, Rueschemeyer, D and Skocpol, T (eds) (1985) *Bringing the State Back In*, Cambridge: Cambridge University Press.

Fadel, M (2002) 'La Auditoría General de la Nación', in L Despouy *et al* (eds) *El control público en la Argentina*, Buenos Aires: AGN: 117–24.

Faundez, J (2007) 'The Fragile Foundations of Administrative Legality in Chile between 1932 and 1973', *Journal of Comparative Law* 2(2): 1–18.

Ferreira Rubio, D (2000) 'El presidente argentino: ¿de la decisión al consenso?', *Contribuciones* 1/2000: 1–12.

Ferreira Rubio, D and Goretti, M (1998) 'When the President Governs Alone: The Decretazo in Argentina, 1989–1993', in J Carey and MS Shugart (eds) *Executive Decree Authority*, Cambridge: Cambridge University Press: 33–61.

Figueiredo, A (2003) 'The Role of Congress as an Agency of Horizontal Accountability: Lessons from the Brazilian Experience', in S Mainwaring and C Welna (eds) *Democratic Accountability in Latin America*, Oxford: Oxford University Press: 170–98.

Figueiredo, A and Limongi, F (2002) 'Incentivos Electorais, Partidos e Política Orçamentária', *Dados* 45(2): 303–44.

________ (1997) 'O Congreso e as Medidas Provisórias: Adbicação ou Delegação?', *Novos Estudos CEBRAP* 47: 127–54.

Figueroa Neri, A (ed) (2005) *Cuenta pública en México. Evaluando el laberinto legal de la fiscalización superior*, México, Universidad de Guadalajara and Angel Editor.

Garretón, M (1989) *The Chilean Political Process*, Boston, MA: Unwin Hyman.

Geddes, B (1994) *Politician's Dilemma: Building State Capacity in Latin America*, Berkeley, CA: University of California Press.

________ (1990) 'Building "State" Autonomy in Brazil, 1930–1964', *Comparative Politics* 22(2): 217–35.

Goetz, AM and Jenkins, R (2004) *Reinventing Accountability: Making Democracy Work for the Poor*, London: Palgrave Macmillan.

________ (2001) 'Hybrid Forms of Accountability', *Public Management Review* 3(3): 363–83.

Gonçalves, F (1991) 'O controle que o Tribunal de Contas precisa practicar', *Revista do Tribunal de Contas da União* 22(48): 33–36.

________ (1984) *Relatório sobre as Contas do Governo da República 1983*, Brasilia: TCU.

González de Rebella, LC (2001) 'El control externo del sector público: la Auditoría General de la Nación', paper presented at CLAD VI International Congress, Buenos Aires, Argentina, 5–9 November.

Grindle, M (1996) *Challenging the State: Crisis and Innovation in Latin America and Africa*, Cambridge: Cambridge University Press.

Guimarães Souto, H (2002) 'Control de la administración pública: El modelo brasileño,' in L Despouy *et al* (eds) *El control público en la Argentina*, Buenos Aires: AGN: 221–38.

Gutiérrez, G, Lujambio, A and Valadés, D (2001) *El proceso presupuestario y las relaciones entre los órganos del poder*, México: Instituto de Investigaciones Jurídicas.

Gutiérrez, R (1997) 'Hacia una administración financiera más transparente', *Revista de la ASAP* 29: 43–50.

Gutiérrez, R. (2002). 'Activos y pasivos de una cultura del presupuesto,' in L. Despouy et al. *El control público en la Argentina* (Buenos Aires, Argentina: AGN):89-97.

Guzmán, M (2005) *Systems of Management Control and Results-based Budgeting: The Chilean Experience*, Santiago, Chile: DIPRES.

Haggard, S (2000) 'Interests, Institutions, and Policy Reform, Economic Policy Reform in Latin America', in A Krueger (ed) *Economic Policy Reform: The Second Stage*, Chicago, IL: The University of Chicago Press: 61–98.

Haggard, S and Kaufman, R (1995) *The Political Economy of Democratic Transitions*, Princeton, NJ: Princeton University Press.

________ (eds) (1992) *The Politics of Economic Adjustment*, Princeton, NJ: Princeton University Press.

Haggard, S and McCubbins, M (eds) (2001) *Presidents, Parliaments and Policy*, Cambridge: Cambridge University Press.

Henisz, WJ (2004) 'Political Institutions and Policy Volatility', *Economics & Politics* 16(1): 1–27.

________ (2000) 'The Institutional Environment for Economic Growth', *Economics and Politics* 12(1): 1–31.

Heredia, B and Schneider, B (2003) 'The Political Economy of Administrative Reform in Developing Countries', in B Schneider and B Heredia (eds) *Reinventing the Leviathan: The Politics of Administrative Reform in Developing Countries*, Miami, FL: North South Centre Press: 1–32.

Hjalmarsson, Å and Jonsson, G (2003) *Accountability and Control: Case Study of Sweden*, Paris: OECD PUMA.

Hommes, R (1996) *Evolution and Rationality of Budget Institutions in Colombia*, Washington, DC: Inter-American Development Bank, Office of the Chief Economist, Working Paper 317.

Inter-American Development Bank (2005) *Evaluación de la Gobernabilidad Democrática en el Perú*, Washington, DC: IDB RG-P1043.

________ (2003) *Modernization of the State*, Washington, DC: Inter-American Development Bank, Strategy document.

International Monetary Fund (2003) *Chile: Report on the Observance of Standards and Codes – Fiscal Transparency*, 03/237 Washington, DC: IMF.

________ (2001) *Brazil: Report on the Observance of Standards and Codes – Fiscal Transparency*, Washington, DC: IMF Country Report 01/127.

Iturriaga Ruiz, O (1995) 'Discurso en el acto de inauguración', in CGR, *Proceedings of the Seminar: ¿Qué Contraloría General de la República Necesita el Chile de hoy y del futuro? Santiago, Chile, 13–14 November 1995*, Santiago: CGR 17–23.

Ivanega, M (2004) 'Reflexiones entorno al control externo de la administración pública y sus consecuencias', unpublished manuscript.

Jones, M (2001) 'Political Institutions and Public Policy in Argentina: An Overview of the Formation and Execution of the National Budget', in Haggard and McCubbins (eds) *Presidents, Parliaments and Policy*, Cambridge: Cambridge University Press: 149–82.

Jones, M, Saiegh, S, Spiller, P and Tommasi, M (2000) *Professional Politicians, Amateur Legislators; The Argentine Congress in the 20th Century*, Buenos Aires: CEDI Working Document 45.

Kaufmann, D and Kraay, A (2003) *Governance and Growth: Causality Which Way?*, Washington, DC: WBI unpublished mimeo.

________ (2002) 'Growth Without Governance', *Economía* 3(1): 169–215

Kaufmann, D, Kraay, A and Mastruzzi, M (2005) *Governance Matters IV: Governance Indicators for 1996–2004*, Washington, DC: WBI Working Paper.

Kaufmann, D, Kraay, A and Zoido-Lobatón, P (1999) *Aggregating Governance Indicators*, Washington, DC: World Bank Policy Research Working Paper 2195.

Kaufmann, D, Recanatini, F and Biletsky, S (2002) *Assessing Governance: Diagnostic Tools and Applied Methods for Capacity Building and Action Learning*, Washington, DC: World Bank Institute.

Keefer, P (2004) *A Review of the Political Economy of Governance: From Property Rights to Voice*, Washington, DC: World Bank Policy Research Working Paper No 3315.

Kenney, C (2003) 'Horizontal Accountability: Concepts and Conflicts', in S Mainwaring and C Welna (eds) *Democratic Accountability in Latin America*, Oxford: Oxford University Press: 55–76.

Kettl, DF (1999) 'The Global Revolution: Reforming Government-Sector Management', in LC Bresser Pereira and P Spink (eds) *Reforming the State: Managerial Public Administration in Latin America*, Boulder, CO: Lynne Rienner: 41–74.

Kiewert, DR and McCubbins, MD (1991) *The Logic of Delegation: Congressional Parties and the Appropriations Process*, Chicago, IL: The University of Chicago Press.

Klitgaard, R (1988) *Controlling Corruption*, Berkeley, CA: University of California Press.

Knack, S (2002) 'Governance and Growth: Measurement and Evidence', paper prepared for the Forum Series on the Role of Institutions in Promoting Growth, Washington DC: USAID and IRIS.

________ (2000) *Aid Dependence and the Quality of Governance: A Cross-Country Empirical Analysis*, Washington, DC: World Bank Policy Research Working Paper 2396.

Knack, S and Keefer, P (1997) 'Why Don't Poor Countries Catch Up? A Cross-National Test of an Institutional Explanation', *Economic Inquiry* 35: 590–602.

________ (1995) 'Institutions and Economic Performance: Cross-Country Tests Using Alternative Institutional Measures', *Economics and Politics* 7: 207–27.

Kopits, G and Craig, J (1998) *Transparency in Government Operations*, Washington, DC: IMF Occasional Paper 158.

Kuczynski, PP and Williamson, J (eds) (2003) *After the Washington Consensus: Restarting Growth and Reform in Latin America*, Washington, DC: Institute for International Economics.

Lamberto, O (ed) (2005) *La Cuenta de inversión*, Buenos Aires: CPMRC.

Lamberto, O (2002) 'Salir del Laberinto' in L Despouy *et al* (eds) *El Control Público en la Argentina – Jornadas 2002*, Buenos Aires, Argentina: AGN: 31–4.

Laranjeira, C (1999) *A Verdadeira História do Rouba, mas Faz*, São Paulo: Fundação Biblioteca Nacional.

Larraín, H (1995) 'Intervención', in CGR, *Proceedings of the Seminar: ¿Qué Contraloría General de la República Necesita el Chile de hoy y del futuro? Santiago, Chile, 13–14 November 1995*, Santiago: CGR 57–70.

Lavielle, B, Pérez, M and Hofbauer, H (2003) *Latin America Index of Budget Transparency*, Mexico and Washington DC: IBP.

Lederman, D, Loayza, N and Reis Soares, R (2001) *Accountability and Corruption: Political Institutions Matter*, Washington, DC: World Bank Policy Research Working Paper 2708.

Lillo Valenzuela, JC (2002) *Sobre la toma de razón y la facultad dictaminadora de la Contraloría General de la República de Chile*, paper presented at the 12th assembly of OLACEFS, Mexico, 24–28 September.

Llanos Campos, P (2003) *Antecedentes institucionales de la Contraloría General de la República de Chile*, Santiago: CGR.

Llanos González, H, and García Yerkovis, O (2002) *La función de auditoría en la Contraloría General de la República*, Santiago: CGR.

Longo, F (2005) *Diagnóstico institucional comparativo de sistemas de servicio civil: Índices de 21 países*, Washington DC: IDB Regional Policy Dialogue.

________ (2003) 'La calidad de los sistemas de servicio civil en América Latina y el Caribe: Una metodología de evaluación', paper presented at the 7th International Congress of CLAD, Panamá, 28–31 October.

Lopes Meirelles, H (1989) *Direito Administrativo Brasileiro*, São Paulo: Revista dos Tribunais.

Lora, E (2001) *A Decade of Structural Reform in Latin America: What Has Been Reformed and How to Measure It*, Washington: IADB Research Department Working Paper WP-446.

Lora, E and Panizza, U (2002) *Structural Reforms in Latin America under Scrutiny*, Washington: IADB Research Department Working Paper WP-348.

McCubbins, M and Schwartz, T (1987) 'Congressional Oversight Overlooked: Police Patrols versus Fire Alarms', in M McCubbins and T Sullivan (eds) *Congress: Structure and Policy*, Cambridge: Cambridge University Press: 426–40.

McGee, D (2002) *The Overseers: Public Accounts Committees and Public Spending*, London: Commonwealth Parliamentary Association and Pluto Press.

Machado, L, Beirão, AF and Giacobbo, M (1996) 'Análise do processo decisório de julgamento das contas do governo', *Revista do Tribunal de Contas da União* 27(69): 51–65.

Mainwaring, S (2003) 'Introduction: Democratic Accountability in Latin America', in S Mainwaring and C Welna (eds) *Democratic Accountability in Latin America*, Oxford: Oxford University Press: 3–33.

Mainwaring, S and Shugart, MS (eds) (1997) *Presidentialism and Democracy in Latin America*, Cambridge: Cambridge University Press.

Mainwaring, S and Welna, C (eds) (2003) *Democratic Accountability in Latin America*, Oxford: Oxford University Press.

Makón, M (2002) 'Ley 24.156 de Administración Financiera y Sistemas de Control del Sector Público Nacional', in ASAP, *XVI Seminario Nacional de Presupuesto Público*, Buenos Aires, Argentina: ASAP: 140–52.

________ (1997) 'La reforma del sistema presupuestario nacional', *Revista de la ASAP* 29: 51–64.

Manning, N and Matsuda, Y (2000) *Difficulties with Autonomous Agencies*, Washington, DC: World Bank Governance and Public Sector Reform.

Marcel, M and Tokeman, M (2002) 'Building a Consensus for Fiscal Reform in Chile', in OECD, *Public Sector Transparency and Accountability: Making it Happen*, Paris: OECD: 107–24.

Matsuda, Y (1997) 'An Island of Excellence: Petróleos de Venezuela and the Political Economy of Technocratic Autonomy', Pittsburg: University of Pittsburgh, unpublished doctoral dissertation.

Mauro, P (1995) 'Corruption and Growth', *Quarterly Journal of Economics* 110(3): 681–712.

Monks, RAG, and Minow, N (1991) *Power and Accountability*, New York, NY: Harper Collins.

Montecinos, V (2003) *Economic Policy-Making and Parliamentary Accountability in Chile*, Geneva: UNRISD Democracy, Governance and Human Rights Programme Paper 11.

Moreno, M (2001) 'La Ley Orgánica de Aministración Financiera del Sector Público: Contenido, Alcance, Limitaciones', *Revista Venezolana de Análisis de Coyuntura* VII(2): 11–50.

Moreno, E, Crisp, B and Shugart, M (2003) 'The Accountability Deficit in Latin America', in S Mainwaring and C Welna (eds) *Democratic Accountability in Latin America*, Oxford: Oxford University Press: 79–131.

Morgenstern, S and Manzetti, L (2003) 'Legislative Oversight: Interests and Institutions in the United States and Argentina', in S Mainwaring and C Welna (eds) *Democratic Accountability in Latin America*, Oxford: Oxford University Press: 132–69.

Moynihan, D (2003) *Performance-based budgeting: beyond rhetoric*, Washington, DC: World Bank PREM Note No 78.

Muruzabal Lerga, J (1999) 'Los órganos de control externo ¿sirven para algo?', *Revista Auditoría Pública* 19: 6–10.

Naím, M (1995) 'Latin America: The Second Stage of Reform', in L Diamond and M Plattner (eds) *Economic Reform and Democracy*, Baltimore, MD: John Hopkins University Press: 28–44.

Naranjo Gálvez, R (2002) 'La responsabilidad fiscal en Colombia ¿instrumento para combatir la corrupción o estímulo a la misma?', paper presented at CLAD VII International Congress, Lisbon, Portugal, 8–11 October.

Newell, P and Bellour, S (2002) *Mapping Accountability*, Brighton: IDS Working Paper 168.

North, D (1990) *Institutions, Institutional Change and Economic Performance*, Cambridge: Cambridge University Press.

O'Donnell, G (2003) 'Horizontal Accountability: The Legal Institutionalization of Mistrust', in S Mainwaring and C Welna (eds) *Democratic Accountability in Latin America*, Oxford: Oxford University Press: 34–54.

________ (1999) 'Horizontal Accountability and New Polyarchies', in A Schedler *et al* (eds) *The Self-Restraining State: Power and Accountability in New Democracies*, Boulder, CO: Lynne Rienner: 29–52.

________ (1998) 'Horizontal Accountability in New Democracies', *Journal of Democracy* 9(3): 112–26.

________ (1994) 'Delegative Democracy', *Journal of Democracy* 5(1): 55–69.

OECD (2004) *Budgeting in Chile*, Paris: OECD Working Party of Senior Budget Officials GOV/PGC/SBO(2004)7.

________ (2003) *Budgeting in Brazil*, Paris: OECD Working Party of Senior Budget Officials GOV/PUMA/SBO(2003)10.

Orrellana Vargas, P (2003) 'Chile: La Contraloría ¿baluarte de la probidad?', *Revista Probidad 21*, available at: www.revistaprobidad.info/021/003.html (accessed 20 September, 2006).

Osborne, D and Gaebler, T (1992) *Reinventing Government*, London: Addison-Wesley Publishing Company.

Oxhorn, P and Ducatenzeiler, G (1999) 'The Problematic Relationship Between Economic and Political Liberalization: Some Theoretical Considerations' in P Oxhorn and P Starr (eds) *Markets and Democracy in Latin America: Conflict or Convergence?*, Boulder, CO and London: Lynne Rienner Publishers: 43–60.

Panizza, U (2001) 'Electoral Rules, Political Systems and Institutional Quality', *Economics & Politics* 13(3): 311–42.

Payne, M, Zovatto, D, Carrillo Flórez, F and Allamand Zavala, A (2002) *Democracies in Development: Politics and Reform in Latin America*, Washington, DC: IDB.

Pereira, C and Muller, B (2004) 'The Cost of Governing: Strategic Behavior of the President in Brazil's Budgetary Process', *Comparative Politics Studies* 37(7): 781–815.

Persson, T (2001) *Do Political Institutions Shape Economic Policy?*, Cambridge: NBER Working Paper 8214.

Persson, T and Tabellini, G (2001) *Political Institutions and Policy Outcomes: What are the Stylized Facts?*, London: CEPR Discussion Paper 2872.

________ (2000) *Political Economics: Explaining Economic Policy*, Cambridge: MIT Press.

________ (1999) *Political Economics and Public Finance*, Cambridge: NBER Working Paper 7097.

Persson, T, Tabellini, G and Trebbi, F (2002) *Electoral Rules and Corruption*, Stockholm: Stockholm University, unpublished mimeo.

Pessanha, C (2003) 'O Congresso Externo sob Controle das Contas', *Inteligência* 21: 120–9.

________ (2000) 'The National Congress and External Control in Brazil: The Federal Court of Accounts, 1946–1998', paper presented at the 18th IPSA World Congress, Quebec, Canada, 1–5 August.

________ (1999) 'O Controle externo do Legislativo sobre o Executivo no Brasil: 1946–1998', unpublished manuscript.

Petrei, H (1998) *Budget and Control: Reforming the Public Sector in Latin America*, Washington, DC: IDB.

Polity IV (2003) *Political Regime Characteristics and Transitions, 1800–1999*, Washington, DC: University of Maryland, available at www.cidcm.umd.edu/inscr/polity (accessed 20 September, 2006).

Pontes, JB and Pederiva, JH (2004) *Contas Prestadas pelo Presidente da República: Apreciação do Congresso Nacional*, Brasilia: Consultoria Legislativa do Senado Federal, Textos para a Discussão 14.

Premchand, A (1999) 'Public Financial Accountability', in Salvatore Schiavo-Campo (ed) *Governance, Corruption and Public Financial Management*, Manila: Asian Development Bank: 145–92.

Przeworski, A (1999) 'On the Design of the State: A Principal-Agent Perspective', in LC Bresser Pereira and P Spink (eds) *Reforming the State: Managerial Public Administration in Latin America*, Boulder, CO: Lynne Rienner: 15–40.

Ramírez Aluja, A (2002) *El proceso de reforma del Estado y la modernización de la gestión pública en Chile. Lecciones, experiencias y aprendizajes (1990–2003)*, Madrid: INAP.

Rejtman, M (2005) 'El Tratamiento de la Cuenta de Inversión: Una Obligación Constitucional', in O Lamberto (ed) *La Cuenta de inversión*, Buenos Aires: CPMRC: 63–89.

Rocha, A (2003) 'Especialização e Autonomia Funcional no Âmbito to Tribunal de Contas da União', *Revista de Informação Legislativa* 40(157): 223–51.

Rodríguez, H (2002) 'Comentarios', *Revista ASAP* 29: 159–67.

Rodríguez, J and Bonvecchi, A (2006) *El papel del poder legislativo en el control presupuestario: La experiencia argentina en perspectiva comparada*, Santiago: CEPAL Working Paper 51.

Rodrik, D, Subramanian, A and Terbi, F (2002) *Institutions Rule: The Primacy of Institutions over Integration and Geography in Economic Development*, Washington, DC: IMF Working Paper WP/02/189.

Roque Citadini, A (1995) *O controle externo da administração pública*, São Paulo: Max Limonad.

Rose-Ackerman, S (1999) *Corruption and Government: Causes, Consequences and Reform*, Cambridge: Cambridge University Press.

________ (1978) *Corruption: A Study in Political Economy*, New York, NY: Academic Press.

Sánchez de Lozada, A (1999) 'In Pursuit of Public Accountability in Bolivia', in R Stapenhurst and SJ Kpundeh (eds) *Curbing Corruption: Toward a Model for Building National Integrity*, Washington, DC: World Bank, Economic Development Institute: 67–87.

Santiso, C (2008a) 'Keeping a watchful eye? Parliaments and the politics of budgeting in Latin America', in R Stapenhurst *et al* (eds) *Legislative Oversight and Government Accountability*, Washington, DC: World Bank: 243-266.

________ (2008b) 'Parlements et démocratie budgétaire en Amérique latine' in S Bellina (ed) *Gouvernance démocratique: Un nouveau paradigme pour le développement?*, Paris, France: Ministry of Foreign and European Affairs, MAEE-DCID: 223-236.

________ (2008c) 'Eyes Wide Shut? Reforming and defusing checks and balances in Argentina', *Public Administration and Development* 28(1): 67–84.

________ (2007a) 'Comme un tango amère? L'économie politique du contrôle des finances publiques en Argentine', *Revue française d'administration publique*, 2007/3: 337–51.

________ (2007b) *Eyes wide shut? The politics of autonomous audit agencies in emerging economies*, Buenos Aires, Argentina: CIPPEC Working Paper 5/2007.

________ (2007c) 'Strengthening Checks and Balances in Financial Governance: The Evolving Role of Multilateral Banks in Latin America', in S Bracking (ed) *Corruption and Development: The Anti-Corruption Campaigns*, London: Palgrave Macmillan: 273–92.

________ (2007d) 'Auditing, accountability and anticorruption: How relevant are autonomous audit agencies', in Transparency International *Global Corruption Report 2007*, Cambridge: Cambridge University Press: 358–62.

________ (2006a) 'Banking on Accountability? Strengthening budget oversight and public sector auditing in emerging economies', *Journal of Public Budgeting and Finance* 6(2): 66–100.

________ (2006b) 'Combattre la corruption et améliorer la gouvernance financière: Les institutions financières internationales et le renforcement du contrôle budgétaire dans les pays en développement', *Revue française d'administration publique* 119: 459–92.

________ (2006c) 'Pour le meilleur ou pour le pire? Le rôle du parlement dans le processus budgétaire dans les pays en développement', *Revue française d'administration publique* 117: 149–83.

________ (2006d) 'El día que me quieras: Parlamentos y presupuestos en América Latina', in M Braun, L Diaz Frers and G Uña (eds) *Cada cual; ¿atiende su juego? El rol del Congreso en el Presupuesto Nacional de Argentina*, Buenos Aires: CIPPEC.

________ (2006e) 'Improving Fiscal Governance and Curbing Corruption: How Relevant are Autonomous Audit Agencies', *International Public Management Review* 7(2): 97–108.

________ (2005a) *Budget Institutions and Fiscal Responsibility: Parliaments and the Political Economy of the Budget Process*, Washington, DC: WBI Working Paper No 37253.

________ (2005b) 'Parliaments and Budgeting: Understanding the Politics of the Budget', paper presented at the Annual Meeting of the Governance for Development Network of the IDB, Hamburg, Germany, 12–13 December.

________ (2004a) 'The Contentious Washington Consensus: Reforming the Reforms in Emerging Markets', *Review of International Political Economy* 11(4): 827–43.

________ (2004b) 'Re-forming the State: Governance Institutions and the Credibility of Economic Policy', *International Public Management Journal* 7(2): 271–98.

________ (2004c) 'Lending to Credibility: The Inter-American Development Bank and Budget Oversight Institutions in Latin America', *CEPAL Review* 83: 171–90.

________ (2004d) 'Legislatures and Budget Oversight in Latin America: Strengthening Public Finance Accountability in Emerging Economies', *OECD Journal on Budgeting* 4(2): 47–77.

________ (2003) 'Another Lost Decade? The Future of Reform in Latin America', *Public Administration and Development* 23(4): 297–305.

________ (2001a) 'Gobernabilidad democrática y política económica insular: Paradoja de las reformas de segunda generación en la Argentina de los 1990', *Revista Contribuciones* 4/2001: 109–36.

________ (2001b) 'Nuevos tiempos, viejas manías. Gobernabilidad democrática y reformas económicas en la Argentina', *Revista Pensar Hacer* 2/2001: 81–108.

________ (2001c) 'Gobernabilidad democrática y reformas económicas de segunda generación en América Latina', *Revista Instituciones y Desarrollo* 8–9: 325–66.

Saporiti, A and Streb, J (2003) 'Separation of Powers and Political Budget Cycles', mimeo.

Scartascini, C and Stein, E (2004) *The Bolivian Budget: A Year Long Bargaining Process*, Washington, DC: IDB.

Schedler, A (1999) 'Conceptualizing Accountability', in A Schedler *et al* (eds) *The Self-Restraining State: Power and Accountability in New Democracies*, Boulder, CO: Lynne Rienner: 13–28.

Schedler, A, Diamond, L and Plattner, M (eds) (1999) *The Self-Restraining State: Power and Accountability in New Democracies*, Boulder, CO: Lynne Rienner.

Schiavo-Campo, S and Tommasi, D (eds) (1999) *Managing Government Expenditure*, Manila: Asian Development Bank.

Schick, A (2003) 'The Performing State: Reflection on an Idea Whose Time has Come but Whose Implementation Has Not', *OECD Journal on Budgeting* 3(2): 71–103.

________ (2002) 'Can National Legislatures Regain an Effective Voice in Budget Policy?', *OECD Journal on Budgeting* 1(3): 15–42.

________ (2001) 'The Changing Role of the Central Budget Office', *OECD Journal on Budgeting* 1(1): 9–26.

________ (2000) *The Federal Budget: Politics, Policy, Process*, revised edition, Washington DC: Brookings.

________ (1998) 'Why Most Developing Countries Should Not Try New Zealand Reforms', *World Bank Research Observer* 13(1): 123–31.

________ (1990) *The Capacity to Budget*, Washington, DC: Urban Institute.

Schmitter, P (1999) 'The Limits of Horizontal Accountability', in A Schedler *et al* (eds) *The Self-Restraining State: Power and Accountability in New Democracies*, Boulder, CO: Lynne Rienner: 59–62.

Sciolla Avendaño, G (2003) 'Rol de la Contraloría General de la República', *Revista Chilena de Administración Pública* 2(5): 121–31.

________ (2002) 'Se debe estar atento a cualquier atisbo de corrupción', *La Semana Jurídica* 97: 8–9.

Shugart, MS and Mainwaring, S (1997) 'Presidentialism and Democracy in Latin America: Rethinking the Terms of the Debate', in S Mainwaring and MS Shugart (eds) *Presidentialism and Democracy in Latin America*, Cambridge: Cambridge University Press: 12–54.

Siavelis, P (2002) 'Disconnected Fire Alarms and Ineffective Police Patrols: Legislative Oversight in Postauthoritarian Chile', *Journal of Interamerican Studies and World Affairs* 42(1): 71–98.

________ (2000) *The President and Congress in Postauthoritarian Chile*, University Park, PA: Pennsylvania State University Press.

Silvera e Silva, JM (2002) 'O Réquiem do TCU', *Correio Braziliense*, 30 September.

Solares Mendiola, M (2004) *La Auditoria Superior de la Federación: Antecedentes y perspectiva jurídica*, Mexico DF: UNAM, Instituto de Investigaciones Jurídicas.

Sour, L, Ortega, I and San Sebastián, S (2003) *Política presupuestaria durante la transición a la democracia en México: 1997–2003*, Mexico: CIDE.

Speck, B (2000) *Inovação e Rotina no Tribunal de Contas da União*, São Paulo: Fundação Konrad Adenauer.

________ (1999) 'The Federal Court of Audit in Brazil', paper presented at the 9th International Anti-Corruption Conference, Durban, South Africa, 10–15 October.

Spiller, P and Tommasi, M (2000) 'The Institutional Foundations of Public Policy: A Transaction Approach with Application to Argentina', unpublished mimeo.

Spink, P (1998) *The Saga of Public Administration Reform in Latin America 1925–1995*, Stockholm: Swedish International Development Cooperation Agency.

Stapenhurst, R and Titsworth, J (2001) *Features and Functions of Supreme Audit Institutions*, Washington, DC: World Bank PREM Note 59.

Stein, E, Tommasi, M, Echeberría, K, Lora, E and Payne, M (eds) (2005) *The Politics of Policies: Economic and Social Progress in Latin America*, Washington, DC: IDB.

Stein, E, Talvi, E and Grisanti, A (1998) *Institutional Arrangements and Fiscal Performance: The Latin American Experience*, Washington, DC: IDB OCE Working Paper 367.

Straface, F (2005) 'El Rol del Estado y la Gestión Pública en la Promoción del Desarrollo Económico', presentation at the CAD Internacional Congress on Good Government Practices, Lima, 1 June.

Taliercio, R (2004) *Designing Performance: the Semi-Autonomous Revenue Authority Model in Africa and Latin America*, Washington, DC: World Bank Policy Research Working Paper 3423.

________ (2003) 'Administrative Reform as Credible Commitment: The Impact of Autonomy on Revenue Authority Performance in Latin America', *World Development* 32(2): 213–32.

Tanzi, V (2000a) 'Rationalising the Government Budget: Or Why Fiscal Policy is So Difficult' in A Krueger (ed) *The Second Stage*, Chicago, IL: The University of Chicago Press: 435–52.

________ (2000b) *The Role of the State and the Quality of the Public Sector*, Washington, DC: IMF Working Paper WP/00/36.

TCU (2003) *TCU Annual Report – Fiscal Year 2002*, Brasilia: TCU.

________ (2000a) *Referencial Estratégico do TCU*, Brasilia: TCU.

________ (2000b) *Pesquisa sobre o TCU Frente às Tendências do Control de Gestão Pública: Uma proposta de Mudança Instituticional*, Brasilia: TCU.

________ (2000c) *Proceso de Exame e Julgamento de Tomada e Prestação de Contas*, Brasilia: TCU.

________ (2000d) *Principais Trabalhos do Tribunal de Contas da União na Década 1990–1999*, Brasilia: TCU.

Tendler, J (1997) *Good Government in the Tropics*, Baltimore, MD: Johns Hopkins University Press.

Tsebelis, G (2002) *Veto Players: How Political Institutions Work*, Princeton, NJ: Princeton University Press.

________ (2000) 'Veto Players and Institutional Analysis', *Governance* 13(4): 441–74.

Tsebelis, G and Chang, E (2004) 'Veto Players and the Structure of Budgets in Advanced Industrialized Countries', *European Journal of Political Research* 43(3): 449–76.

Uña, G (2004) 'Un enfoque alternativo para el diseño del Institutional and Governance Review (IGR): la experiencia de Argentina', paper presented at the 9th International Congress of CLAD, Madrid, 2–5 November.

Uña, G, Cogliandro, G, Bertello, N and Labaqui, J (2005) *El Congreso y el Presupuesto Nacional: Desempeño y Condicionantes de su Rol en el Proceso Presupuestario*, Buenos Aires: Fundación Konrad Adenauer.

Uña, G, Bertello, N and Cogliandro, G (2004) *Delegación de facultades del Jefe de Gabinete de Ministros: evolución e impacto en el contexto fiscal actual*, Buenos Aires: Fundación Konrad Adenauer.

United Kingdom National Audit Office (2005) *Annual Report 2005*, London: UK NAO.

________ (2001) *State Audit in the European Union*, London: UK NAO.

United Nations Development Programme (2004) *Democracy in Latin America*, New York, NY: UNDP.

United States Government Accountability Office (2005) *Performance and Accountability Highlights 2004*, Washington, DC: US GAO.

Vial, J (2001) 'Institucionalidad presupuestaria y desempeño fiscal: Una Mirada a la experiencia chilena en los 90', unpublished manuscript.

Von Hagen, J and Harden, IJ (1995) 'Budget Processes and Commitment to Fiscal Discipline', *European Economic Review* 39: 771–79.

Waissbluth, M (2001) 'Un organismo para el siglo XXI', *Revista La Tercera*, 8 May.

Walker, D (2004) 'Addressing Fiscal Risks: A Case for Greater Truth and Transparency in Government Financial Reporting', *International Journal of Government Auditing* 31(1): 10.

Wehner, J (2004) 'Determinants of Legislative Financial Scrutiny', paper presented at the roundtable on the Role of Parliament in the Budget Process at the Southern Political Science Association Conference, New Orleans, 6–8 January.

Weingast, B, Shepsle, K and Johnsen, C (1981) 'The Political Economy of Benefits and Costs: A Neoclassical Approach to Distributive Politics', *Journal of Political Economy* 89: 642–64.

Weldon, J (2002) 'Legislative Delegation and the Budget Process in Mexico', in S Morgenstern and B Nacif (eds) *Legislatures and Democracy in Latin America*, New York, NY: Cambridge University Press: 377–412.

Wildavsky, A (1992) 'Political Implications of Budget Reform: A Retrospective', *Public Administration Review* 52: 594–9.

________ (1964) *The Politics of the Budgetary Process*, Boston, MA: Little Brown.

Wildavsky, A and Caiden, N (2000) *The New Politics of the Budgetary Process*, 4th edn, New York, NY: Addison Wesley.

Wildavsky, A and Swedlow, B (eds) (2001) *Budgeting and Governing*, Somerset, NJ: Transaction Publishers.

Williamson, J (1993) 'Democracy and the 'Washington Consensus', *World Development*, 21(8): 1329–36.

Willis, E (1996) 'Explaining Bureaucratic Independence in Brazil: The Experience of the National Economic Development Bank', *Journal of Latin American Studies* 27: 625–61.

World Bank (2005) *Chile: Study of Evaluation Program-Impact Evaluation and Evaluations of Government Programs*, Washington, DC: World Bank.

________ (2004) *Chile: Evaluación de la responsabilidad financiera pública*, Washington, DC: World Bank.

________ (2002) *Brazil: Country Financial Accountability Assessment*, Washington, DC: World Bank.

________ (2001) *Anti-corruption Diagnostic for Argentina: An Overview of Three Reports and Recommendations*, Washington, DC: World Bank Report No 20133-AR.

________ (2000) *Bolivia: from Patronage to a Professional State* Washington, DC: World Bank Report No. 20115-BO.

________ (1997) *World Development Report 1997: The State in a Changing World*, New York, NY: Oxford University Press.

World Economic Forum (2002) *Global Competitiveness Report*, Geneva: World Economic Forum.

Zanella di Pietro, MS (1996) 'Coisa julgada – aplicabilidade a decisões do Tribunal de Contas da União', *Revista do Tribunal de Contas da União* 27(70): 23–36.

Index

www.ingramcontent.com/pod-product-compliance
Ingram Content Group UK Ltd.
Pitfield, Milton Keynes, MK11 3LW, UK
UKHW011012180926
475701UK00004B/701
* 9 7 8 1 1 3 8 9 8 9 6 6 5 *